Contents

Cover: Water lilies, Okefenokee National Wildlife Refuge *Page 1:* Great blue heron, Everglades National Park *Pages 2-3:* Bicyclists, Cumberland Island National Seashore *Opposite:* Fishing at sunrise, Hobe Sound National Wildlife Refuge

Treading Lightly in the Wild

Little grass frog

NATIONAL GEOGRAPHIC GUIDE TO AMERICA'S OUTDOORS: SOUTHEAST takes you to the wildest and most beautiful natural areas of a region renowned for its forested mountain slopes, rocky gorges, lush swamps and wetlands teeming with wildlife, sunbaked sandy beaches, and jewel-like keys sheltering coral reefs ablaze with color.

Visitors who care about this region know they must tread lightly on the land. Ecosystems can be damaged, even destroyed, by thoughtless misuse. Many have already suffered from the impact of tourism. The marks are clear: litter-strewn acres, polluted waters, trampled vegetation, and disturbed wildlife. You can do your part to preserve these places for yourself, your children, and all other nature travelers. Before embarking on a backcountry visit or a camping adventure, learn some basic conservation dos and don'ts. Leave No Trace, a national educational program, recommends the following:

Plan ahead and prepare for your trip. If you know what to expect in terms of climate, conditions, and hazards, you can pack for general needs, extreme weather, and emergencies. Do yourself and the land a favor by visiting if possible during off-peak months and limiting your group to no more than four to six people. To keep trash or litter to a minimum, repackage food into reusable containers or bags. And rather than using cairns, flags, or paint cues that mar the environment to mark your way, bring a map and compass.

Travel and camp on solid surfaces. In popular areas, stay within established trails and campsites. Travel single file in the middle of the trail, even when it's wet or muddy, to avoid trampling vegetation. Be particularly sensitive in boggy or coastal areas, and avoid stepping on mussels, sea stars, and the like. When exploring off the trail in pristine, lightly traveled areas, have your group spread out to lessen impact. Good campsites are found, not made. Travel and camp on sand, gravel, or rock, or on dry grasses, pine needles, or snow. Remember to stay at least 200 feet from waterways. After you've broken camp, leave the site as you found it.

Pack out what you pack in—and that means *everything* except human waste, which should be deposited in a hole dug away from water, camp, or trail, then covered and concealed. When washing dishes, clothes, or yourself, use small amounts of biodegradable soap and scatter the water away from lakes and streams.

Be sure to leave all items—plants, rocks, artifacts—as you find them. Avoid potential disaster by neither introducing nor transporting nonnative species. Also, don't build or carve out structures that will alter the environment. A don't-touch policy not only preserves resources for future

Guide to America's Outdoors

Southeast

Guide to America's Outdoors
Southeast

By John Thompson
Photography by Raymond Gehman

NATIONAL
GEOGRAPHIC
WASHINGTON, D.C.

generations; it also gives the next guy a crack at the discovery experience.

Keep fires to a minimum. It may be unthinkable to camp without a campfire, but depletion of firewood harms the backcountry. When you can, try a gas-fueled camp stove and a candle lantern. If you choose to build a fire, first consider regulations, weather, skill, and firewood availability. At the beach, build your fire below the next high-tide line, where the traces will be washed away. Where possible, employ existing fire rings; elsewhere, use fire pans or mound fires. Keep your fire small, use only sticks from the ground, burn the fire down to ash, and don't leave the site until it's cold.

Respect wildlife. Watch animals from a distance (bring binoculars or a telephoto lens for close-ups), but never approach, feed, or follow them. Feeding weakens an animal's ability to fend for itself in the wild. If you can't keep your pets under control, leave them at home.

Finally, be mindful of other visitors. Yield to fellow travelers on the trail, and keep voices and noise levels low so that all the sounds of nature can be heard.

With these points in mind, you have only to chart your course. Enjoy your explorations. Let natural places quiet your mind, refresh your spirit, and remain as you found them. Just remember, leave behind no trace.

MAP KEY and ABBREVIATIONS

National Park	N.P.
National Battlefield Park	N.B.P.
National Memorial	NAT. MEM.
National Military Park	N.M.P.
National Monument	NAT. MON.
National Preserve	
National Recreation Area	N.R.A.
National Seashore	N.S.
National Forest	N.F.
State Forest	S.F.
National Wildlife Refuge	N.W.R.
Heritage Preserve	H.P.
National Estuarine Research Reserve	N.E.R.R.
Wildlife Management Area	W.M.A.
State Park	S.P.
State Conservation Park	
State Cultural Site	S.C.S.
State Preserve	
State Recreation Area	S.R.A.
State Reservation	
State Wildlife Park	S.W.P.
Indian Reservation	I.R.
Military Reserve	
Air Force Base	A.F.B.
Naval Air Station	N.A.S.
United States Marine Corps	U.S.M.C.
National Wild & Scenic River	N.W.& S.R.

U.S. Interstate
(95)

U.S. Federal or State Highway
(17) (20)

Other Road
[162]

Trail

Ferry

Canal

Intracoastal Waterway

Wilderness Waterway

BOUNDARIES

STATE

FOREST	I.R.	N.P.	WILDERNESS
N.P. in water	N.W.R. in water	S.P. in water	NATIONAL MARINE SANCTUARY

POPULATION

● **JACKSONVILLE** above 500,000
● **Charleston** 50,000 to 500,000
● Selma 10,000 to 50,000
● Darien under 10,000

ADDITIONAL ABBREVIATIONS

Cr.	Creek
DR.	Drive
Info.	Information
I.-s.	Island-s
L.	Lake
MEM.	Memorial
Mt.-s.	Mount-ain-s
N.M.S.	National Marine Sanctuary
N.S.T.	National Scenic Trail
Pres.	Preserve
Pt.	Point
Rec.	Recreation
RD.	Road

□ Point of Interest ⊣⊢ Falls
⊛ State capital ⚲ Spring
+ Elevation ⊤ Dam
⤨ Pass Swamp, Marsh
△ Campground

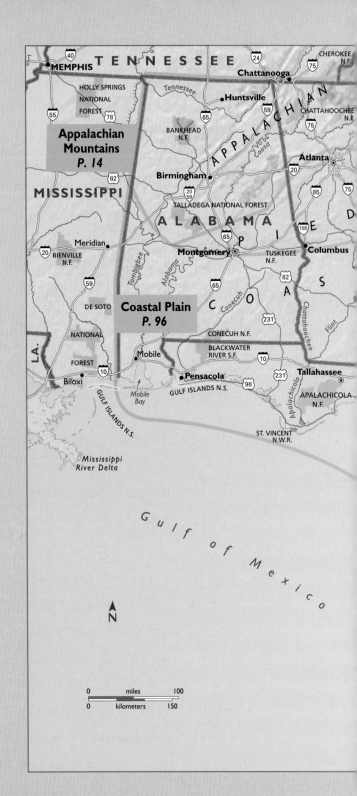

NANTAHALA N.F.
Charlotte
Piedmont P. 62
NORTH CAROLINA
26 85
77
Greenville
385 SUMTER
CAROLINA SANDHILLS N.W.R.
95
23
85
NATIONAL
SOUTH
20
Athens
FOREST
Columbia
OCONEE N.F.
20
O **Augusta**
CAROLINA
26
GEORGIA
1
Santee
26
FRANCIS MARION N.F.
95
Macon
Oconee
Savannah
Edisto
Charleston
16
ACE BASIN N.W.R.
Altamaha
Ocmulgee
Savannah
ATLANTIC
Broxton Rocks Reserve
1
75
Waycross
82
CUMBERLAND NATIONAL SEASHORE
Coast P. 166
OKEFENOKEE N.W.R.
St. Marys
OSCEOLA N.F.
10
JACKSONVILLE
OCEAN
Suwannee
19 98
FLORIDA
95
St. Johns
LOWER SUWANNEE N.W.R
75
OCALA N.F.
Daytona Beach
19
Orlando
Titusville
4
Melbourne
Tampa
95
St. Petersburg
Kissimmee
Sarasota
MYAKKA RIVER S.P.
Lake Okeechobee
Grand Bahama Island
ARTHUR R. MARSHALL LOXAHATCHEE N.W.R.
Boynton Beach
Naples
BIG CYPRESS NATIONAL PRESERVE
Fort Lauderdale
BAHAMAS
Miami
South Florida P. 214
EVERGLADES N.P.
BISCAYNE N.P.
The Everglades
Florida Bay
Andros Island
FLORIDA KEYS N.M.S.
DRY TORTUGAS N.P.
Key West
1
Florida Keys
Straits of Florida

Southern Beauty

I'VE SPENT NEARLY HALF MY LIFE living and traveling in the Southeast, and it amazes me how many places of incredible beauty I keep stumbling upon every time I go back out in the field. The region seems to grow bigger and bigger the more I learn about it. It could be that my memory is faulty; maybe I *did* see breathtaking Tallulah Gorge or that wild stretch of Cumberland Island ten years ago. But certainly never with the same kind of light, or in the same weather. Perhaps last time it was autumn and there was a rainbow, and now it's spring and wildflowers are out and a red-tailed hawk cries while its shadow races silently across the gorge walls.

While researching this book, I revisited a lot of favorite old haunts, but I also discovered many places that were new to me. The resulting medley of parks, preserves, refuges, and other sites included in this guide will give you a good idea of the great variety of southeastern landscapes that await your visit. Every book of this type reflects the biases of its author. Here's one: There are few things better in life than a whole day to waste and a seashore or mountain park to spend it in. Finding a brand-new vista—or bird, or flower—adds an exclamation point to the day. And in the Southeast, the possibilities for exclamatory days are endless.

On some sites I went into a lot of detail, often because they were big, but sometimes for other reasons. There might have been a particularly attractive trail, or an unusual species of plant or animal that caught my attention. You would have written a different book; my hope is that this one will make you eager to get outside and help you identify and appreciate the natural beauty of this region once you get there.

Redbud trees in bloom, Crockford-Pigeon Wildlife Management Area

If you had picked up a natural history guide to the Southeast written 300 years ago, you might have read, "Walk outside your door and you're there." A guide published a century later would have noted farms and small towns springing up all over. By 1900, much of the old-growth forest was falling to the ax, but you still could have found wilderness without much trouble. Now, instead of pockets of civilization, we have pockets of open space, gardens strung together by miles of highway. But they are lovely gardens nonetheless. One of the longest settled and most exploited regions of the country, the Southeast still has the heartwarming ability to renew itself, to put on a fresh suit of green and attract worshipers.

The astounding thing is what we still do have—stunning mountain vistas, lush forests, protected shorelines, and animals ranging from alligators and sea turtles to wood storks and bears. There are places in the Southeast where you can lose yourself in immense and timeless landscapes—the dizzying ledges of Little River Canyon, the primeval waters of Okefenokee Swamp, the bird havens of the South Carolina Sandhills and the Everglades, the kaleidoscopic coral reefs in the keys, to name a few. In almost every case, these great preserves and animals are still there because one person or group decided they were worth saving.

Even if you don't know the names of these preservationists, you can thank them in your heart as you are walking that trail, or paddling that rapid, or focusing on that rare bird. The southeastern outdoors remains a treasure because we will it so. I'd love to see a copy of an outdoor guide written a century from now, to open it and read of even more wilderness areas than I ever dreamed of.

John Thompson

Southeastern Biogeography: A Short Course

STEPPING DOWN FROM THE HIGHLANDS, the Southeast embraces a vast coastal plain that funnels south into the long runway of Florida, dividing the Atlantic Ocean from the Gulf of Mexico. Here on the lush fringe of the continent is where many journeys end—rivers find the sea, birds nest on nourishing wetlands, and people come for sun, springs, and salt water. Life's source and destination are one. In the thick forests, fertile marshes, and warm waters of the Southeast the natural world finds its full voice.

The total area of the Southeast—which, for the purposes of this guide, includes South Carolina, Georgia, Alabama, and Florida—is about equal to that of France. Within it you will find a stunning diversity of landscapes and habitats. Yet the region possesses a defining unity that makes it unmistakable from any other in the United States. Plants such as yucca and magnolia grow all the way from the coast up to the mountains. In all four states you'll see such standards as wild lilies, moss-dripping oaks, rustling marsh grasses, elegantly plumed herons, and bellowing alligators.

There is also a softness to the weather and the land that tells you, for instance, that the rolling mountain panorama you behold could lie only at the southern end of the Appalachians, and the vine-snarled subtropical forest a day's drive away has to be near the coast of Georgia or Florida. Sure, you could mistake a cypress swamp here for one in Louisiana, or a stretch of wide beach in South Carolina for a similar view farther north. Even so, a distinctive bird call or frog trill would soon set you straight.

Geologically, the Southeast claims some of the newest and the oldest land on the continent. The Appalachians rose to life some 500 million years ago, gradually eroding from Andean stature to the cloaked ridges and secluded hollows we think of as distinctly Appalachian. The sea began receding about 50 million years ago, dropping back nearly one hundred miles from the fall line to its present shore and leaving a fertile plain overgrown with cypress, tupelo, and longleaf pine. Not until 10 million years ago did the Florida peninsula emerge from the retreating sea.

With more than 1,000 miles from northwest Alabama to Key West, the Southeast holds several biogeographic regions, bands that generally run northeast to southwest. Though much of the flora and fauna overlaps from one region to the next, subtle changes become apparent as you move from the mountains, across the littoral, and down to the coast.

Guarding the Southeast's perimeter, the Appalachian Mountains (Chapter 1) climb to nearly 5,000 feet. Their rugged peaks offer thrilling lookouts; their cool coves and shaded streams cradle waterfalls, rare ferns, and wildflowers. The Piedmont (Chapter 2), a region of forested foothills, rolls out to the fall line, where rivers drop sharply to the soft, loamy soil of the Coastal Plain (Chapter 3). Here are found swamps and marshes that shelter a breathtaking abundance of bird and animal life.

Although technically part of the Coastal Plain, the Coast (Chapter 4) is so distinctive as to merit its own chapter. The region comprises a narrow strip of marsh, maritime forest, and Atlantic beach running from South Carolina to northern Florida; think of "barrier islands" as a subtitle, since most of the coast is strung together by these long, thin isles. Likewise, South Florida (Chapter 5) is a continuation of the Coastal Plain's slow drainage, but its complex pattern of subtropical plants and animals renders it unique not only to the Southeast but also to the world. Within all five chapters, sites have been handpicked for their ecological significance and scenic value.

Great blue heron at sunset, Arthur R. Marshall Loxahatchee National Wildlife Refuge

When packing for outings in the Southeast, keep in mind that heat and humidity are the rule for at least half the year. In winter, snow is possible in the mountains. Spring and fall are probably the best times for outdoor adventuring, with low crowds, relatively cool temperatures, peak bird migrations, and changing foliage. Essentials, then, include sturdy hiking boots, short sleeves, a sun hat, bug and sun lotions, a water bottle, and binoculars. A good guide to southeastern birds will add immeasurably to your appreciation of each site.

Try to imagine how it would have been to walk through the great forests of the Southeast before they were cleared and settled. We might well envy William Bartram, a botanical explorer with a keen eye, who traversed the region in the 1770s. Bartram was ahead of his time in viewing the wilderness not as an obstacle to civilization but as an infinite source of amazement. His drawings and writings give us a tantalizing picture of the paradise we lost: wetlands brimming with birds and alligators; tremendous tracts of longleaf pine forest so mature that the grassy floor was like a prairie, each huge tree looming over its own half-acre of ground; unbroken realms of nature with irresistible views and drinkable streams.

But all is not lost. Most of the flora and fauna Bartram saw across the Southeast still exists, albeit in reduced—and sometimes dangerously low—numbers. And though the wilderness has been fragmented, there are still long, unblemished vistas aplenty, especially in the mountains and on protected strands. At Cumberland Island National Seashore, a line of dunes gives way to a wide promenade of untamed beach that stretches as far as the eye can see. Even now, as you read this, pelicans may be flying in tight chains between breakers awash in moonlight, or dolphins may be roiling the dark surface of a sea rose-tinted with the dawn of a new day. ■

Appalachian
Mountains

Morning fog in Chattahoochee National Forest, Georgia

ON A CRISP SPRING DAY at the top of Brasstown Bald in the Chattahoochee National Forest you can see wave after wave of blue-green mountains rippling off into the hazy distance, 50 to 60 miles away. All over the wooded slopes glorious blooms of rhododendron, laurel, and azalea waft their sweetness through the woods. Here at 4,784 feet above sea level, the highest point in Georgia, the Appalachian Mountains hardly appear to be making their final stand. Yet only a couple of hundred miles to

the southwest, they bow toward the coastal plain of Alabama. Running in a widening band through the northern fringes of South Carolina, Georgia, and Alabama, the southern Appalachians rear up sharply from the Piedmont some 2,000 feet below, creating a distinctly mountainous terrain that holds a diversity of habitats. Although the term "southern Appalachians" also includes the mountains of West Virginia, Virginia, Kentucky, Tennessee, and North Carolina, this chapter spotlights only the extreme southern end of the chain.

Among the oldest mountains on the planet, the Appalachians date back more than a billion years. Four major periods of faulting, folding, and uplifting occurred between 250 and 500 million years ago, when tremendous pressure from shifting continental plates pushed up the landmass here until it stood perhaps as high as the Himalaya. The steady work of wind and water over millions of years created the softened contours of the Appalachians you see today.

The Blue Ridge defines the northwestern edge of South Carolina and pushes into northern Georgia. Rocky summits, roaring falls, deep gorges, and fern-lined streams are reference points within thick forests of oak, hickory, and magnolia. Down within the cool recesses of ravines and valleys, mighty hemlocks grow at their southern extremity, their soft leaves adding a pine-fresh scent to the air. Springtime within the Chattahoochee

National Forest or along the muscular Chattooga River brings a medley of blue, gold, pink, and white wildflowers. Understory trees such as dogwood, redbud, serviceberry, and hawthorn also burst forth in bloom, providing fruit for wildlife. In the fall, the leaves put on their own spectacular show. Wintertime can glaze the hills with ice or powder them with 8 inches of snow, then suddenly deliver a week of springlike weather.

Just west of the Blue Ridge, a ridge and valley zone angles through northwest Georgia and northeast Alabama with its contorted triple-decker of limestone, shale, and sandstone. Creeks running through this rugged country have created such not-to-be-missed features as Cloudland Canyon, Russell Cave, and Little River Canyon on Lookout Mountain. Bordering this zone, the Cumberland Plateau thrusts out of the north, framing the once wild and reckless Tennessee River, tamed by TVA dams in the 1930s. Highlights here include Wheeler National Wildlife Refuge, with its multitudes of migratory waterfowl, and Bankhead National Forest, which shelters the no-wheels-allowed Sipsey Wilderness.

Plan to spend some time in this region of rough beauty, but remember that getting from one site to another is slow going, dictated by the rising and falling contours of the land. You'll also find yourself slowing for scenic overlooks, high ledges, waterfall trails, boulder-studded swimming holes, and sacred little coves that will remain in your memory forever. ■

Mountain Bridge Wilderness Area

■ 10,883 acres ■ Northwest South Carolina, 25 miles northwest of Greenville off US 276 (Jones Gap); or 37 miles northwest of Greenville on US 276 (Caesars Head) ■ Year-round ■ Hiking, backpacking, fishing, wildflower viewing ■ Contact Caesars Head State Park, 8155 Geer Hwy., Cleveland, SC 29635, phone 864-836-6115; or Jones Gap State Park, 303 Jones Gap Rd., Marietta, SC 29661, phone 864-836-3647

JUST SOUTH OF the North Carolina border, the mountains abruptly drop 2,000 feet to the rolling hills of the Piedmont. Bridging Greenville's two watersheds and including high rock escarpments and lush valleys, the Mountain Bridge area offers spectacular vistas, spritely waterfalls, burbling streams, and a dazzling array of wildflowers and rare plants.

Comprising more than two-thirds of the wilderness area, Caesars Head State Park sprawls over the high country, its namesake granite outcrop standing 3,266 feet above sea level. To the east, adjacent Jones Gap

Blue Ridge at sunset

State Park covers the Middle Saluda River Valley, a haven for more than 600 plant species, including ash, basswood, red maple, and birch, and such colorful wildflowers as grass-of-Parnassus, yellow-fringed orchids, bluets, and red-flowering columbines.

In the 1840s a mountain man named Solomon Jones laid out a road along the steep slopes and gorges, eyeballing the grades and contours instead of using instruments. The Jones Gap toll road followed the Middle Saluda from River Falls up to Cedar Mountain, North Carolina, and stayed in business until around 1910. A horse-drawn wagon driver in 1895 complained that "the way up is torturous, and possibly could be improved," but he admitted that the road was quite an engineering feat and that the views made the trip worthwhile. In 1877, another traveler on the road described the breathtaking outlook from Caesars Head: "The magnificent height dwarfing the giant trees hundreds of feet below us, the far reaching view extending to the horizon miles on miles away, the solemn mountains rearing their verdured crests on either hand, all combined to make an impression I will carry through life."

Bird-watching in Caesars Head State Park

What to See and Do

Some 50 miles of trails lace the two state parks, luring day-hikers and backpackers to a rugged, unspoiled mountain wilderness. **Jones Gap** is the place to go for views of cliff faces towering more than 1,500 feet above the valley floor. From the parking lot a short path crosses the splashy **Middle Saluda** and winds past a former fish hatchery; rainbow, brook, and brown trout swim in the pools, evidence of what anglers can look forward to in the shaded streams all around. For exhibits and trail maps, stop at the **Environmental Education Center.** Outside the building, the stone rising sheer to the north is Cleveland Cliff.

The 4.4-mile **Hospital Rock Trail** twists sharply up **Standing-stone Mountain,** offering good views within the first mile or so. You walk through a classic southern forest of rhododendron, mountain laurel, magnolia, pine, and oak. Indian pink, violet showy orchids, and other wildflowers bloom in spring and summer.

You're apt to startle (and be startled by) ruffed grouse, exploding from nearby bushes as you tramp past. Big turkey buzzards inhabit these woods, too, gathering in trees and shady glens like lost colonies of mountaineers. The trail is steep and can be stiflingly hot in summer, so bring plenty of water. At 1.2 miles you arrive at Hospital Rock, a 30-foot-wide overhang where Confederate soldiers are said to have stored medical supplies. Soon the trail levels off; in another 3 miles you come to the intersection with **False Creek Trail** atop Standingstone Mountain. This trail descends to Friddle Lake, where you can pick up the road back to the parking lot.

For the best views, make a 6-mile loop by connecting **Rim of the Gap Trail** with **Pinnacle Pass Trail** (via connector #22). The easiest way up to Caesars Head from Jones Gap is by the **Jones Gap Trail.** Tracing the old Jones Gap Road, the trail follows the Middle Saluda; about halfway along you can branch left for a total 5-mile walk to Caesars Head. Unless you're prepared for a long march back, have someone drive around and meet you at the top. In either case, you'll have fine views of the mountains to the north.

Vistas to the south and west are splendid from **Caesars Head** at the top of twisty US 276, which continues into North Carolina. From the visitor center, you can take a short stroll out to the promontory for dramatic panoramas of the hills to the south and the vertically scarred face of Table Rock to the southwest. Ravens and hawks soar here in thousands of feet of empty space. To see the Caesars Head profile, take the stairway down through a damp, shoulder-wide crevice in the rock called the **Devil's Kitchen** and look up to the left. The chin fell off some 50 years ago, making it difficult to discern the outline of the face.

The best hike in the area lies just over a mile farther up the road. The 2.2-mile walk (one way) to **Raven Cliff Falls** takes you through a forest of hickory, oak, tulip poplar, black locust, dogwood, and thick rhododendron. Within about 15 minutes you round the head of a small valley and come out on wonderful views to the south. Along the trail look for jack-in-the-pulpits, cardinal flowers, trilliums, fire pink, flame azaleas, and little white pussytoes. As a suitable reward at hike's end, the falls drop a total of 420 feet in a lovely series of water slides and free-falling cascades. ■

Rhododendron

Table Rock State Park

■ 3,083 acres ■ Northwest South Carolina, 16 miles north of Pickens on S.C. 11 ■ Year-round ■ Camping, hiking, boating, swimming, fishing, wildlife viewing ■ Adm. fee ■ Contact the park, 158 E. Ellison Ln., Pickens, SC 29671; phone **864-878-9813**. www.southcarolinaparks.com

ONE OF THE MOST STRIKING landmarks in the South Carolina Blue Ridge, the tremendous bulk of Table Rock slams up like an extruded stone fist. Its curved sides rise to a tree-crowned summit that stands at 3,124 feet. Cherokee legend holds that the ancients sat at the adjoining rock "stool" while dining at the Table and admiring the majesty of creation. At the **Carrick Creek Interpretive Center** you can learn more about the rock and the park's flora and fauna. The gentle 1.9-mile **Carrick Creek Trail** introduces you to the area's natural wonders as it loops past small waterfalls, rhododendrons, and mountain laurels.

The trail offers views through the canopy to the distant ridge, but for a truly spectacular vista take at least part of the 3.5-mile trek (one way) up to Table Rock. In the spring and summer irises, bloodroots, violets, trout lilies, and sweet shrubs add pinpoints of color and whiffs of perfume along your route. Songbirds and chipmunks scold from trailside thickets in a forest of oak and hickory, with hemlocks in the lower, wetter areas. You may see squirrels or deer, although most of the park's mammals—gray foxes, bobcats, skunks, and bears—are nocturnal. Water and garter snakes are fairly common, copperheads and timber rattlers less so.

The trail climbs to the top of the rock, so be prepared for several hours of tough walking if you go all the way. Bring a lunch and plenty of water. Or make a full day of it by adding 3,425-foot **Pinnacle Mountain** for about a 10-mile loop. From the top of either of these peaks you can see the 3,560-foot summit of Sassafras Mountain, South Carolina's highest point, to the north. From Pinnacle Mountain, you can pick up the 84-mile **Foothills Trail,** which runs from Jones Gap and Caesars Head parks, up Sassafras Mountain, and southwest to Oconee State Park.

After a tough, exhilarating hike, you can cool off in 36-acre **Pinnacle Lake,** which features summertime swimming and year-round fishing. Rental kayaks, canoes, paddle boats, and fishing boats are available in summer at the park. For a quieter fishing experience, the larger **Lake Oolenoy** lies just across S.C. 11; non-gas-powered boats are allowed. For those who don't want to work that hard for their dinner, the park has a nice restaurant in an old CCC building; it's open for noon and evening meals in summer, dinner only the rest of the year. ■

Ashmore Heritage Preserve

■ 560 acres ■ Northwest South Carolina, west on S.C. 11, 3.9 miles from Marietta, then right 0.9 mile on Persimmon Ridge Rd. to parking area on the right ■ Year-round ■ Hiking, wildlife viewing ■ Contact Heritage Trust Program, S.C. Dept. of Natural Resources, Box 167, Columbia, SC 29202; phone 803-734-3893

WHERE A PREVIOUS LANDOWNER once envisioned a housing development, a special mountain habitat referred to as a "cataract bog" has been preserved. Cataract bogs can exist only on southern-exposed rock outcrops steep enough for a constant flow of water. On these water slides several unusual species are to be found, such as sundews, grass-of-Parnassus, and Indian paintbrush—all plants that thrive on the "bog's" plentiful sun and generous moisture. Two animal species of special concern also live here. The green salamander slithers among the outcrop's crevices, and Rafinesque's big-eared bat roosts in hollow trees, coming out at night to hunt insects. The big-eared bat can hover like a butterfly, allowing it to distinguish moths from tree foliage.

A **trail** of a little over a mile follows the road built for the development that never came to fruition. It crosses a stream and loops around small **Lake Wattacoo,** where you have great views of outcrops, a slick water slide, and a beaver dam. Within the surrounding forest live white-tailed deer, ruffed grouse, wild turkeys, and black bears.

A recent 30-acre addition to the preserve west of Persimmon Ridge Road connects to the **Chandler Heritage Preserve** and thus provides a vital linkage for plant and animal migration. The mostly south-facing property includes chestnut oaks and other dry community trees, as well as some pines and hickories. Augmenting the Mountain Bridge Wilderness Area (see pp. 18-21), the tract also helps protect the Saluda River watershed. The area is subject to periodic feral hog problems, often caused by hog owners who release their animals for hunting. The hardy creatures can wreak havoc on fragile wetland ecosystems. ■

Eastatoe Creek Heritage Preserve

■ 373 acres ■ Northwest South Carolina, off US 178, 8 miles north of S.C. 11
■ Year-round ■ Hiking, fishing, wildlife viewing ■ Contact Heritage Trust Program, S.C. Dept. of Natural Resources, Box 167, Columbia, SC 29202; phone 803-734-3893

HIDDEN AWAY IN THE BLUE RIDGE and allowed to grow wild since the last logging in the mid-1900s, a rugged section of the Eastatoe (EAST-a-towhee) Creek drainage preserves a number of rare plants and provides sanctuary for migratory birds, various reptiles, small mammals, and a nonstocked population of rainbow trout. Within the nearly 3-mile stretch of the creek embraced by the preserve, the Eastatoe drops more than 1,000 feet, meaning that hikers will find the terrain fairly steep in places. But the sheer cliffs, rock outcrops, bouldery flumes, and riffling tributaries you pass on the way down keep the walk interesting.

The 2.5-mile **trail** (one way) begins on an old logging road just off the parking area. Open areas along here provide good habitat for rabbits, white-tailed deer, prairie warblers, Eastern towhees, indigo buntings, and cardinals. Maple saplings, yellow poplars, and small pines are filling in, taking advantage of their day in the sun, while blackberry vines grow in thickets around old stumps and by the wood's edge.

In winter and early spring you'll have good open views through the trees to distant ridges and peaks, including 3,560-foot-high Sassafras Mountain, South Carolina's tallest, to the northeast. But as you begin descending toward the brawling noise of the creek, the forest closes in

Dragonfly on a forest fern

with a dense canopy of oaks, hickories, and beeches. Under these giants grow flowering dogwoods, pawpaws, and hollies, and in cool, spray-moistened glens you'll find some virgin stands of old hemlock. Left alone because of the trees' inaccessibility and low market value, the feathery-limbed hemlocks freshen the air with their zesty scent.

As the trail sweeps around a small ravine it drops into an area thick with rhododendron. In the spring, when the blooms are out, listen for the fluting of the wood thrush, which annually migrates north from rain forests in Central America. Pileated woodpeckers hammer away high overhead, and ruffed grouse drum their wings together in the underbrush. You may also surprise a wild turkey or bobcat. Try to avoid surprising a copperhead: Common in the area, this poisonous snake averages some 2 feet long and is distinguished by its brown, hourglass pattern. Though painful, its bite is rarely life-threatening.

Down by the creek, the trail levels out into a parklike clearing, where you can picnic and camp. There are several places along the bank of the stream where you can stand and count dozens of different kinds of wild-flowers, including purple ginger, galax, saxifrage, Carolina geranium, foamflower, trilliums, and 16 kinds of violets. The birdlife here is particu-larly active; a pair of binoculars and trained ears will help you locate downy woodpeckers, chickadees, tufted titmice, ruby-throated hum-mingbirds, and red-eyed vireos. Moderate temperatures and a constantly humid environment enable Tunbridge and dwarf filmy ferns to grow here. A bit farther downstream, the 15-foot-wide creek narrows into a chute only 3 feet across as it roars through a rock cataract, creating a beautiful waterfall known to few people. ■

Early morning cast

Devils Fork State Park

■ 622 acres ■ Northwest South Carolina, 4 miles northeast of Salem off
S.C. 11 ■ Year-round ■ Hiking, boating, swimming, fishing, wildlife viewing,
wildflower viewing ■ Contact the park, 161 Holcombe Circle, Salem, SC
29676; phone 864-944-2639. www.southcarolinaparks.com

ONE OF THE HALF DOZEN attractive parks strung along the **Cherokee
Foothills Scenic Highway** (S.C. 11), Devils Fork State Park nestles along
the southwestern shore of scenic **Lake Jocassee,** a 7,565-acre reservoir
created by the Duke Energy Company in 1973 to generate hydroelectric
power. The name "Devils Fork" has been applied to this area since at least
1780 in reference to a creek, perhaps specifically to the confluence of
Corbin, Howard, and Limber Pole Creeks.

Stop at the **park headquarters** where rangers will furnish information
and a trail map. Then you can take the easy 1.5-mile **Oconee Bell Nature
Trail** through a mixed forest of pines, oaks, and hickories. More than 90
percent of the world's rare Oconee bell wildflowers grow here, blooming
in February or March with white petals and yolk yellow centers.

For a bit more exercise, pick up the 3.5-mile **Bear Cove Trail** at the
picnic area. The shaded route passes through mixed forest and offers
good views of the lake and surrounding hills. Among the wildflowers
you can see along the path are clublike jack-in-the-pulpits, yellow trout
lilies, showy white bloodroots, and violets. You have a good chance of
spotting white-tailed deer and wild turkeys and of hearing, if not actually
seeing, scarlet tanagers, red-eyed vireos, and various warblers. The once

endangered peregrine falcon was reintroduced into the area after decades of decline throughout the East due to pesticides.

The deep, clear waters of Lake Jocassee make for fine boating, fishing, and swimming—although you should note that no lifeguard is on duty. The 75-mile shoreline holds numerous quiet nooks and coves, where you can enjoy a picnic lunch in total seclusion. You can rent boats just outside the park from Fish, Inc. *(864-944-9292)* or Hoyetts Bait and Tackle *(864-944-9016)*. The most likely prizes are rainbow and brown trout, white bass, largemouth and smallmouth bass, bluegill, and black crappie. A South Carolina fishing license is required.

To save a vast tract of land near Devils Fork State Park from potential development, South Carolina's Department of Natural Resources recently completed the **Jocassee Gorges** purchase. This farsighted measure placed 33,000 acres of mountain land valued at about 55 million dollars under permanent protection as a wildlife management area. In so doing, the state of South Carolina has vouchsafed the area's forested hills and steep gorges as a legacy to future generations.

Serene pleasures, such as primitive camping and hiking, await the dedicated visitor. More than 20 miles of the scenic **Foothills Trail** course through the expansive acreage, which includes the 2,500-foot-high Jumping Off Rock and its fine views over Lake Jocassee and into the mountains of North Carolina. Other than the existing trails and old logging roads, there is no development in the tract—nor is any planned. An additional 7,000 to 8,000 acres of conservation easements, plus the U.S. Forest Service lands to the west and the watershed projects and state parks to the east, mean that a large piece of Appalachian wilderness will remain wild. ■

Essence de Polecat

Two inhabitants of the southeastern woodlands—the striped and eastern spotted skunks—are among the most elegant of animals. Their black-and-white coats make them stand out in the forest; they have little need for camouflage because of their nocturnal nature and their notorious scent.

When threatened, the skunk faces its enemy and raises its tail. Sometimes, this warning step is cut, and the skunk adopts a shoot first policy: It pivots around and sprays a stream of yellow musk from its anal glands. The slightly larger and more common striped skunk can spray up to 15 feet away, with the mist carrying an additional 30 feet. The smell itself is detectable for a mile or more. Although the skunk can shoot five or six rounds of musk, one is usually enough. A single jet of this remarkably potent liquid equals only about one-fifth of a teaspoon.

A hit to the eye causes intense pain and temporary blindness. Tomato juice and ammonia are the best agents for removing the overpowering smell. It may sound incredible, but some commercial perfumes are made by deodorizing the oily musk and using it as a base.

Chattahoochee National Forest

■ 750,000 acres ■ Northeast Georgia ■ Year-round ■ Camping, hiking, walking, canoeing, fishing, wildlife viewing, wildflower viewing ■ Contact forest supervisor's office, 1755 Cleveland Hwy., Gainesville, GA 30501; phone 770-297-3000. www.fs.fed.us/conf

SPLASHED ACROSS THE GREEN and mountainous north part of Georgia, this vast forest holds a treasury of southern Appalachian natural history. Cool streams tumble from high rocky gorges, cutting steep defiles, and gathering momentum as they plunge to rivers lined with hemlock and oak. Trout-filled lakes dot the highlands like sparkling beads. In the fall the worn and rugged hills flare gold and scarlet, succeeded after a chilly winter by spring's even more impressive display. Tender new leaves and buds begin to clothe the bare limbs; blushes of redbud and orange-tinted maple appear, then swathes of shrubby white hawthorn, yellow jasmine, and lacy dogwood. Brilliant wildflowers begin blooming low on dormant meadows and beside trails and creeks, and wild bursts of pink azalea and mountain laurel announce the long, warm days of summer. Vireos and warblers return to the forest, and the liquid flute of the wood thrush resounds once again deep in the heart of the woods.

The healthy forest you see today was not always so verdant and wild. A gold rush originating near Dahlonega drew thousands of white settlers in the 1830s, displacing the Cherokee who had been here for centuries. With the rush over, the miners moved on but farmers stayed and began working and depleting the land. They often planted on steep slopes, failed to rotate crops, relied too much on burning, and did not plant cover crops in winter. Pretty soon they, too, sold out and left. Timber companies came in and from the 1880s to the 1920s took out just about everything the forest had to give. A charred, eroding land of stumps and gullies remained when the federal government stepped in. With the establishment of the national forest in 1936, the Civilian Conservation Corps and others began replanting trees and restoring the forest.

Today black bears, deer, turkeys, raccoons, hawks—in all, more than 500 species of animals—find shelter in the Chattahoochee. More than 500 miles of trails, 10 sizable lakes, 1,770 miles of trout streams, numerous waterfalls, scenic roads, state parks, and a national wild and scenic river give visitors ample opportunity to explore.

What to See and Do

The **Chattooga National Wild and Scenic River** *(864-638-9568 or 803-561-4000)* flows wild and free for 50 undammed miles, torquing through narrow passages, frothing up in constant rapids and flumes, swishing past truck-size boulders, and occasionally gentling to deep pools. The first 10 miles pass through dense forests and old

Tallulah River, Tallulah Gorge State Park

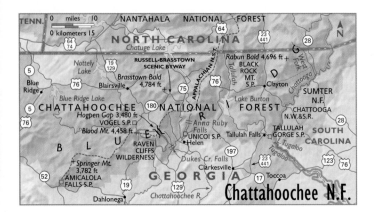

fields in North Carolina; the river then becomes the boundary line between Georgia and South Carolina, twisting and turning its way down to Lake Tugaloo, just north of Tallulah Falls.

The river made an indelible impression on the American public in the 1972 movie *Deliverance,* about a canoe trip that turns into a test of survival. Running the river by canoe, kayak, raft, or inner tube has become ever more popular over the years. Rapids all the way up to a Class VI offer challenges for all skill levels. Because of the river's remoteness from main highways, you should plan at least half a day for an excursion.

If you prefer walking, there are more than 50 miles of trails along the river. At the Russell Bridge (Ga. 28), you can pick up the **Bartram** and **Chattooga River trails,** which together travel north about 4 miles on the South Carolina side of the river before the Bartram splits to the east. Southward, the trails run 10 miles along the Georgia side to Sandy Ford, where the Bartram Trail heads west. Heading south takes you past more rapids and rif-

fles, but in either direction you get a taste of the Chattooga landscape—its cool, ferny coves and steep, rocky ridges.

The easiest place for a quick look at some exciting white water is just off the US 76 bridge. A short trail on the South Carolina side takes you to **Bull Sluice,** a Class V rapid that few paddlers attempt. North of here the river constricts to a 15-foot-wide channel, then screams around a blind curve to the Sluice. To the south lies a hazardous series of Class IV rapids. The 7 miles from here to the lake are a minefield of undercut rocks, standing waves, steep drops, and swirling eddies—off-limits to all but the best boaters.

One theory on local geology posits that millions of years ago the Chattooga and Tallulah Rivers joined with the Chattahoochee. In this scenario the nearby Tugaloo-Savannah River system kept cutting back up into the hills and "captured" the two rivers, forming a waterfall at the junction. The Tallulah, which drops even more precipitously than the Chattooga, began knifing its way sharply into its hard quartzite bed, eventually digging out the spectacular gorge on display at **Tallulah Gorge State Park** (*Tallulah Falls, US 441. 706-754-7970. Adm. fee*). In less than a mile, the river drops 500 feet through a breathtaking chasm of sheer walls resounding with cascades and pounding waterfalls.

The **Jane Hurt Yarn Interpretive Center** is packed with exhibits and a 70-seat theater. A bird-watching station outfitted with binoculars and information sheets helps you identify local birds. Outside, a short trail takes you to the **North Rim,** where you have thrilling views out into a vast cathedral of space. Hawks swoop up and down on elevators of air, and water slides and falls plunge through the gorge 750 feet below. The .75-mile **North Rim Trail** is nice and flat and takes you to several awe-inspiring overlooks. The dam is visible to the right (west), but you can imagine what the area looked like before the dam's construction. A few weekends a year (April and November), the power company releases enough water to turn the river into a roiling cauldron of white water, a test of nerve and skill for expert kayakers (*call the park for more information*).

Tallulah Gorge Hike

Hiking both the North and the South Rims gives you an appreciation for Tallulah's magnitude and its various ecosystems. This 3-mile walk starts at the interpretive center. Follow the North Rim Trail to the left to station #1 and take in the vertiginous views of the gorge and Oceana and Bridal Veil Falls.

Tallulah Falls

In the late 1800s, Tallulah Falls was one of the most popular resorts in the South, its little town holding 20 hotels. To supply energy to Atlanta and other urban areas, the river was dammed just above the falls in 1912, an early marvel of engineering that drew sharp criticism from many locals who claimed the wild nature of the gorge would be forever lost. The resort business did decline, and by the early 1920s fires had claimed most of the hotels.

One of the most vocal gorge advocates, Helen Dortch Longstreet, wife of Confederate hero Gen. James Longstreet, fought to keep the gorge wild and protected by a state park. She lost her battle, but finally in 1992 the Georgia Power Company leased land to the state for the creation of a new 3,000-acre park; the rim trail system is named for Mrs. Longstreet.

The sun dries out the cliffs on this south-exposed side, leaving a harsh environment where only a few hardy oaks and pines, dwarfed to bonsai shapes, can exist. Small plants like birds-foot violets, blueberries, and mountain laurels send roots into the shallow soil.

Now take the trail west toward the dam, stopping at the various overlooks. Back in the woods to your right, woodpeckers nest in tree cavities and tree frogs trill

Following pages: Mayapples in Fort Mountain State Park

after a good rain. When you reach the dam, you'll need to take the stairway up to the US 441 bridge and then the bridge sidewalk to the south end. Off to your right is **Tallulah Falls Lake,** a good habitat for green herons, mallards, kingfishers, and beavers. Fewer people venture over to the **South Rim,** yet some of the best views are on that side. Standing at the pavilion (station #6), look at the way the gorge not only slopes down in the direction of the river but also tilts north to south, creating a disorienting fun house illusion that the eye tries in vain to resolve. It's as though a giant stacked rock layers on either side, then yanked them down. The path, at any rate, is level.

Between stations #7 and #8, you will pass **Hurricane Falls Trail,** one of two descent trails into the gorge. (*This hike is rated as very strenuous and a special permit is required for entry into the gorge.*) Environmental damage to the terrain and accidents to humans are thus kept to a minimum.

Within the gorge bloom purple asters, as well as white flowers of persistent trillium. Other rare floral gems, such as roundleaf sundews and monkey-face orchids, grow in hidden, protected nooks. In lush shade, green salamanders slink among mosses and ferns; skunks and foxes sneak out onto exposed rocks.

Near the bottom drape lacy boughs of hemlocks, which are at their southern limit here in northern Georgia. At the bottom of the gorge lies the rushing river with its rocky pools. Continue along the South Rim all the way to station #10 and take in another angle on the 1,000-foot-wide gorge. From here you can retrace your steps back to the interpretive center.

Unicoi State Park

Heading west from Tallulah Gorge in the rumpled hills just north of Helen, this park (*706-878-3982. Adm. fee*) holds more than 1,000 acres of forest. Some 12 miles of trails wander through bottomland woods and around a small lake.

The half-mile **Frog Pond Nature Trail** has markers along the route identifying oaks, maples, hemlocks, and sweet gums. The 4.6-mile (one way) **Smith Creek Trail** heads up to **Anna Ruby Falls** (*706-754-6221*), or you can drive up (*parking fee*). A quarter-mile paved footpath brings you to the base of these twin falls, whose water comes from springs high on Tray Mountain. The Curtis Creek falls plummets 153 feet, while the one on York Creek makes a quieter counterpoint at 50 feet.

Brown and brook trout live in the streams. In the early spring look for wildflowers such as birdsfoot violet, sessile trilliums, and foamflowers. Later on, rhododendron and mountain laurel produce beautiful pink blooms. Spring through fall listen for the melodious repeated phrases of the brown thrasher, Georgia's state bird, in the poplars, white pines, and feathery hemlocks all about.

Russell-Brasstown Scenic Byway

This 38-mile loop begins in the tourist center of Helen, rolls through the forested highlands, and ascends Georgia's highest peak. Take Ga. 75 north from Helen through a thick forest of hemlock, poplar, oak, sumac, and pine. In 5 miles you can pull over on the right side for a stop at **Andrews Cove,** by the cool, clear waters of Andrews Creek. You can picnic here or hike a 2-mile trail that follows a logging road up to the Appalachian Trail. You'll cross the famous Georgia-to-Maine trail in any case once you get back on the main road.

Continue north, forking west at Ga. 180. In a few miles, look on the right for the spur road that climbs **Brasstown Bald.** The 3-mile road makes a steep, zigzagging assault on the state's highest point, hacking its way through rhododendron and laurel. From the parking lot *(fee)* near the top, you'll need to get out and either take a shuttle (operating seasonally) or walk a strenuous half-mile trail to the tip-top. If you come on a clear day—preferably in spring or fall—the view from the 4,784-foot summit is gorgeous.

The Appalachians tumble away in gentle crests of brown and blue in all directions, allowing you to see Georgia, Tennessee, and the Carolinas. The high peak located about 35 miles to the east is Rabun Bald, at 4,643 feet the second highest peak found in Georgia. The mountains are a dense mass off to the south, in the heart of the Chattahoochee National Forest. There is an excellent visitor center up here *(706-896-2556)*, and you have access to a number of worthwhile hiking trails.

Back on the road, continue west on Ga. 180 through the undulating countryside, passing picturesque farmsteads and homes, then turn left (south)

Summer fun along the Chattooga River

on the Richard B. Russell Scenic Highway (Ga. 348). The road now begins climbing, dipping around contours, then climbing again to 3,480-foot Hogpen Gap on the Blue Ridge Divide. Water flowing west of here drains into the Tennessee River and thence to the Mississippi; to the east, streams join with the Chattahoochee, which weaves its way south to the Gulf of Mexico via Florida.

Stay with Ga. 348, pulling to the right for a superb overlook of the 9,113-acre **Raven Cliffs Wilderness** and the sleeping-bear profile of Yonah Mountain to the south. You then descend toward Helen again. In 4.5 miles, the parking lot for **Dukes Creek Falls** *(Parking fee)* lies on the right. A 1-mile trail takes you close to the 300-foot-high falls, or, alternately, you can get a pretty good look

An old barn framing a pond near Brasstown Bald

from the platform just off the parking lot. In about another 2 miles, turn right onto Ga. 75A for the 5,555-acre **Smithgall Woods-Dukes Creek Conservation Area** *(706-878-3087)*, which has 4 miles of woodsy trails. From here it's 3 miles back to Helen.

Vogel State Park

One of Georgia's oldest parks, **Vogel State Park** *(northwest of Helen, and 11 miles S of Blairsville via US 129. 706-745-2628. Adm. fee)* nestles into the base of Blood Mountain upon which, legend holds, a ferocious battle between Creek and Cherokee made the mountain streams run red. Though fairly heavily developed—with a lake, swimming beach, and miniature golf course—the park does offer more than 17 miles of trails. Not far from the camping

area the 1-mile **Byron Herbert Reece Nature Trail** makes a nice soft loop through stands of towering hemlocks, oaks, and hickories with interpretive markers to help you find order in the seeming chaos of the woods.

The sheer number of tree species in the forest gives you an appreciation for the ingenuity of nature; red maple, sweet birch, black cherry, mockernut hickory, black locust, American holly, wild dogwood, sourwood, black gum, musclewood, persimmon, Fraser magnolia, and others all have an important place here. Run your fingers through the feathery branches of a hemlock and inhale the delicious resiny odor. Bluebirds make brilliant azure flashes against the forest greenery; woodpeckers hammer away high above; and in high summer scarlet tanagers and

Hiking trail bear warning, Fort Mountain State Park

rose-breasted grosbeaks blend their voices with the year-round denizens. For more walking, take on the 4-mile **Bear Hair Gap Trail,** which also starts near the camping area. It affords captivating views of Brasstown Bald on clear days.

Each year during March and April some 2,000 hikers set off from Springer Mountain with the goal of hiking all 2,150 miles of the **Appalachian Trail** to Maine. But to get to the start of the trail on Springer, they have an 8.3-mile walk from **Amicalola Falls State Park** (*15 miles NW of Dawsonville on Ga. 52. 706-265-4703. Adm. fee*). Amicalola, from the Cherokee word for "tumbling waters," features a 729-foot-high waterfall—the highest east of the Rockies.

A short footpath takes you to the base of the falls, which cascade over a series of lovely rock terraces. Nearby hillsides remain thinned out from 1995's Hurricane Opal, which toppled hundreds of local hardwoods. Wander off the path to find wild iris and pink lady's slipper blooming in spring. Also look for belted kingfishers hunting salamanders, crayfish, and insects along the creek and reflecting pool, and try to spot the drill holes of sapsuckers in trees along the trail.

Several other trails explore the 1,021-acre park, including a 5-mile walk to the new **Len Foote Hike Inn** (*Reservations, 800-864-7275*), a rustic lodge accessible only by foot. Of the backpackers who set off fresh and fully loaded from Amicalola Falls for the famed AT, only 10 percent complete the five-month trek all the way to Maine; some 20 percent call it quits after the first week. Hike some of the steep trails around here, and you will understand why.

About 40 miles west of Amicalola, **Fort Mountain State Park** (*8 miles E of Chatsworth on Ga. 52. 706-695-2621. Adm. fee*) harbors a mysterious 855-foot-long rock wall, likely dating back 2,000 years to Woodland Indians who used it either as a fortification or a ceremonial site. Several other theories have been advanced, including the remote possibility that an early group of whites built the wall and were later killed or adopted by local tribes. Supporters point to Cherokee tales of "moon-eyed people" and to the legendary 12th-century Welsh Prince Madoc, who supposedly landed with 200 countrymen near Mobile.

What is certain is that the fort now anchors a beautiful 3,520-acre parcel atop Fort Mountain. The quarter-mile **Old Fort Trail** ascends from the parking area through a hardwood and shortleaf pine forest to the wall, much of it covered with vegetation. Walk past a stone lookout tower and take a short path to the left, which brings you to a wonderful overlook of mountains rippling away in topographical detail to the north and the farmlands and broad valley surrounding Chatsworth and Dalton to the west.

Off in the distance is the long back of Lookout Mountain. The 1.3-mile **Old Fort Loop** will carry you around the front of Fort Mountain, or you can walk back the same way you came.

One of the Chattahoochee's most valuable assets is the 36,977-acre **Cohutta Wilderness** (*Cohutta Ranger District, 706-695-6736*) in the northwest part of the forest. Coupled with the contiguous 8,082-acre Big Frog Wilderness in Tennessee's Cherokee National Forest, the Cohutta offers more than 70 square miles of roadless designated wilderness.

Only hikers and horses are allowed to enter this tract—no motorized vehicles or equipment and no bikes, carts, or wagons. Timber harvesting is not allowed, although 70 percent of the area was logged between 1915 and 1930. Many of the current trails traverse old railbeds and logging roads. But in keeping with a primitive environment, there are few signs or markers. You're on your own in these big, wild woods. It's advisable to obtain a map from the ranger district office before you wander in too far. ■

American Chestnuts

Once the king of the forest, the great American chestnut so dominated eastern woodlands that one in four trees was a chestnut. It grew to more than 100 feet tall; its nuts provided food for wildlife, and its wood was used for cabins, fence posts, and tool handles. In 1904 an Asian fungus hit chestnuts in the New York City area. Within a span of 20 years the blight had ravaged trees in a 1,000-mile radius. Two decades later the chestnut was virtually eliminated from the forest.

Yet the American chestnut has not completely vanished. Saplings still sprout from the stumps of long-dead chestnuts, sometimes growing to a height of 20 feet before succumbing to the blight. Researchers have had some success in crossing the American chestnut with Asian species to produce a blight-resistant hybrid suitable as an ornamental shade tree and nut provider. Though they may never again dominate the forest, these chestnut trees carry on the genetic inheritance of their forerunners.

Cloudland Canyon State Park

■ 2,500 acres ■ Northwest Georgia, 8 miles southeast of Trenton on Ga. 136
■ Year-round ■ Hiking, wildlife viewing ■ Adm. fee, except Wed. ■ Contact
the park, 122 Cloudland Canyon Park Rd., Rising Fawn, GA 30738; phone
706-657-4050. www.georgiastateparks.org

ONE OF THE MOST DRAMATIC VISTAS in the southern Appalachians is preserved at this state park, where you have an opportunity to see the work
wrought by geologic forces over hundreds of millions of years. On the
western lip of Lookout Mountain, streams slowly eroded layers of shale
and sandstone laid down when this area was at the bottom of an ancient
sea. The resulting 1,000-foot-deep canyon is a wonder of craggy cliffs,
exposed rock layers, and roaring waterfalls. Cloudland Canyon sits on
the southeast corner of the Cumberland Plateau, which parallels the Blue
Ridge off to the east. It is so rugged that until Ga. 136 was completed in
1939, the only way in was by roads from Tennessee or Alabama.

Park in the main lot and stroll out to the **Canyon Overlook** for the
finest views in the park. The ledge forms a point, from which you can
see how Bear Creek (on the right) joins with Daniel Creek to form Sitton
Gulch, which cleaves its way off the west side of Lookout Mountain,
forming a great U-shaped valley. Notice the steep sandstone bluffs up on
the valley shoulders; the floor of Lookout Valley is limestone. Walk along
the low fence around both sides of the point, drinking in the changing
views to the north and west. Scrub pines cling to ledges at dizzying
heights, cliff swallows dart from rocky perches, and the noise of falling
water is lofted up from Daniel Creek on your left. It's nearly impossible
to resist the siren call of the waterfalls.

A newly rebuilt **trail** of a little more than half a mile takes you into
the canyon, under an overhanging rock, and down to a creek bed lined
with rhododendron, laurel, and hemlock. The waterfall off to the left
drops 50 feet into a bouldery amphitheater of cold, limpid water. Mosses
and ferns, well watered by the constant mist, grip the damp rock walls. A
swift stream, **Daniel Creek** splashes down from here over mini-falls and
into curling eddies. In spring and summer look closely for yellow marsh
marigolds, violet wild geraniums, white trilliums, blue morning glories,
azaleas, mayapples, and purple columbines. The second waterfall lies
0.4 mile down the creek, reached by an amazing series of stairways that
seem to go on forever. It's well worth the huffing and puffing, though,
because this waterfall is even louder and more dramatic.

Plunging 100 feet, a giant's faucet pours out into a giant's tub, huge
clouds of spray boiling up and floating all the way to the observation
platform some 200 feet away. Over time, the waterfalls have cut back into
the soft layers of sedimentary rock, receding uphill as their ledges wear
away. Eventually, the slopes will smooth out and the creek will run without the defining punctuation of the falls.

Spring blooms, Cloudland Canyon State Park

On the way back up the hill you can pick up the 4.8-mile **West Rim Trail,** which crosses the creek above the falls and continues to the west rim for more fine views from a different perspective. The trail loops around to a view from the west side of the mountain, where you can see Lookout Valley, the town of Trenton, and an almost infinite space.

When you get back to the parking lot, drive down to the swimming pool and take the short trail out to the **wildlife viewing area.** Clover, wheat, and rye have been planted around a small pond to attract deer, rabbits, turkeys, foxes, quail, and other animals. You can watch them from a 15-foot observation tower. The food plots supplement the soft mast available in the Appalachian forests—the vitamin- and carbohydrate-rich fruits and berries from dogwood, persimmon, holly, and muscadine—and the protein-loaded hard mast from acorns, beechnuts, walnuts, and hickory nuts. While watching for animals, listen for others that might be in the verge of the woods—the scratchy whooing of the barred owl, the tapping of the pileated woodpecker, and the repeated whistling of cardinals, Eastern towhees, and tufted titmice. Late afternoons often bring nibblers out to this lovely garden spot. ■

Crockford-Pigeon Wildlife Management Area

■ 16,396 acres ■ Northwest Georgia, west of LaFayette 2.5 miles on Ga. 193, then left on Chamberlain Rd. 3 miles, and right on Rocky Lane Rd. for 0.5 mile to check station ■ Year-round ■ Hiking, wildlife viewing ■ Contact Georgia Wildlife Resources Division, 2592 Floyd Springs Rd., N.W., Armuchee, GA 30105; phone 706-295-6041

THIS PRIMITIVE CUMBERLAND PLATEAU area has some of the wildest, most gorgeous scenery around and is well worth the extra effort it takes to get there. More than 30 miles of trails traverse the steep, timbered hills of Pigeon Mountain, a thumblike extension on the east side of Lookout Mountain. Pick up a map at the **check station** and head out on the mile-long **Rock Town Trail** through a forest of hardwoods and Virginia pines; deer browse on blueberries and wild turkeys strut through the openings.

Within a short time, you will come to Rock Town, a 40-acre maze of sandstone formations, some as high as 30 feet. Like nearby Rock City—minus the development—this giant playland offers plenty of room for scrambling, exploring, and overlooking. In spring the blooms of mountain laurel, iris, and other flowers add pizzazz to the scene.

An unadvertised karst area at the base of the mountain features several flowery coves and deep caves, the latter suitable for experienced spelunkers only. Also, be aware that the wildlife management area is a hunting preserve: Call ahead to find out about hunting seasons, and pay attention to postings at the check station kiosk. ■

Herbal Healing

Many of the plants you see on walks through the southern forests have been used for countless generations, first by Native Americans and later by settlers, to cure illness. Some early explorers were impressed by the effectiveness of Indian curatives; others have been more skeptical. Working for the U.S. Bureau of American Ethnology, James Mooney in 1890 compared Cherokee medicinal plants with those listed in the *United States Dispensatory,* the standard pharmaceutical directory. Most were either not listed or used incorrectly according to the *Dispensatory.* But the number of plants he compared was very small—only 20.

Black cherry tree

A Cherokee medicine man, or shaman, on the other hand, had a working knowledge of hundreds of plant species. Medical practice for the Cherokee, Catawba, and others was not merely a matter of doling out remedies to the sick. They had no germ theory. Their healing arts were closely entwined with religion, ceremony, and legend.

Disease came about, according to a Cherokee story, because men grew so populous they began crowding out other species. The animals then got together and decided to inflict people with sickness; the plants sided with people, offering cures. So the job of the medicine man was to figure out which animal spirit was responsible for a particular illness, then to match it with the appropriate plant remedy. A rabbit spirit, for example, might cause dysentery and worms; a drink made from the boiled root of wild roses—rabbit food—could help. The way the medicine was collected, prepared, and administered also played a vital role in the cure. Incantations, crystals, and masks comforted patients and increased their faith in the healer.

There were remedies for everything from rattlesnake bite and paralysis to hemorrhoids, dandruff, sore nipples, and warts. For backaches, the Cherokee and other Indians drank a tea made from the aromatic herb spikenard. Inner bark of the black cherry, boiled in water, was prescribed for labor pains. So effective was this cure that it was listed in another official reference book, *Pharmacopoeia,* in 1820 and is still recognized as a sedative.

Also making the *Pharmacopoeia* was the persimmon fruit, for treating bloody stools. Boiling geranium root with wild grape made a good mouthwash tonic for thrush, yet another cure adopted by whites. Other common plants found in a Cherokee medicine man's kit included sassafras root, elm leaves, cedar chips, and cockleburs.

Russell Cave National Monument

■ 310 acres ■ Northeast Alabama, 8 miles northwest of Bridgeport via
Cty .Rds. 75 and 98 ■ Year-round ■ Hiking, spelunking ■ Contact the
monument, 3729 Cty. Rd. 98, Bridgeport, AL 35740; phone 256-495-2672.
www.nps.gov/ruca

FOR THOUSANDS OF YEARS the green valleys and wooded slopes of the
southern Appalachians have provided people with bounteous resources:
mushrooms from the forest floors, wild grapes, red mulberries, the fruits
of dogwood and basswood, roots, bulbs, sun-dried lichens, chestnuts and
beechnuts, the flesh of deer, squirrels, rabbits, and myriad other creatures.
A rich harvest year after year made the living good for the early Indians
who entered the Russell Cave area about 10,000 years ago. Besides food,
the forest provided everything else they needed—clothes, medicine, stone
tools, wooden implements, and weapons.

Tucked into a remote, hilly corner of Alabama, Russell Cave National
Monument is one of the region's smaller parks, but a visit will leave you
with a real appreciation for early humans' dependence upon their imme-
diate surroundings. Russell Cave was perfectly situated to house 15 to 30
people. A spring-fed creek flows into the adjacent cave, providing a ready

Family of hikers at Russell Cave National Monument

source of water; 6 miles away, the Tennessee River is thick with fish. The cave mouth faces east, letting in morning sunlight and warmth. The ceiling is about 20 feet high, allowing for good ventilation of air and smoke, and the floor measures a comfortable 100 by 150 feet.

Outside was a veritable grocery and hardware store: In addition to trees and plants, there was chert for spear points, scrapers, and knives. Harder stones served for grinding seeds or roots, cracking nuts, and sharpening bones. Countless generations of cave dwellers merely covered over their refuse, leaving layers of treasure for future archaeologists.

In the 1950s, excavations by the Smithsonian Institution and the National Geographic Society to a depth of 32 feet uncovered thousands of stone and bone tools, bits of pottery, and other artifacts indicating that the cave had been occupied off and on for some 9,000 years, often as a winter hunting camp. Parts of nine skeletons have been unearthed, from an infant to a mature woman. The cave provides one of the most complete records of prehistoric Indian culture from the Paleo-Indian period up through the Archaic and Woodland and into the Mississippian period, though by this time (A.D. 1000) cave use was sporadic. Other than a 30-foot-square excavation area, this breathtakingly long record of human occupation has been preserved intact. And nearly all the same plants and animals still live on the surrounding wooded bluffs.

Archaic Indian culture diorama, Russell Cave National Monument

What to See and Do

Begin your visit with a film and a look at the exhibits in the small but informative **visitor center.** Original artifacts and reproductions of drills, baskets, atlatls, and many other tools offer a good introduction to Archaic Indian culture. Then take the **boardwalk** outside that leads to the cave.

Try to forget the modern trail and picnic area; instead imagine approaching the cave as it was thousands of years ago—wood smoke coming from the mossy overhang, the smell of cooking venison, the bubbling of the stream, the chipping sound of stone on stone. Within the cave, mannequins posed in various activities may help you travel back

in time. A ranger is also on hand to answer your questions.

Russell Cave is one of 1,527 caves in Jackson County, where porous limestone created 300 million years ago at the bottom of an inland sea has been gradually eaten away by streams and trickling rainwater. Formerly at stream level, the floor of the cave was raised by rock falls from the ceiling, leaving it high and dry. Over the millennia, the floor has risen in this way some 30 feet. Spelunking permits, available from a park ranger at the visitor center, allow cavers to explore about 2 miles of an extensive cave system.

A 0.6-mile interpretive **nature trail** courses around a sinkhole strewn with boulders and into the woods, with panels outlining the ways prehistoric Indians utilized the forest resources. They made tea from sassafras roots and beer by soaking and fermenting the seed-pods of black locusts. From hickories came nuts, as well as a tough dense wood for shelter poles, spear shafts, and tool handles.

Continue zigzagging up the side of the mountain on the 1.2-mile **hiking trail,** lined in spring with wildflowers and blooming redbuds. A view of the verdant valley to the east gives you an idea of the kind of land that awaited nearby when hunting-gathering culture slowly shifted to a more settled, agricultural lifestyle.

Upon request, rangers demonstrate skills such as fire building, flint knapping, fishhook crafting, grinding, and cordage making to illustrate the challenges that early residents faced. Visitors are allowed to try their hand with a pump drill or a bow. A junior ranger program adds excitement for children, who enjoy a chance to throw the spear and can earn a badge and certificate by answering questions related to Russell Cave and its inhabitants. ■

Sequoyah Caverns

■ Northeast Alabama, 6 miles north of Valley Head on US 11, then 1.5 miles west ■ Year-round; open weekends only, Dec.-Feb. ■ Cave tour ■ Adm. fee ■ Contact the caverns, 1438 Cty. Rd. 731, Valley Head, AL 35989; phone 256-635-0024 or 800-843-5098. www.sequoyahcaverns.com

RUNNING FROM NORTH ALABAMA up into Kentucky is a jumbled, hilly zone of karst topography—a region of caverns, springs, sinks, arches, and underground streams. This porous, potholed countryside is the handiwork of acidic groundwater trickling through the limestone bedrock for thousands of years. The commercially operated Sequoyah Caverns is an easy place to sample some of the fantastic world beneath the surface.

On the 45- to 60-minute guided tour visitors pass through a series of lighted rooms spread over a quarter mile. The caves stay a constant 60°F; the highest point on the ceiling is about 120 feet up. Stalagmites, stalactites, columns, curtains, and flowstone are among the more noteworthy formations. But the most remarkable feature of the caverns is the presence of pools containing pure mineral water so still and reflective that it creates optical illusions. A waterfall appears to flow upward; a bridge seems to cross a space with a vast room both above and below; a canyon looks as if it extends hundreds of yards. Smaller, rimmed pools resemble little fairy landscapes that mirror ancient formations.

The original name, Looking Glass Caverns, was changed to honor Cherokee scholar and alphabet-inventor Sequoyah, who taught in the area in the early 1800s. A cave column bears the inscription "Sam Houston, 1830," although it has never been conclusively linked to the famous frontiersman, Indian agent, and President of the Republic of Texas. ■

Falls at DeSoto State Park

DeSoto State Park

■ 3,000 acres ■ Northeast Alabama, 8 miles northeast of Fort Payne on Cty. Rd. 89 ■ Year-round ■ Hiking, bird-watching, wildflower viewing ■ Contact the park, 13883 Cty. Rd. 89, Fort Payne, AL 35967; phone 256-845-0051. www.mentone.com/desoto

BEGINNING AT CHATTANOOGA, TENNESSEE, the flat-topped ridge of **Lookout Mountain** runs 100 miles, its sandstone cap supporting a vibrant pine- and hardwood forest. DeSoto State Park is located just north of Little River Canyon National Preserve atop Lookout Mountain, whose eastern side falls away into the deep gorge of the Little River. Hernando DeSoto and his expedition passed through this region in 1540 on their quest for gold. During the Civil War, Union troops on the way to join General Sherman in Georgia found the canyon an unwelcome challenge.

The area has remained relatively peaceful since then, a rough beauty hidden away from the reach of high-gloss tourism. The **Lookout Mountain Parkway** passes through the north part of the park, bringing with it some vacation cottages and stores, but not enough to spoil the genuinely rural feel of this old-fashioned state park. You may find the forest still recovering from a January 2000 ice storm that snapped hundreds of trees, offering competing species a chance to have their time in the sun.

Pick up maps and information at the lodge or country store. Adjacent to the store you'll find a **nature center** with mounted animals, live snakes, and other displays. From here you can step out onto a 12-mile network of hiking and biking trails. Boardwalks, bridges, and paths wind through the forest, past unusual rock formations and by some 15 waterfalls. In May and June, banks of rhododendron and mountain laurel turn the woods into a rosy, sweet-smelling garden. Wild dogwood and redbud contribute tones of white and purple. More than 650 species of wildflowers add to the symphony of color, including yellow-flowering jasmine, pink lady's slipper, blue iris, and golden club. In secluded little havens, bogs of sphagnum moss grow endangered green pitcher plants, whose champagne-flute mouths lure insects to their death.

Across the road, wander along the West Fork Little River and find a picnic spot next to a quiet, rockbound pool or a bubbling rapid. All kinds of birds use the updrafts for soaring and the wetland habitats for feeding. Look for hawks, ravens, and eagles, as well as herons. The most spectacular waterfall, **DeSoto Falls,** is 6 miles north of the country store, just a mile off County Road 89 at the end of Cty. Rd. 613. It spills 100 feet from a fern-draped upper terrace to its rock-rimmed plunge pool. ∎

Little River Canyon National Preserve

∎ 14,000 acres ∎ Northeast Alabama, just south of DeSoto State Park via Ala. 35 ∎ Year-round ∎ Hiking, rock climbing, kayaking, fishing, bird-watching ∎ Contact the preserve, 2141 Gault Ave. N., Fort Payne, AL 35967; phone 256-845-9605. www.nps.gov/liri

SLICING ITS WAY ALONG the east side of the Lookout Mountain plateau, the Little River is considered the nation's longest mountaintop river. Through layers of sandstone, shale, and limestone, the river has cut a 500-foot-deep canyon, the deepest one in the South. Little River Canyon, which is difficult to reach, easily ranks as one of the South's great untouched wild places, a burly paradise of high bluffs cut by tributary creeks, rock outcrops that offer views of roaring rapids and reclusive waterfalls, and woods where rare plants grow unseen.

Established in 1992, the national preserve still has a rough-edged feel, but with more facilities and trails planned for the future, a good time to visit is right now. In this raw wilderness, you can get a whiff of the untamed southern forests and rocky gorges of precolonial America.

Flowing for 30 undammed miles, the Little River collects water from approximately 200 square miles in northwestern Georgia and northeastern Alabama, and funnels it into the Weiss Lake impoundment below the south end of the preserve. The river's showcase, the canyon measures 12 miles long and contains several very different habitats. Along the rim spreads an upland forest of pine, oak, and hickory, understoried by dogwood, sassafras, sourwood, viburnum, and black gum.

You can't miss the springtime bouquets of rhododendron, but you'll have to hunt a bit to find the low-bush blueberries. Come fall, the colors burnish the cliff tops to a deep fiery glow. In the cliffs and rock outcrops, Virginia pines and vaccinium have spread roots into the thin soil. Rare green salamanders hide in rock crevices or rotting trees during the day; you'll have an easier time spotting prickly pear and yucca.

Down on the lower slopes and bottomlands, yellow poplar, sycamore, white ash, and white oak grow in abundance, shading an understory of red maple, birch, beech, and magnolia. Masses of royal ferns create lacy, miniature forests along the stream banks, while hatpins, pimpernels, and other unusual wildflowers peer above the moist humus. In secluded coves up and down the river, endangered blue shiners swim, and Kral's water plantain—an aquatic perennial found only in northern Alabama—grows in its small but enviably scenic niche.

What to See and Do

There is no visitor center yet; you can start wherever you like. One obvious point of entry is from the north side, about 10 miles south of DeSoto State Park via County Road 89 and Ala. 35. Cross the Little River bridge and pull into the parking lot on the right for a visit to the impressive **Little River Falls.** A short paved trail leads to the pounding 45-foot-high cataract, its mist clouds illuminated by streaming shafts of sunlight.

Drive back to the west side and turn left (south) onto Ala. 176 to begin the 23-mile **Canyon Rim Scenic Drive,** a narrow, twisting, turning high road with ebullient canyon vistas. The road is paved, but the going is often steep and slow. The sheer walls and churning rapids are a blessing for rock climbers and kayakers. The lower portion of the river is a special challenge. Contact the preserve for more information, as the rapids are Class III to VI and therefore suitable for experts only.

Numerous overlooks offer varying vantage points on the big boulder-tossed river, the frothy chutes, and the canyon walls with their multicolored layers of sedimentary rock. About 2 miles down, pause for **Mushroom** (or Needle Eye) **Rock,** a 15-foot-high slotted rock formation in the middle of the road. Among the marked points of interest, **Canyon View** is a must stop for some of the most breathtaking views into the roiling river and a good angle on the steep cut-in made by Wolfe Creek, to your right. Hawks, vultures, and the occasional bald eagle

Bat Cave

The newly renamed **Sauta Cave National Wildlife Refuge** (just W of Scottsboro, off US 72. 256-350-6639) helps preserve an age-old phenomenon. Go there at dusk during the summer and behold the sky around the cave speckled with endangered gray and Indiana bats: Up to a quarter million fly out to hunt insects.

Bats maneuver in the dark by means of echolocation; they emit a series of supersonic sounds (up to 60 squeaks per second) that bounce off objects and come back like sonar signals to the bats' highly evolved ears. They sometimes scoop insects into their wings or tail, then do midair somersaults to gobble them up while flying. Hundreds of thousands of tons of crop-destroying pests are eradicated in this way every year.

Elf orpine, Little River Canyon National Preserve

glide and circle up here, their shadows racing along the canyon walls. A little farther on, pull over for a view of **Grace's High Falls,** which (seasonally) spills 200 feet from a nook far above Bear Creek. The road now swings some distance to the west to skirt the Bear Creek side canyon.

At the halfway point, **Eberhart Point,** you have the option of heading back to civilization on Ala. 176 or pressing on. The final 11 miles are steeper and rougher. This part of the route should not be attempted by trucks, trailers, or RVs. But if you have the time and the car, go ahead. Way down below the blue-green river curls like a great undulating serpent.

Eberhart Point is also a good place for a view of colorful kayaks far below, and for a quick walk down to the river. The .75-mile (one way) **Eberhart Point Trail** drops through the woods to an old access road that soon becomes thickly carpeted with grass. It's a short, but quite steep trail, punctuated with benches if you feel yourself in need of a rest.

Notice how the roar of the wind dwindles as you descend, replaced by the riffling flow of the river. An unmarked trail of sorts heads downriver from here, an adventurous scramble over rocks and roots and vines; sample it for an idea of the possibilities in the wilderness all around.

Back at your car, continue down the canyon, following the river as it widens. **Canyon Mouth Park** at the southern end has a big picnic area and plenty of space for rambling along the river. A trail heads north to **Johnnies Creek,** an easy mile away. Here you can fish for bass, bluegill, crappie, and catfish. Or if you find yourself in a more reflective mood, just sit back and listen to the songbirds above your head and the steady rhythm of the river at your feet. ■

Wheeler National Wildlife Refuge

■ 34,700 acres ■ Northern Alabama, between Decatur and Huntsville; visitor center 2 miles west of I-65 on Ala. 67 ■ Year-round ■ Hiking, boating, fishing, bird-watching, wildlife viewing ■ Contact the refuge, 2700 Refuge Headquarters Rd., Decatur, AL 35603; phone 256-353-7243. wheeler.fws.gov

EVERY WINTER TENS OF THOUSANDS of migrating ducks, geese, and other waterfowl come flapping and honking into this Tennessee River refuge to eat, nest, and idle. Cupped within the Tennessee River Valley, the area stays warmer than the highlands all around. One of Alabama's largest refuges, the Wheeler encompasses wetlands, hardwood bottomlands, pine uplands, shorelines, and fields—a great variety of managed ecosystems that attract 285 bird species, 47 mammal species, and numerous reptiles, amphibians, and fish. Ten federally threatened or endangered species regularly visit the refuge. Farmers who lease the refuge fields leave part of their wheat and other grain for the hungry birds. The sheer variety and abundance of the migrating birds that hole up here for the winter is astounding. Among the 32 kinds of waterfowl to be found in fall and winter are Canada geese, snow geese, mallards, wood ducks, black ducks, green-winged teal, wigeons, mersangers, pintails, and buffleheads.

After the waterfowl have gone, migratory songbirds begin piling in. By April, wildflowers are at their peak. In the slow, hot days of summer, only resident animals remain; among the more notable are turtles, alligators, deer, great egrets, and green herons. Purple martins and other swallows begin the fall migration in August. Headed ultimately to South America, they zip and swirl through the air in flocks, swooping to catch insects. Look for their glossy purple bodies and forked tails. Then, as early as late September, arriving geese signal the annual mass meeting of waterfowl, which will peak in late December.

What to See and Do

The **visitor center** (*Closed Sun.-Mon., March-Sept.*) is a good first stop. Displays, handouts, and a video will help you plan your outing. An **observation building** and the short **Atkeson Trail** just outside offer a chance to spot wildlife in the wetlands and forest edges.

The one-way viewing window in the observation building makes you invisible to the 10,000 ducks that enliven the scene every winter evening. Canada geese come in impressive numbers as well, along with a few sandhill cranes. In other seasons look for butterflies and hummingbirds in the specially planted areas; purple martins find shelter in hanging gourds, and red-tailed hawks make use of unoccupied osprey platforms.

Across the road, the 1.5-mile **Flint Creek Environmental Trail** makes a nice easy loop lined with pond cypresses, tulip poplars, and silver maples. You'll likely see wading birds, songbirds, turtles, and fish. Just ten minutes south of the visitor center, look for the 2-mile (one way) **Dancy Bottoms Trail** *(N side of Redbanks Rd.)* through a little-visited hardwood floodplain full of 150-year-old trees. On the north side of the refuge, just off I-565, the 1-mile **Beaverdam Swamp Boardwalk** courses through the state's northernmost tupelo-cypress swamp. ■

Bankhead National Forest

■ 180,000 acres ■ Northwest Alabama, district office in Double Springs ■ Year-round ■ Camping, hiking, fishing ■ Adm. fee ■ Contact Bankhead Ranger District, P.O. Box 278, S. Main St., Double Springs, AL 35553; phone 205-489-5111

ROLLING OVER THE FOOTHILLS just west of the Appalachians, this big national forest holds limestone canyons, sandstone bluffs, purling streams, lakes hidden within deep woods, the state's largest designated wilderness, and its only wild and scenic river. Sprawling over former agricultural lands, a healthy forest grew here and was managed for timber production. Recent years, however, have seen a shift away from timber management and toward restoration of the native ecosystem. Hardwoods are now growing on erstwhile loblolly plantations, shortleaf pines have been preserved, and rare tracts of longleaf pine have been not only maintained but even expanded. Within the Bankhead's sheltering arms, deer, raccoons, wild turkeys, neotropical songbirds, beavers, otters, and other animals find refuge. Among rare animals that live here are threatened Indiana and gray bats, which swarm from the mouths of caves at dusk.

Tree lichen, Bankhead National Forest

Waterfall and sinkhole, Sipsey Fork

What to See and Do

The 25,000-acre **Sipsey Wilderness** harbors stands of hardwoods that line twisting creeks, craggy coves, and bluffs. The picnic area 5 miles west of Ala. 33 on County Road 60 makes a fine place for a day or half-day excursion into the wilderness, which spreads north of the road. The **Sipsey River Trail** skirts the right side of the wild and scenic **Sipsey Fork,** crosses Borden Creek, and hooks to the northwest for several miles, through a forest of yellow poplar, hemlock, beech, oak, hickory, and stunning wild azalea and laurel.

In spring and fall you can hear the warbles and flutes of songbirds and thrushes. The rare Alabama streak-sorus fern noses out of rock crevices. A pileated woodpecker taps a dead branch for beetles while the sun spangles coins of light on the quiet forest floor and braids golden threads into the whispering river, sluicing its way around the next bend. Outcroppings provide vantage points and rock shelters give off refreshing blasts of cool air as you pass.

You can also walk along the riverbank south of the road. Not recognizing the wilderness boundaries, the forest here looks the same. The Sipsey widens as it journeys south. At this point, though, you could easily throw a stone across its 50- to 75-foot width.

The picnic area serves as a point of entry for delightful canoe trips; the river meanders for several scenic miles before crossing Ala. 33. To visit a less frequented section of the wilderness, drive about 5 miles west on Ala. 33 to the **Randolph Trailhead** for the **Randolph** and **Rippey trails.** You can make a loop by heading out on the Randolph, picking up the Sipsey River Trail, then returning along the Rippey. You'll almost certainly have long stretches of wild woods all to yourself. During hunting season, it's a good idea to wear a bright orange jacket.

Another pretty area is found on the western edge of the wilderness, north of County Road 60 about 3 miles on County Road 23. Just beyond the county line and Hubbard Creek lie a waterfall and swimming hole at **Kinlock Spring.** It takes more effort to get to the 33-acre **Brushy Lake** area, 5 miles east of Ala. 33 on Pine Torch Road. But you'll be rewarded by this heart-of-the-forest jewel tucked amid rock bluffs and shaded trails.

Several developed areas south of US 278 are easily accessible for visitors who want a taste of the Bankhead's more civilized attractions. The **Clear Creek** and **Corinth Recreation Areas** offer trailer camping, fishing, and skiing on **Lewis Smith Lake.** A somewhat quieter respite is available at the **Houston Recreation Area** (*via Cty. Rd. 63*), located on one of the many arms of the lake.

About 15 miles west of Double Springs on US 278, you'll find **Natural Bridge** (*205-486-5330; Adm. fee*), an impressive 148-foot sandstone arch thousands of years old. A trail winds through gardens of wild mountain laurels, magnolias, hemlocks, ferns, and snowball bushes to explore the base and top of the six-story-tall bridge. ∎

Cheaha State Park

■ 2,799 acres ■ Northeast Alabama, 29 miles south of Anniston on Ala. 281
■ Year-round ■ Hiking, rock climbing, swimming, fishing, wildlife viewing
■ Adm. fee ■ Contact the park, 19644 Ala. 281, Delta, AL 36258; phone 256-
488-5111. www.dcnr.state.al.us/Parks/state_parks_index_1a.html

AS THE APPALACHIANS FADE AWAY in northern Alabama, they make a final
thrust skyward on Cheaha Mountain. From a Creek Indian word for
"high," Cheaha (CHEE-HA) rises to 2,405 feet, the highest point in the
state. Lofty perches within the park let you see far beyond the low-lying
hills all around. And because the park lies within Talladega National Forest, the views are unadulterated by evidence of civilization. To gaze at
nothing but forest and plains disappearing into a distant haze in every
direction has become a rare privilege in the Southeast.

The Civilian Conservation Corps turned the mountaintop into a state
park in the 1930s and '40s, building a lodge, cabins, reservoir, observation
tower, and winding road using only native stone, hand tools, and mules.
Other than that, there's almost no commercial development up here, a
fact you'll greatly appreciate on the trails or over a plate of mountain
trout at the lodge's restaurant with an unobstructed view to the west. A
new observation deck offers the same splendid views alfresco.

What to See and Do

You can pick up a park brochure
and map at the country store, then
begin driving the 2.5-mile **Bunker
Loop,** which circles the top of the
mountain. Pull over for the **observation tower** and climb up to add
about 65 feet to Cheaha's height.
The timbered hills stretch far away
in panoramic splendor, shifting
from a dark green to a smoky blue
near the horizon because of the
volume of water vapor released by
the miles of dense vegetation.

On extremely clear days in fall,
winter, and early spring the air
may be sharp enough for you to
see for more than 50 miles from
the top of the tower. This venera-
ble structure—as well as the ten
rustic cabins—is slated for renova-
tion, a project that will adhere to

the original CCC plans without
neglecting modern comforts.

Continue on the one-way
counterclockwise road until you
come to the quarter-mile **Bald
Rock Trail,** an easy loop through
a scrubby, boulder-dotted forest
of pines, chestnut oaks, and hickories. Within a few minutes you'll
have breathtaking westward views
of lush green hills and vales. A new
1,520-foot handicap-accessible
boardwalk parallels the old Bald
Rock Trail, making it a bit easier
to obtain the same fine views. The
park also plans to renovate the
nearby Bald Rock Lodge.

Drive on around and park for
the half-mile (one way) **Pulpit
Rock Trail,** offering more topflight
views to the west and south. You

Rappelling at Cheaha State Park

Death Cap

Most of the hundreds of species of mushrooms found in the Southeast are innocuous if not edible. Some species—artist's fungus and shaggy mane, for example—are quite beautiful. Several others, however, are poisonous, even deadly!

If you plan to do any mushroom hunting, you should familiarize yourself with these right off. Unlike most plants, mushrooms and other fungi do not photosynthesize; instead, they draw carbohydrates from living or decaying vegetation. In return, they furnish their hosts with minerals. To reproduce, the mushroom releases single-celled spores, in many species located in the gills or in microscopic tubes underneath the cap. The spores travel on air currents and, finding suitable ground, put down a network of tiny filaments that can last for years as a kind of root structure for the growing of mushrooms.

The mushroom kingdom's most notorious family, the amanita, have such a benign appearance that they are often mistaken for edible mushrooms. They have caused more deaths than any other kind of mushroom. They grow about half a hand high, have an umbrella-shaped cap with gills, and often have a skirtlike ring around the stalk. The aptly named destroying angel has a lovely pure-white color and can be found in oak and pine woods, especially after heavy summer rains. A white-stippled orange cap gives the fly agaric a fairyland appearance. Chewing a small amount causes hallucinations; too much can kill. Oddly, the Caesar's mushroom—

Death cap mushroom

also an amanita—looks much like the fly agaric, yet it makes a nice addition to salads.

The most lethal of all the mushrooms, *A. phalloides,* or death cap, is distinguishable by its grayish green to pale white color; it grows commonly in fertile soil under deciduous trees from summer to fall. Cooking or drying the death cap does not destroy its toxins, and there is no known antitoxin.

What would happen if you ate half a cap? For the first several hours, nothing. Then you would begin feeling sick to your stomach. After two or three days of terrible vomiting and diarrhea, your condition would actually improve somewhat. But meanwhile, your liver and kidneys would start to fail. After a week in the hospital, which could involve convulsions, coma, a liver transplant, and massive doses of penicillin and other drugs, you might live—although probably with some permanent impairment. Advances in medical treatment in the last few decades have increased the survival rate from a mere 10 percent to about 75 percent.

Wild mushrooms, anyone?

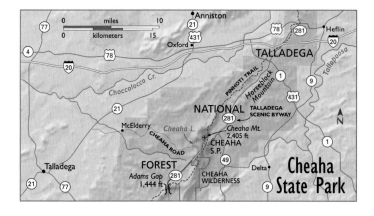

can sit or lie out on a cliff and take vicarious flight while watching hawks and buzzards ride the updrafts welling from the valley floor. On cloudless days you almost feel as if you're floating in a warm universe of blue and green.

The very short **Rock Garden Trail,** just off the native wildflower garden, takes you to an overlook of a cliff that's good for rock climbing. You can also continue down the hill about a mile to **Cheaha Lake.** In spring you'll pass by blooming thickets of laurels and patches of bluebells, wild indigos, and fragrant goldenrods. The trail is quite steep, descending about 1,000 feet, but bring along your bathing suit and reward yourself with a dip in the lake and a relaxing spell on the sandy beach.

The lake was hand-dug by CCC workers using pickaxes and mule-drawn carts; some of the original tools are on display in the CCC museum beside the observation tower. The nature center across the road from the park store is closed for the time being, but you can arrange for ranger-led walks and talks if staffers are available.

To the south of the park stretches the 7,500-acre **Cheaha Wilderness,** off-limits to vehicles and logging. One of the best ways to get to it is by foot on the **Pinhoti Trail,** which runs 105 miles through the national forest from Talladega to Piedmont; more than 14 miles traverse the Cheaha, climbing up and down wooded hills and bluffs and offering plenty of spectacular photo opportunities. There are other trails in the wilderness, but getting to them takes a bit of maneuvering. If you want just a sample of the Pinhoti, start at Adams Gap, at the end of the Talladega Scenic Byway, and hike north. Within a few miles you'll reach some of the best overlooks in the wilderness.

In season, golden asters, blazing stars, and the white flower-clusters of wild hydrangea will brighten your way. Feathery mountain spleenwort peeks from rock crevices and low blueberry bushes grow in clumps on the hillsides. In fall, the red maples and black gums blush to a deep red, standing out against the Virginia pines that cling to ridges and outcrops.

Sunrise, Talladega Scenic Byway

Along creek banks grows a profusion of ferns, including southern lady, royal, and cinnamon. Here and there a flowering dogwood seems to add a touch of civilization to the wilderness. Among animal denizens are deer, bobcats, foxes, weasels, and wood rats. Most of the snakes are nonpoisonous, but you should remember that venomous copperheads, cottonmouths, and timber and pygmy rattlers also live here.

A less intimate but certainly worthwhile way to experience the majestic Cheaha area is to drive the 27-mile **Talladega Scenic Byway,** which runs along Ala. 281 from just west of Heflin to Adams Gap. Twisting up the narrow spine

of Horseblock Mountain, you'll have expansive views of rolling hills to the east, then to the west, across the Coosa River Valley. The route crests at Cheaha State Park, then continues another 7 beautiful miles to Adams Gap, where the pavement finally ends.

At this point, you can reverse direction and go all the way back up to Ala. 281, or pick up curvaceous Cheaha Road, just below the state park, and head west to McElderry and Talladega. This road also makes a dramatic approach to Cheaha Mountain, which looms ever closer as you crest the hills; sometimes the mountaintop plays hide-and-seek with heaps of windblown clouds. ■

Piedmont

Hikers atop Stone Mountain, Georgia

THE PIEDMONT—that supposedly unspectacular zone between the coast and the mountains, the region where everybody lives and works but then leaves for vacation elsewhere—holds a surprising number of green spaces large and small in which wildlife flourishes and the natural order remains in balance. These beauty spots, from precious pocket-sized heritage preserves to sensational 500-square-mile national forests, offer some of the most memorable outdoor escapes in the Southeast. You won't

get high mountaintop views or sunny walks on the beach, but you will see stands of longleaf pine forest tousled by gentle breezes, rivers that gather strength as they run coastward, and broad rock outcrops tucked like hidden gardens into hillsides. And who can forget the sight of a swallowtail butterfly alighting on a bouquet of Queen Anne's lace or the sound of a white-throated sparrow calling at dusk in the autumn woods?

The Piedmont—literally the "foot of the mountain"—runs in a curving band from New Jersey southwest to eastern Alabama, a 70- to 100-mile-wide swath of verdant forests, frothing rivers, trickling streams, and sun-sprayed lakes, as well as highways, cities, towns, fields, and orchards. A vast uplifted peneplain being constantly eroded by streams and rivers, the Piedmont comprises about one-third of South Carolina and Georgia. The eastern slope of the Blue Ridge defines its northwestern border at about 1,500 feet in elevation; the Fall Line, at around 500 feet above sea level, marks its southeastern limit.

If you were to drag your finger along the above map from Cheraw to Columbia, Augusta, Macon, and Columbus, you'd approximate the Fall Line. Within a "fall zone" about 10 miles wide, the region's rivers tumble over rock outcrops, churning into white water, then slowing and calming as they reach the softer soils of the Coastal Plain. These wide rivers—the Great Pee Dee, Santee, Savannah, Ocmulgee, and Chattahoochee, among

others—stream like parallel northwest-to-southeast ribbons, slaking the land and draining into the sea. The Chattahoochee is the only major river to end in the Gulf of Mexico; the others run to the Atlantic.

Just below the Fall Line rise the Sandhills—large remnant windblown dunes created 5 to 65 million years ago when the sea lapped this far inland. At Carolina Sandhills National Wildlife Refuge, you can drive or walk these ancient forested hills. The Piedmont is less sandy and loamy than the Coastal Plain. Hardscrabble farmers in the early 19th century tried to wrest a living from the clay-heavy soil, but it was a losing battle. Ditches became gullies, slopes eroded, and crop returns spiraled downward. Cotton, which did well on the Coastal Plain, fared poorly here. By 1900, the economy had started switching over to textile mills, taking advantage of the region's abundant waterpower. Land that wasn't already farmed was cleared for its timber. In the 1930s the federal government began restoring the forests, and the earth slowly came back to life.

The southern Piedmont is now covered with healthy woodlands that shelter a great variety of songbirds, migratory birds, mammals, and rare plants. In the region's preserves, refuges, forests, and state parks you can walk, paddle, bike, or drive for an hour or several days, discovering intimate details about your natural world that often go unnoticed by travelers intent on the dramas of mountain and shore. ■

Anne Springs Close Greenway

■ 2,000 acres ■ North-central South Carolina, near Fort Mill, 2 miles north of S.C. 160 off US 21 bypass ■ Year-round ■ Hiking, horseback riding, camping ■ Adm. fee ■ Contact the greenway, 250 Springfield Ln., Fort Mill, SC 29716; phone 803-548-7252

DONATED BY A FAMILY that traces its local heritage back to the early 1800s, this jewel-like parcel of forests, lakes, and pastures offers outdoor respite from the hectic pace of nearby Charlotte, North Carolina. In 1780, British General Lord Cornwallis compared the area to an English park, and the same sense of peacefulness pervades the greenway's gentle woods and fields today. In addition to protecting a piece of the Steele Creek watershed, the greenway preserves a section of the old Nation Ford Road, a wagon route built over a key trade artery of the Catawba tribe. A 1780s log cabin and two early 19th-century houses complement the property's natural beauty with reminders of its settler history.

Flowering dogwoods in the fog, Anne Springs Close Greenway

Start out at the **nature center**, where you can touch a video screen or examine photos and mounted animals to help you identify the plants and wildlife outside. Then take the quiet 1.25-mile **Lake Haigler nature trail**, which loops a 30-acre lake fringed by cedars, pines, oaks, and hickories. Geese honk loudly as they swim away, and songbirds chatter in hidden perches. You may catch fleeting glimpses of white-tailed deer, raccoons, and red and gray foxes. Also secreted within the forest, but less visibly, are opossums, beavers, and otters. In the springtime flowering dogwood laces the meadows with white blossoms, while bloodroot paints little snow-white dollops along the ground. All told, more than 200 species of wildflowers bloom here in abundance, including the splashy red of wild azaleas and the pale purple of muscadine grapes.

Leading north, three parallel 1-mile trails cater separately to hikers, cyclists, and horseback riders. Running on or next to the old Nation Ford Road, these paths wind their way past a renovated 1946 dairy barn. A total of more than 32 miles of trails explore the greenway, taking in Steele Creek as well as several wildflower-rimmed ponds. ■

Forty Acre Rock Heritage Preserve

■ 1,567 acres ■ North-central South Carolina, 8 miles south of Pageland on US 601, then right 1.5 miles on Taxahaw Rd. and follow signs to left ■ Best seasons spring and fall ■ Hiking, nature study ■ Contact South Carolina Dept. of Natural Resources Heritage Trust, P.O. Box 167, Columbia, SC 29202; phone 803-734-3894. water.dnr.state.sc.us

IN THE TRANSITION ZONE between the Coastal Plain and the Piedmont, oak forests intermingle with piney uplands and cool winding creeks. Dotting this region are fissured granite outcroppings, the exposed portions of 450- to 500-million-year-old magma domes. One such outcropping, Forty Acre Rock—it actually covers only 14 acres—supports a great abundance of plants, including about a dozen rare, threatened, or endangered species. Adapted to thin soil and dry conditions, some of these plants are found only in these specialized southeastern environments.

A figure-eight loop **trail** of approximately 4 miles takes you past the major biological communities in the preserve. From the parking area, head out on an old logging road that now makes for a nice, wide, needle-strewn path. The cutting of pines through here once opened up niches for cottontail rabbits and red-tailed hawks, as well as indigo buntings and bright yellow prairie warblers. New growth has transformed it into

White-tailed deer

an inviting home for other species, such as opossums, mockingbirds, and pine warblers.

The trail then skirts a placid pond with views of the beaver dam that created it; you'll see wood ducks and, if you are very lucky, beavers swimming near their lodge. White-tailed deer frequent the viny shrubs and briar patches found along the stream floodplain. After crossing a bridge at the base of a water slide, the trail enters the granite community.

The stream below Forty Acre Rock is home to diminutive fish and leopard frogs. Near a shallow cave, a small waterfall (dry in summer) makes soothing woodland music that serenades passing hikers. Emerging onto the rock itself, you have wonderful long views of an upward sloping granite slab that feels almost like a high mountaintop. Here and there are solution pools, shallow depressions created over millennia as the granite is dissolved by rainwater. They are filled in with delicately swirled color—the tiny plants that gain a toehold in the meager amount of soil caught by the shallow holes.

If you're here in spring, you'll see the succulent diamorpha spread like tiny red beads across the solution pools. By summer the red plant has turned into a shriveled, black, seed-bearing stem. This pioneering plant is among the first to colonize the bare rock. The endemic pool sprite is another small plant; it grows only during the brief period of late winter rains. As more soil builds up in the depressions, herbs and shrubs begin to take root, to be followed at last by scrubby red cedars and other species of trees.

Scattered all about the granite face of Forty Acre Rock are a wide assortment of mosses and lichens, varying from the lush black rock moss to the bristly reindeer moss. Run your hand lightly over the distinct textures and see how many different kinds you can count. Look up and you may see turkey vultures gliding over the rock or rising on warm updrafts to become distant specks in the sky. Unfortunately, though, it's not all pristine beauty up here: Over the years untold thoughtless visitors have left their marks—graffiti, fire scars, and broken glass—that detract from the small-scale natural wonders of the rock.

The trail loops back along the south side of the beaver pond through a forest of shortleaf pine and tangled honeysuckle to reach **Flat Creek.** Look carefully for the lightly speckled leaves of trout lilies, which bloom yellow in spring; Easter lily, jack-in-the-pulpit, and creeping phlox may also brighten the path as you make your way back to your car.

A new 141-acre addition on the northwest side of the preserve protects the headwaters of Flat Creek and three endangered freshwater mussels. This stately tract contains mature hardwoods, rich bottomlands, a prairie remnant, and a field of boulders. ■

Fawns

The sight of a speckled fawn bounding along behind its mother is a sure sign that summer has arrived in the Piedmont. After about seven months of gestation, the doe drops one to three fawns, hiding them in separate patches of high grass to reduce the odds of a predator wiping out an entire litter.

For the first month, the fawns venture out only a few hours a day in short intervals. They spend the rest of the time lying motionless, their spots helping camouflage them. People who encounter a concealed fawn often assume—incorrectly—that it has been abandoned. The best thing is to leave it alone; the mother is probably nearby.

Another note of caution: Slow down when you see a single deer near the road, even if it has already passed. Deer travel in family groups, so there could be more about to jump out.

Carolina Sandhills National Wildlife Refuge

■ 45,348 acres ■ Northeastern South Carolina, on US 1, 4 miles north of McBee ■ Best months April-May, Sept.-Oct. ■ Hiking, bird-watching, auto tour ■ Contact the refuge, Route 2, Box 100, McBee, SC 29101; phone 843-335-8401. southeast.fws.gov/carolinasandhills

IT IS 200 YEARS AGO and you are riding a horse through one of the virgin forests of longleaf pines that cover broad swaths of the South. Thousands of straight, brown-barked columns soar 120 feet or more into the sky. Yet they are spaced so far apart that you can see a mile down the avenues of trees. Great tubes of sunlight collect in warm pools on the thick, tawny wire grass of the forest floor; scattered pine straw lies underfoot, damp-ening the steps of animals; and behind the silence a persistent breeze sweeps the woodland like the sound of a distant sea. Some of these giant pines are 400 years old and measure more than 3 feet in diameter. Pan-thers, bison, red wolves, and black bears roam the open forest, adding a further thrill and a hint of danger to your solitary intrusion.

Of the 90 million acres of longleaf pine forest that once graced the Southeast, only about 2 million are left in severed parcels. The rest disap-peared as the trees were logged; the land was either cleared for other uses or replanted with different species, primarily slash pine. The suppression of natural fires has also contributed to the demise of longleaf pines by allowing hardwoods to move in and take over.

Situated just below the Fall Line between the Atlantic Coastal Plain and the Piedmont, Carolina Sandhills National Wildlife Refuge preserves one of the few remaining large stands of longleaf pine as well as inter-laced stretches of wetlands and fields. The refuge contains a remarkable diversity of flora and fauna: more than 750 plant species, 190 bird species, 42 species of mammals, 41 of reptiles, and 25 of amphibians. Among the rare or endangered ones are the red-cockaded woodpecker, the pine barrens tree frog, the southern bald eagle, Bachman's sparrow, Sandhills pyxie moss, American chaffseed, rough-leaved loosestrife, Michaux's sumac, and several species of pitcher plants and sundews.

The Sandhills region began millions of years ago as a delta plain formed by rivers running from the mountains and foothills, depositing sediments, and fanning out into the sea. In the past 50 million years wind and water have eroded the area into the hills you see today. Dominating the uplands are the magnificent longleaf pines, their monumental boles shooting up to crowns of sunlit needles. The needles can grow up to 18 inches long, and the cones vary from 6 to 10 inches. To hold one of these giant cones, the largest of all the eastern pines, is to hold a true piece of Southern history, as potent as an Indian totem or a Civil War relic.

Red-cockaded woodpeckers make nests high in cavities of older long-leaf and loblolly pines; the birds can easily penetrate the soft, rotten wood of 80- to 100-year-old trees that have red heart disease (see sidebar, p. 75). For protection, the woodpeckers drill holes that release a stream of pine resin, which deters snakes and other predators from climbing to the nests. Naturalists at the refuge are doing their best to save this tightly niched endangered species that is so dependent on longleaf pines for sur-vival. The forest itself receives a payback of sorts when the red-cockaded woodpecker moves from one cavity to another, leaving a potential home for screech owls, wood ducks, raccoons, flying squirrels, or bees.

When the refuge was established in 1939, the area was a wasteland of eroded hills, denuded of trees and devoid of much wildlife. Beaver, wild turkey, and white-tailed deer were restocked and have since grown to healthy populations. You can see turkeys crossing roads and fields, espe-cially on spring mornings. Red-cockaded woodpeckers nest in late spring, when neotropical songbird migration reaches its peak. On early summer evenings listen for the nasal honk of the rare pine barrens tree frog, a bright green creature more often heard than seen. The hot days of late summer are good times for spotting wildflowers and white-tailed does with new fawns (see sidebar, p. 69). In the fall, sharp-eyed observers have a good chance of seeing hawks and bald eagles. Ducks and Canada geese arrive at Carolina Sandhills after the first frost. At any time of the year you have the opportunity to view the small resident population of great blue herons, particularly at the refuge's many ponds and lakes.

Following pages: Reflection on Pool D, Carolina Sandhills NWR

Cycling at Carolina Sandhills NWR

What to See and Do

Start out at the refuge office, then proceed north on the 9-mile (one-way) **Wildlife Drive.** The quiet road also makes for a nice bike ride. Near the refuge office, look for the large cones of longleaf pines all over the ground.

A short way up on the left, pull over for the 1-mile **Woodland Pond Trail** around **Pool A,** which feeds into **Little Alligator Creek.** A catwalk crosses the quiet stream edged by pond pine and tulip poplar, the understory bristling with thickets of titi and impenetrable stands of bamboo. Sphagnum moss and carnivorous pitcher plants and sundews dapple the banks of the stream. Two geese come honking overhead, set their wings, and glide onto the pond with a light splash.

Continue driving or cycling to the middle of the refuge, where you have your choice of ponds and lakes for fishing or bird-watching. **Tate's Trail,** a 3-mile footpath, wends alongside **Martins Lake** and up to **Lake Bee.** Farther along, near the end of the route, pull off to the right and drive about half a mile up a sandy road to the 15-foot-tall wooden **observation tower.** You'll see prickly pear cactus growing in the dry, sandy soil around the base, and from the top there are views of fields of broom sedge and tree-fringed ponds. Off in the trees, barred owls cackle, shriek, and call in a raspy voice that sounds like *"Who cooks for you? Who cooks for you-all?"*

To maintain the open pine forests and fields at desired successional stages, the refuge selectively thins the woods by harvesting timber and periodically sets prescribed burns. Persimmon, sassafras, blackberry, and other shrubs and trees thrive on the edges of clearings, waiting for the opportunity to spread. ■

Red-cockaded Woodpecker

With the reduction of the vast southern pine forests to about 2 percent of their original acreage, the numbers of red-cockaded woodpeckers have likewise dwindled precipitously. Some 10,000 to 14,000 individual birds are all that stand between this endangered species and extinction.

It takes a lot to keep the red-cockaded woodpecker happy. Males excavate cavity nests with their strong beaks high up the trunks of living, mature—though preferably diseased—pines. Each family group of four to nine birds requires on average 200 acres of territory. But the very presence of the demanding red-cockaded woodpecker speaks wonders for the general health of an old pine forest.

About the size of a cardinal, the red-cockaded woodpecker is distinguished by its black cap and nape and its white cheeks. On males, a small red streak—the cockade—extends on either side of the cap from behind the eye down toward the white cheek patch. Breeding pairs remain together for several years, raising one brood a year.

But parents don't get stuck with all the hard work: Young males from previous years stay in the area to help incubate the next season's eggs and raise the fledglings. Young females, on the other hand, leave home to look for mates, ideally ones who already have cavity nests.

Red-cockaded woodpecker at its cavity nest in a longleaf pine

Congaree Swamp National Monument

■ 22,200 acres ■ Central South Carolina, southeast of Columbia, 14 miles west of US 601 (follow signs off S.C. 48)J ■ Best months March-May, Sept.-Nov. ■ Camping, hiking, canoeing, fishing (state license required) ■ Contact the monument, 200 Caroline Sims Rd., Hopkins, SC 29061; phone 803-776-4396. www.nps.gov/cosw

PRESERVING THE LARGEST INTACT expanse of old-growth floodplain forest in the country, Congaree Swamp National Monument has been designated an International Biosphere Reserve. In this waterlogged woodland, giant loblolly pines and hardwoods rise to a canopy higher than in the

Boardwalk loop trail in Congaree Swamp National Monument

Amazon rain forest. Loblolly pines thrust up 150 to 170 feet to reach the sunlight, and some majestic old bald cypresses measure more than 25 feet in circumference, their leafy crowns shuttering the world below into a landscape of liquid echoes in shades of brown and green.

The Congaree Indians once hunted and fished in this swamp as their prehistoric forerunners had done since time immemorial. But after Hernando de Soto journeyed through the area in 1540, a wave of European settlers followed. By 1715 the Congaree had suffered near extinction from a combination of warfare and the foreign-introduced smallpox virus, against which they had no natural immunity.

For the next hundred years, the bottomland hardwood forests changed only a little; more than a million acres of old-growth floodplain still cloaked South Carolina's riverine lands. Then the region's growing human population began needing more room and more things that the forest could give. Mounds were built within the Congaree Swamp in the

Bald cypress knees

Bald Cypress

Surrounded by an entourage of knobby knees and rising from dark water to a tapered waist, a twisted trunk, and a sky full of branches with feathery leaves, the bald cypress is a symbol of the vanishing southeastern wetlands. Throw on some swags of Spanish moss and put a heron in the water and you have the quintessential Southern swamp backdrop.

Ranging from southern Delaware to Texas, the bald cypress spends several months of the year in watery conditions that would adversely affect most other trees. This adaptability gives the bald cypress its highly valued rot-resistant property and its nickname, "wood eternal." Only the heartwood, though, is resistant to decay, and over the years it has been used in bridges, docks, and other structures that take heavy weathering. You can also find it in boats, pilings, fences, and decorative paneling. Fairly easy to work with, the wood is only moderately heavy and hard.

When the floodplain forests were logged in the late 19th and early 20th centuries, a lot of the old-growth bald cypresses went down. But some glorious, 500-year-old specimens measuring up to 10 feet in diameter still exist today. Most of these survivors are found in state and national preserves.

What are the knees for? Though no one knows for sure, the best answer is that they help support the tree in the soupy ground. They may also provide some kind of gas exchange between the air and the water- and mud-bound roots, similar to the fingerlike roots of the black mangrove. The cypress itself rises from a flared base with ridges that look like buttresses or rocket fins; the reddish brown to gray bark peels in long strips. Small cones are surrounded by stems of short, soft, needle-like leaves that turn from green to rusty brown in fall.

Its shedding behavior has given the cypress the "bald" part of its name. One of four members of the redwood family native to North America, the bald cypress grows as tall as 125 feet—nowhere near its 300-foot cousins in California, but inch for inch every bit as appealing.

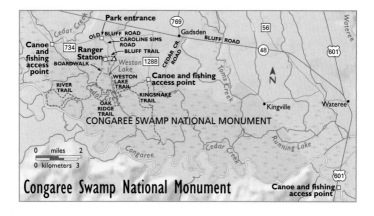

Congaree Swamp National Monument

mid-19th century to provide safe ground for cattle during floods, and though the frequent high water level left the area unsuitable for farming, the huge old trees looked like pots of gold.

Logging began in swamps across the Southeast in the 1880s, and soon thereafter it focused on the old-growth bald cypress. During the next two decades all the stands within easy reach were cut, and South Carolina's floodplain forests suffered a drastic reduction. The 11,000 acres of old-growth bottomland hardwood forest now preserved in the monument account for nearly 90 percent of the state's remaining total. Lack of accessible waterways for removing timber and the heaviness of the constantly soaked logs helped save this irreplaceable tract. In 1969 a new market for timber once again threatened the swamp. Quick action by local citizens and environmental and civic groups led to the establishment of Congaree Swamp National Monument in 1976.

Fierce winds from Hurricane Hugo in 1989 put a dent in the old-growth forest, toppling some of the national and state champion trees harbored here. But the storm also opened up holes in the dense canopy, clearing the way for fresh growth. Dead trees, meanwhile, became homes for various birds, bats, reptiles, insects, and fungi. About ten times a year the floodplain is inundated, usually following dam releases and heavy rains upcountry. Sloughs and guts (narrow creeks) overflow, carrying nutrients that enrich the soil. Shallow-rooted hardwoods occasionally fall, but cypresses with far-reaching roots and supportive knees as tall as 7 feet rarely topple. Animals seek higher ground—bobcats, for example, climb trees—and some even find refuge on floating logs.

On a topographical map you will see very few contour lines within the monument's boundaries; the elevation dips only about 20 feet from the west side to the east, so excess water can slosh all over the swamp. Yet even that slight, seemingly insignificant change of elevation produces dramatically different biological communities: At the higher, drier levels of the monument live sweet gums, cherrybark oaks, and hollies, whereas cypresses, water tupelos, and water ashes thrive at the lower, wetter levels.

What to See and Do

Stop in at the **visitor center** for trail maps, information, and suggestions on hikes. Most people meander at least some of the 2.5-mile **Boardwalk** loop trail, which has interpretive markers keyed to an informational handout. As you gradually enter the floodplain forest, the vegetation changes from upland pines and hardwoods to the old-growth loblolly pines and mixed hardwoods of the swamp.

During floods, the water level can rise as high as the elevated boardwalk—or even higher. Thick vines of scuppernong and climbing hydrangea hug the trunks of ancient trees, adding to the primordial atmosphere. The hairy vines belong to the poison ivy, and it's worth noting that not only the leaves but also the vines and dormant stems can irritate the skin.

Farther along, tupelos and cypresses grow in standing black water, stained by the tannin in decayed vegetation. A light rainfall is an especially evocative time for a walk through here—raindrops ping the reflective water, a gauzy mist envelops the forest primeval, and the birdsong seems to come from far away in time. It's little wonder that sightings of the presumably extinct ivory-billed woodpecker surface every now and again; back in these penumbral depths you almost expect to find creatures from another age.

Continue down the boardwalk toward **Weston Lake.** Fanlike dwarf palmettos just off the walk lend a tropical accent to the surroundings. The riddled trunks of sweet gums and other trees bear the marks of woodpeckers, including yellow-bellied sapsuckers.

In summer, hummingbirds zoom for the showy orange flowers of the trumpet vine, while sparrows dart about for berries and seeds. Fallen logs lie moldering in puddles of wet vegetation—life renewing itself. Small-scale communities are built upon the pits and mounds of overturned trees.

River otters frolic in Weston Lake, and red-bellied turtles line up on floating logs. The small oxbow lake, measuring 25 feet deep, was once a bend in the Congaree River; thousands of years ago, the river changed course—leaving the bend as a lake—and now lies 2 miles away. Near here stand dwarf forests of gnarled cypress knees; the farther you walk around to the east, the more old-growth cypress you encounter.

The boardwalk then takes you through a forest of tupelos, hollies, loblolly pines, and, above all, cypresses. Touch the rippling bell-bottom trunks of the older cypresses—their mossy surface feels like velvet. Extend the Boardwalk Loop by taking the 2.5-mile **Weston Lake Trail,** which follows a cypress-tupelo slough down to Cedar Creek. In this largest of the park's creeks, you have the best chance of spotting herons and otters.

For an even longer outing, the **Oak Ridge Trail,** accessible off the Weston Lake loop, pushes farther south into the old-growth forest and makes for a 7.5-mile round-trip hike from the visitor center. If you want to walk to the river

Beauty berries, Congaree Swamp National Monument

and back, plan to spend most of the day on a 10.5-mile trek starting with the boardwalk, then taking the western sections of the Weston Lake loop and Oak Ridge Trails; the **River Trail** takes you the rest of the way, but it will be underwater during a flood. The 11-mile round-trip **Kingsnake Trail** offers further opportunities for wildlife watching and secluded exploration in the park's little-visited eastern section. The trailhead is off the Cedar Creek parking area.

The **Cedar Creek canoe trail** within the park slips through sunless channels of black water haunted by reclusive birds and other animals. Once a month, the monument staff offers a guided trip and provides canoes for participants. Otherwise, plan to rent a canoe from one of the many outfitters in nearby Columbia. ■

Diverging trails, Hitchcock Woods

Hitchcock Woods

■ 2,000 acres ■ Western South Carolina, in Aiken, off S. Boundary Ave. ■ Best seasons spring and fall ■ Hiking, horseback riding, bird-watching ■ Donations accepted ■ Contact the Hitchcock Foundation, P.O. Box 1702, Aiken, SC 29802; phone 803-642-0528

ON THE EDGE OF the ballooning town of Aiken sprawls a tract of woods and wetlands much larger than you'd expect to find so close to a bustling urban area. Starting in 1939 with a gift of 1,200 acres from Thomas Hitchcock (a wealthy member of the local gentry) and his daughter, the reserve now covers nearly 2,000 peaceful acres and offers more than 60 miles of trails for quiet strolling and nature observation.

A crazy network of **trails** and **bridal paths** veins the woods. You can map out a good 2- to 5-mile walk, or just stroll aimlessly and enjoy the tranquillity of this remnant longleaf-pine and wire-grass habitat. Starting in the northeast at **Memorial Gate,** you can walk along a sandy-bottomed river lined with bracken and other ferns. To the south around **Bebbington Springs** lie hills dotted with bloodroot, trailing arbutus, and other wildflowers. And there are small streams crossed by quaint bridges, oaks bearded with Spanish moss, and meadows where white-tailed deer bound past wild azaleas and eastern bluebirds perch on flowering dogwoods. Among the dozens of bird species, you may see or hear red-tailed hawks, eastern screech owls, pileated woodpeckers, and wood thrushes.

A former game preserve, the park carries on Aiken's long-standing equestrian tradition with periodic hunts and riding events. Walkers are requested to announce their presence when encountering horses and carriages, especially around blind curves. Throughout Hitchcock Woods you'll notice hunt fences, and in the north section you can find the **Ridge Mile Track,** built by Hitchcock for training horses in the 1920s. Just west of here, **Cathedral Aisle** is a pretty trail traversing an 1830s railbed. ■

Forest Fires

Exploring the wooded hills of South Carolina and Georgia, you may from time to time pass a field or forest billowing with smoke, a line of flame creeping along like an advancing army. Once considered hazards to be snuffed out at all costs, forest fires now are often set deliberately—in carefully planned and controlled programs—to create diverse habitats for flora and fauna and to help protect endangered species. Small burns also rid the forests of excess grasses, leaves, and pine straw that can build up and fuel a conflagration.

For millennia, forests were managed naturally by lightning-strike fires every few years. Native Americans learned to mimic this process in order to clear away brush for game animals and to put nutrients back into the soil. Scientists now understand that by breaking down organic material and supplementing the soil with nitrogen from ash, fires help rejuvenate the ground.

A number of pines and other trees depend on the high temperatures of fire to release their cone-bound seeds; in the Everglades alone, some 33 plant species need fire for long-term survival. Finally, the destructive work of fire can open up new niches in the forest, the extra sunlight stimulating the growth of seedlings. In fact, without fire, many habitats eventually would be lost—for example, pines, which can withstand ground fires, would give way to hardwoods.

Where do animals go during a fire? Some are lost, but in general they fare quite well. Ponds and streams draw numerous species; rodents disappear into their burrows; birds, of course, fly off. Later, they return to feed on fresh sprouts and seeds. For all the good that fires do, people should still take care not to start one by accident. Unplanned fires can quickly spread out of control, causing enormous damage to wildlife, natural habitats, and human beings.

New growth following a fire

Savannah River Bluffs Heritage Preserve

■ 84 acres ■ Western South Carolina, northeast of Augusta, Georgia, south of I-20, west of S.C. 230 ■ Best season fall ■ Walking, wildlife viewing ■ Contact South Carolina Dept. of Natural Resources Heritage Trust, P.O. Box 167, Columbia, SC 29202; phone 803-734-3894

TUCKED BETWEEN AN INTERSTATE and North Augusta, South Carolina, this unpublicized preserve along the Savannah River champions an inordinate number of small gems native to the Piedmont-Coastal Plain nexus. Within these 1,076 feet of unspoiled riverfront grow several extremely rare plants on one of the few remaining shoals of the **Savannah River.** One such plant, the greenish to brownish purple relict trillium, holds an uncoveted position on the federal endangered species list, while the white rocky shoals spider lily grows in the river and blooms briefly in late spring.

Other noteworthy species found in this tiny preserve include the spreading shrub bottlebrush buckeye, yellowwood (also called prickly ash or toothache tree), swamp privet, and the slender white-flowering herb known as false rue anemone. A 0.75-mile-loop **nature trail** parallels

Savannah River

a sluggish stream through a forest of saw palmettos and bald cypresses to reach the river. Along the bluffs and in the water, you'll see interesting rock formations. Many historians think that Native Americans used to string nets between the rocks out in the Savannah to create fishing weirs. The trail then follows an old logging road through the woods before turning off to return to the parking lot via a power-line right-of-way. ∎

Driving the Savannah

Along the eastern bank of the Savannah River, the 120,000-acre **Long Cane Ranger District** *(810 Buncombe St., Edgefield, SC 29824. 803-637-5396)* of Sumter National Forest shines like a dewy emerald of pines and hardwoods. Driving S.C. 28 gives you a pleasant look at forest interspersed with old farmsteads, with wildflowers and hedgerows lining the road. Take S.C. 81 to get deeper into the woods, where hiking trails and fishing holes abound; wild turkeys, deer, raccoons, and waterfowl are the main residents. Heading north, the road presents fine views of island-dotted J. Strom Thurmond Lake and Richard B. Russell Lake, impoundments of the river. Several state parks dot this forest-lake interface, offering recreational and nature-viewing opportunities.

Piedmont National Wildlife Refuge

■ 35,000 acres ■ Central Georgia, 25 miles north of Macon via US 23/S.C. 87
■ Best seasons spring and fall ■ Ticks and chiggers are especially bad in summer
and early fall—use repellent ■ Hiking, fishing (state license required), wildlife
drive, wildlife viewing ■ Contact the refuge, 718 Juliette Rd., Round Oak, GA
31038; phone 912-986-5441. piedmont.fws.gov

LIKE THE CAROLINA SANDHILLS, this area was a victim of intensive logging
in the 19th century. Settlers then planted and replanted cotton year after
year, robbing the soil of its nutrients. A combination of the Civil War,
the boll weevil, and the Great Depression left the land and its occupants
played out. Farms were abandoned, and erosion continued to strip the
land bare. When the wildlife refuge was established in 1939, hardly any
wildlife remained to take advantage of it. But slowly the forest began to
rebound—loblolly pines on the ridge and hardwoods down in the lowlands. Along with the cover and the man-made ponds came animals.

Deer and wild turkeys returned, and several species of migratory
wildfowl added the refuge to their flight schedules. With plenty of habitat
for nesting, resting, feeding, and breeding, the refuge now hosts nearly
200 species of birds, including great blue herons, wood ducks, Bachman's
sparrows, red-tailed hawks, and endangered red-cockaded woodpeckers.
The refuge is surrounded by the 115,483-acre **Oconee National Forest**
(1199 Madison Rd., Eatonton, GA 31024. 706-485-3180).

What to See and Do

First stop by the **visitor center** and
peruse the exhibits pertaining to
the refuge's wildlife and habitats.
Then step out and take a stroll
along the 1.5-mile **Pine/Creek
Loop Trail** as it heads up along a
creek lined with hardwoods; look
for flowering dogwoods in spring.

You can swing back through
pine woods, or add another mile
to your walk by taking the interpretive **Allison Lake Trail** loop. If
you need to conserve energy and
prefer doing only the Allison Lake
Trail, take your car, park in the
lot just before the lake's dam, and
pick up the trail there. In summer
mayapple and wildflowers scent
the air and color the ground. In all

seasons, deer and squirrels forage
along the forest floor; bluebirds
flit though the understory; great
blue herons and belted kingfishers
look for snacks in the marsh at the
edge of the lake. You may also see a
gully or two left over from the bad
old days of exhaustive farming—
nature takes time to heal.

At the end of the lake, look for
a beaver lodge; if you're lucky you
may see an otter swimming away
along the banks with a bass or
bream in its mouth. Sit quietly for
a while on the observation deck
or in the photography blind by
the edge of the lake, and you'll
likely see some wildlife. From late
fall through early winter you can

Old homestead, Piedmont National Wildlife Refuge

observe ring-necked ducks (the white ring, though, is around the bill, not the neck, of both sexes). Throughout the year look for colorful wood ducks; the heads of the males look like they were painted by Picasso. There are special boxes around the refuge's ponds solely for wood-duck nesting.

You'll find the 2.9-mile-round-trip **RCW** (Red-Cockaded Woodpecker) **Trail** across the dam. The trail passes a red-cockaded woodpecker colony, its trees marked with the white resin the birds release from the trunk to protect their nests from predators. Or save yourself from craning and simply look for the stripe of white that refuge workers paint on pines containing woodpecker nests. Mornings in April and May, during nesting season, are the best times for watching the birds.

Pick up a brochure at the visitor center for the 6-mile self-guided **Little Rock Wildlife Drive,** a one-way gravel road that offers a slice of the various habitats found on the refuge. The drive passes an old homesite now poetically covered with wisteria vines and hackberry trees; the rock piles left by settlers as they cleared the land make good refuge for lizards and snakes. You'll also cruise by pine woods, a pond, a mowed field, a controlled burn area, and groves of bottomland and upland hardwoods, each distinct plant community providing corresponding links in the wildlife chain.

A variety of habitats line the route between stops 4 and 5, making this area one of the best in the refuge for bird-watching. It was called Little Rock by early settlers because of its proximity to Rock Creek. Further back in time, Indians camped here. The cornfield off to your right, when flooded in winter, is an ideal feeding ground for ducks and other waterfowl; the impoundment pond left of the road attracts shorebirds, waterfowl, beavers, and otters. ∎

Vines on red clay bank, Piedmont NWR

Panola Mountain
State Conservation Park

■ 862 acres ■ North Georgia, 18 miles southeast of Atlanta on Ga. 155 ■ Best seasons spring and fall ■ Hiking, access to mountain by guided walk only (fee) ■ Adm. fee ■ Contact the park, 2600 Highway 155 S.W., Stockbridge, GA 30281; phone 770-389-7801

SCATTERED ABOUT GEORGIA and the Carolinas are granite outcroppings that welled up more than 300 million years ago as huge bubbles of molten rock. They eventually cooled and began wearing away until, some 15 million years ago, the flat or dome-shaped surface you see today was revealed. The Georgia Piedmont has an especially high concentration of monadnocks, as these residual hills are called. The most famous is Stone Mountain, the recreational and historic park 16 miles east of Atlanta.

Whereas Stone Mountain draws large crowds with its laser show and Rushmore-like Confederate tableau, 13 miles to the south the smaller Panola Mountain has been relatively ignored. Panola has a similar geologic history, but it has been preserved in its natural state. It was family owned until 1970, when it was sold to the state to be safeguarded from commercialization. It has never been quarried, vandalized by graffiti, or trod upon by hundreds of boots a day. The only access onto the granite dome itself is by a guided walk of two to three hours. Each hike is limited to a maximum of 25 people, so relatively few park visitors actually go up on the mountain. Guides request that you walk single file to minimize the impact on the rock's fragile plant life. The result is that Panola has the look and feel of an untouched environment, which is a good thing because several plants, described below, grow only on granite outcrops. For its role in protecting this unique ecological heritage, the park has been declared a national natural landmark.

Very little of the granite itself is exposed; most is covered with lichens and mosses that vary in color from light green to slate gray to black. They take about 100 years to grow a square inch—another reason for treading lightly. Rainwater falling on the lichens forms a carbonic acid that nibbles away at the granite; over thousands of years the acid creates a depression, or solution pool, where bigger plants can start growing.

First comes diamorpha, whose tiny stalk holds the seed just high enough off the rock's hot surface to keep it from cooking. In time enough soil will accumulate to support pineweed grass and broom sedge; then, with a few more inches of dirt, shrubs and pine trees can grow. The fascinating thing here is that you can see each of these stages in process.

Miniature circular gardens of red diamorpha and dark green grimea moss grow in one place, while elsewhere stunted cedars preside over their own little landscapes. In springtime nature's palette of subtle color variations on Panola's gray granite canvas is spectacular. Into this miniature wonderland come snakes, deer, foxes, and bobcats. Black vultures and turkey vultures roost on the mountaintop and fly off at the approach of people. You might also spot a variety of hawks: Cooper's and sharp-shinned hawks hunt the wooded hills, while red-tailed hawks with 5-foot wingspans soar the open fields nearby and cross Panola Mountain. Down on the rock, lizards attempt to blend in with the mottled green lichens, and wolf spiders chase their prey instead of building webs.

What to See and Do

Stop in at the **Henry D. Stauble Interpretive Center** to pick up literature and view the mounted animals and other displays. If you've called ahead, you'll arrive at the right time for the once-daily guided walk up the mountain, a 3.5-mile round trip. It's not a strenuous walk, but it does take some time (about three hours). The naturalists do an excellent job explaining what's what—as well as why you should care about it.

Beginning behind the center, the walk proceeds slowly up the mountain, a vertical climb of only 250 feet. Once out of the woods, you pass a small pond and start traversing the exposed rock. You begin seeing the little islands of plant life that have adapted to the rock's dry, windy environment. Prickly pear cactus vies for attention with dark green forests of pine moss and the creamy throats of Easter lilies. White-flowering sandwort hugs a shallow depression; the rare quillwort grows almost unnoticed under a film of water, going dormant when the water is gone; willow-wort and amphianthus, both state endangered species, add delicate shades of green and white. Orange star-shaped sunnybells, feltlike woolly ragwort, and the aptly named haircap moss grow in fairy gardens that practically beg you to stoop and stare at the miraculously intricate variety of life on the rock.

From the summit you can make out the skyline of Atlanta to the west and the large dome of Stone Mountain to the north. Another granite outcrop, Arabia Mountain, rises to the right of Stone Mountain; part of a county park, it has unfortunately not been

Lichens on exposed granite, Panola Mountain State Conservation Park

Woodland Flutes

Two of the more unremarkable-looking birds haunting the southeastern woodlands produce some of the most beautiful music you can hear in any part of natural America. Both the hermit thrush and the wood thrush are medium in size and rusty brown in color with white eye rings and a whitish, spotted breast. The wood thrush, at 8 inches from bill to tip of tail, is somewhat longer than the hermit. Wood thrushes are summer residents all over the East—look and listen for them in hardwood or mixed pine-hardwood forests. Hermit thrushes are primarily winter residents of the Southeast.

Because the hermit thrush sings primarily at mating time, you may not hear its song, often described as "liquid" or "flutelike," during the winter. If you are lucky enough to catch his—most songsters are male—performance, you will never forget the experience. The melody begins with a long note, then adds several notes in ascending pitch that give an eerie echoing effect, as though the song were swirling through a long, hollow tube.

Perhaps even more enchanting are the solos of the wood thrush, whose clean, ringing tones can send shivers down your back. The songs are often five or six phrases of a few notes each, ending in a trill. There are distinct rest notes between each phrase, then a repetition of the entire song, which can go on and on during an entire day as the thrush calls for a mate. The intervals—minor thirds, minor sixths—are so close to perfection, and the timbre so rich, that the results are breathtaking.

Anyone who spends much time in the Piedmont's forests and who appreciates good music will recognize thrushes as a key element in the sylvan soundtrack.

---

well preserved. Also near the top you can find another threatened species, the tiny emerald green dwarf stonecrop, so highly specialized that it grows only under cedars on granite outcrops in the Southeast—the stonecrop needs the calcium from cedar leaves. Most of the floral show ends by summer, but there are a few late bloomers—the magenta fameflower and the pink and yellow Curtis's milkwort, for example.

If you miss the guided walk or just want to learn more about Panola, take the two short nature walks behind the interpretive center. The 0.75-mile **Rock Outcrop Trail** through a forest of pines, oaks, hickories, poplars, and dogwoods has interpretive signs and gives you a view of an outcrop and the mountain. In spring, tangles of yellow jasmine and white-flowering hawthorn beautify the path. Birds and deer eat the apple-like fruit of the hawthorn. Also found here are the Spanish bayonet, or yucca, usually associated with the coast, and the shrubby sparkleberry tree with small dark edible berries. A 1.25-mile round-trip, the **Microwatershed Trail** wends its way through a small ravine and across a creek, giving you a bit more of a workout. ■

Franklin D. Roosevelt State Park

■ 10,000 acres ■ West Georgia, a short distance south of Pine Mountain off US 27 ■ Best seasons fall and spring ■ Camping, hiking, fishing (state license required), horseback riding ■ Adm. fee ■ Contact the park, 2970 Highway 190, Pine Mountain, GA 31822; phone 706-663-4858

THE LARGEST STATE PARK in Georgia traverses the long, skinny backbone of Pine Mountain in the west-central part of the state. Much of the eastern section of the park was owned by Franklin D. Roosevelt, who first came to nearby Warm Springs in 1921 to treat his polio. At age 39 he had just finished a seven-year stint as assistant secretary of the navy and had failed in his bid to become Vice President. In addition to seeking treatment in the soothing mineral waters, he began visiting for the solace of these gentle rolling hills and eventually bought several parcels of farmland. After he was elected President, Roosevelt built the "Little White House" nearby, where he spent his increasingly rare free time. He died there in 1945.

The park's cabins and lakes were constructed by the Civilian Conservation Corps, the public service labor force launched by Roosevelt during the Great Depression of the 1930s. The president himself reputedly directed some of the CCC's work here. The park today remains a quiet haven of oaks and dogwoods, cool streams and tumbling waterfalls, rock outcrops and long ridgetop views. Some 85 species of birds have been

One of FDR's favorite picnic spots, Dowdell Knob

observed in the park, as well as a varied population of mammals including white-tailed deer, nine-banded armadillos, and coyotes, which sometimes yip and howl deep in the woods at night.

Winters here offer cool, crisp air and clear views with occasional dustings of snow. In spring the roadsides and trails turn into soft symphonies of color: Sweet gums show a rusty red; white-flowering hawthorn and yellow jasmine brighten fences; dazzling mountain laurel follows the tough act of blossoming dogwoods. Wildflowers and ferns peak in summer, and autumn brings a fine display of gold and russet foliage.

What to See and Do

The park office and visitor center is located on Ga. 190 about 3.5 miles northeast of US 27. In the old-fashioned stone building, formerly the Roosevelt Inn, you can buy a trail map and pick up information on the park and its history.

Franklin D. Roosevelt State Park has about 40 miles of hiking trails, including the 23-mile **Pine Mountain Trail,** which is popular with both day hikers and backpackers. Several worthwhile loop trails varying from 3 to 8 miles in length have been designed as excursions off the main line of the Pine Mountain Trail.

One of the prettiest trails, the 6.7-mile **Wolfden Loop,** lies at the eastern end of the park. It can be reached from the WJSP-TV tower parking lot on Ga. 85W, the

Magnificent Magnolias

A gracious hostess with wide green skirts and heavenly perfume, the southern magnolia (Magnolia grandiflora) has long served as a symbol of the South. In the 1770s, the explorer-naturalist William Bartram was struck by the beauty of the southern magnolia, which he called a laurel magnolia: "How majestically stands the laurel, its head forming a perfect cone! Its dark green foliage seems silvered over with milk-white flowers. They are so large as to be distinctly visible at the distance of a mile or more." Over the centuries since then, magnolias have served as standard props in books and movies that call for an antebellum backdrop of lush beauty.

Often planted as an ornamental, the magnolia grows wild throughout the Piedmont and Coastal Plain. The flowers—as big as salad bowls—open in early summer to waft a delicious lemony sweetness into the air. Squirrels and wild turkeys enjoy the bright crimson seeds that appear on oblong pods in the fall. The tree grows to about 80 feet high, and its hard, heavy wood has been used in boxes, cabinets, doors, and rough floors. With evenly spaced branches that grow fairly close to the ground, the magnolia makes a great climbing tree, as many children can attest.

Another species found in the Southeast, the big-leaf magnolia, is conspicuous for its tremendous pear-shaped leaves, which can reach 10 inches in width and 30 inches in length. The bigleaf is somewhat shorter than the southern, but its 10- to 12-inch-wide creamy white flowers possess a similar fragrance.

eastern terminus of Pine Mountain Trail. It winds through a forest of hardwoods, longleaf pines, and shortleaf pines, passing a series of lovely waterfalls less than a mile from Roosevelt's Little White House. Even in daytime you may hear the distinctive, unforgettable call of the barred owl.

Back in the car, head west from the terminus for 1.2 miles on Ga. 190, then take the left fork and drive 1.3 miles to **Dowdell Knob.** Here, at nearly 1,400 feet elevation, you have wide views south to Oak Mountain and the farms and forests of Pine Mountain Valley; turkey vultures float and tilt above the valley floor, while red-tailed hawks let loose with high-pitched screams. This promontory ranked high on FDR's list of picnicking sites, as a memorial attests. From here you can pick up the **Dowdell Knob Loop,** which winds for 4.3 miles around the knob.

The road to the west offers good views over both sides of the ridge, a highlight among the generally low foothills of the Piedmont. At picturesque **Lake Delano** you can fish for catfish, bass, and bream. Ducks and Canada geese are fairly common except in summer, when they fly north, and you may even spot a great blue heron or mallard along the lake's edge. From February to July you'll be treated to the long and varied riffs of the brown thrasher, the state bird, which sings along the edges of the woods. ∎

Fall foliage, Franklin D. Roosevelt State Park

Coastal Plain

Fern Hammock Springs, Ocala National Forest, Florida

THE LOW-LYING COASTAL PLAIN, the broadest ecoregion in the Southeast, sweeps down from South Carolina and Georgia into Florida and southern Alabama, cutting a swath up to 150 miles from the coast to the Fall Line and rising gently from sea level to about 300 feet. The plain encompasses many different habitats, which sustain a great variety of life. Freshwater wetlands function as arks of plant and animal diversity. Wet prairies, peat bogs, and stands of ancient cypress support thousands

of alligators and wading birds. Around small ponds and streams, fresh-water marshes grow rife with giant plume grass, providing good cover for a variety of amphibians, reptiles, and small birds. Pitting the flat-woods and coastal lowlands by the thousands, mysterious oval-shaped depressions called Carolina bays, which can range in length from a few hundred feet to several miles, support their own little communities of dense vegetation.

Though traditionally a fertile ground for the farming of tobacco, cot-ton, and other crops, the Coastal Plain also harbors several noteworthy corners of natural beauty. Landscapes range from the springs of northern

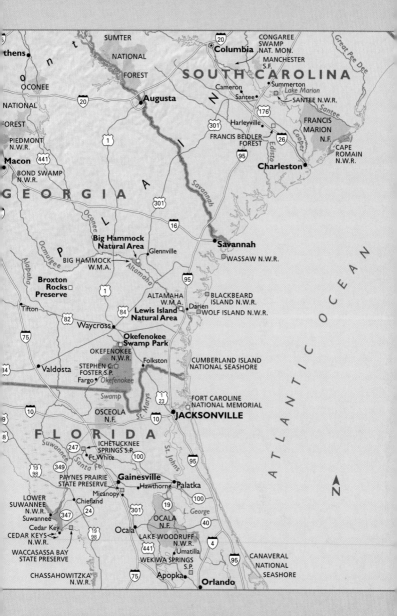

Florida and the talc-smooth Gulf Coast beaches to the deep pine and cypress forests farther inland.

Running from the Atlantic to the Gulf side of the Coastal Plain, a band of pine flatwoods rims the coast. Sliced by river floodplains, the flatwoods continue inland to the sand hills and the Fall Line, where rivers drop sharply enough to power hydroelectric turbines. On the low, wet areas of the flatwoods, slash pines tower over tropical-looking saw palmettos, while in the drier areas, widely spaced longleaf pines dot a tawny carpet of wire grass. Though greatly reduced from their original acreage, glorious stands of giant-coned longleaf pines still survive, particularly in the Conecuh and Blackwater River forests of Alabama and Florida.

Spring and fall wildflowers bloom in abundance within and around the flatwoods: Azaleas, gentians, and lilies vie in loveliness with asters, heaths, and meadow beauties. Wild turkeys, deer, songbirds, turtles, and endangered red-cockaded woodpeckers are some of the animals you are most likely to see on the Coastal Plain.

Northern Florida offers crystal-clear springs and intriguing sinkholes. It also abounds with hills, ridges, and bluffs. Those located along the Apalachicola River shelter rare plants and offer quiet retreats of subtle beauty. Spring-fed pools and rivers in Wakulla Springs and Wekiwa Springs State Parks create lush subtropical Edens where anhingas perch on moss-draped tree limbs and long-nosed gar slip silently through underwater gardens.

Florida's Panhandle offers serene sweeps of Gulf Coast backed by tall-grass marshes, similar to those you find on the Atlantic Coast. The difference is that here the water is calmer, shallower, and warmer, and the beaches have seen less development. Several parks and preserves protect miles and miles of pristine shoreline; on long walks you can watch pelicans flying single file over the surf and herons fishing with utmost patience back in the marshes.

In the southwest corner of the region, Mobile Bay and the four major rivers that flow into it form one of the largest and most productive estuaries in the country. Measuring some 35 miles long, 10 miles wide, and 10 to 12 feet deep, the bay nourishes a teeming chain of marine life from mollusks and crustaceans to fish and birds. Long, thin Dauphin Island is poised at the foot of the bay, acting as a welcome mat for thousands of colorful songbirds that touch down on their annual migration from Central and South America. In the fall and the winter, waterfowl wing their way to Dauphin Island from the north, contributing to a bird list that totals more than 300 species.

In Alabama, the Coastal Plain reaches far inland, especially on the western side, in the lee of the mountains. Tracts of pine forest intermingle with large acreages of rich, dark soil—the so-called black belt—in which cotton has been planted for many generations. To the north, red hills roll out from the Appalachians, veined with iron ore, striped with rivers, and clad with managed forests that provide homes for a representative cross section of southeastern wildlife.

Farmed, logged, and mined for hundreds, even thousands, of years—worked perhaps more than any other land in the Southeast—the resilient Coastal Plain still beckons with its gracefully aging beauty. The sites to visit are numerous, ranging from Georgia's famous Okefenokee National Wildlife Refuge to lesser-known jewels such as the Francis Beidler Forest in South Carolina and the gorgeous but relatively unrecognized spread of St. Marks National Wildlife Refuge in Florida. Have your camera and your binoculars at the ready, as well as a bathing suit and a pair of hiking shoes. This wide and varied region will offer you no end of outdoor pleasures. ∎

Watching the sunset at Gulf Islands National Seashore in Florida

Santee National Wildlife Refuge

■ 15,095 acres ■ Southeast South Carolina, north shore of Lake Marion, 4 miles north of Santee on US 15/301 ■ Year-round ■ Hiking, fishing, wildlife viewing, auto tour ■ Contact the refuge, Rte. 2, Box 370, Summerton, SC 29148; phone 803-478-2217. southeast.fws.gov/santee

IN 1942, SOUTH CAROLINA provided a new hydroelectric power source by damming the Santee and Cooper Rivers and created 96,400-acre Lake Marion in the process. At the same time, officials established the Santee National Wildlife Refuge. Today the lake acts as a much needed stopover for migratory waterfowl, and the refuge—which spreads along 18 miles of the lake's northern shoreline, on either side of the interstate—benefits both local and visiting wildlife.

Wood ducks take advantage of nesting boxes; waterfowl get a share of the wheat and corn planted by contract farmers; and water levels are seasonally adjusted to control plant growth. Hardwoods, pine plantations, fields, and ponds stitch together a tapestry of diverse habitats supporting bobcats, deer, alligators, bald eagles, and the winter influx of thousands of ducks, geese, and swans.

Field of wildflowers, Santee National Wildlife Refuge

Nearly 300 bird species make use of the refuge, but the migratory birds create the most commotion. Trumpeting, honking, whopping the air with tireless wings, the Canada geese, mallard, teal, pintail, wigeons, and mergansers that flock through from November to February make for prime wildlife viewing. Hooded mergansers, with their white swept-back head crests, dive instead of dabble; they fly low, single file, over the water, plunging for fish and crustaceans. In the spring, orioles, tanagers, blue grosbeaks, and other songbirds migrate in from the south. Summer and fall are good times for observing herons, egrets, and other shorebirds, as well as red-shouldered and red-tailed hawks.

A visitor center is located in the refuge's Bluff Unit, the westernmost of the four units. Pick up information at the center and take the 1.5-mile **Wright's Bluff Nature Trail**, which features an **observation tower** for viewing long-legged waders and other birds on an inlet of the lake. You can go on an 8-mile **auto tour route** through the refuge's shrubby wetlands and mixed forests by following the signs north and then southeast to the John C. Land boat ramp to find the Cuddo Unit. There also are two 1.4-mile footpaths off the driving route, which you can combine for a walk of a bit more than 2 miles through the forests and the marshes along the lake. ■

Wild turkey in Francis Beidler Forest

Francis Beidler Forest

■ 11,500 acres ■ Southern South Carolina, 40 miles northwest of Charleston via US 26 ■ Year-round ■ Boardwalk, bird-watching ■ Adm. fee ■ Contact the forest, 336 Sanctuary Rd., Harleyville, SC 29448; phone 843-462-2150. www.pride-net.com/swamp

LIKE THE CONGAREE SWAMP (see pp. 76-81) to the north, the Francis Beidler Forest preserves a vital piece of southeastern natural history—in this case, 1,800 acres of virgin cypress-tupelo river swamp, one of the largest such ecosystems. The Beidler is part of the **Four Holes Swamp**—the name may refer to four lakes fished by the Yemasee Indians, or to four periodically dry passageways traveled by pioneers—which runs for 62 twisty miles from near Cameron down to the Edisto River, which drains into the Atlantic. Unlike the Congaree and other river-bottom swamps, the Four Holes is a braided-stream system, fed by a helter-skelter network of springs and streams flowing slowly through the forest. Just below the Beidler section, the swamp, instead of continuing southeast (the direction of the interstate), makes a curiously sharp right-hand turn to join the Edisto. Geologists believe that before the Pleistocene epoch, when the sea was nearly this far inland, the swamp was part of an estuary aligned to a southwest flow by the prevailing currents. During the American Revolution, "Swamp Fox" Francis Marion is said to have camped here.

In contrast to most of the Four Holes Swamp, the area now known as Beidler Forest was never harvested. The forest's unlikely protector was a lumberman-conservationist from Chicago named Francis Beidler, who bought up vast tracts of swampland in the late 19th century. While trekking in the West, Beidler developed an appreciation for natural beauty. Then, after studying forestry and conservation in Europe, Beidler decided he would keep a portion of his extensive holdings in their original state.

In the 1960s, the Audubon Society and the Nature Conservancy bought from the Beidler family the acreage that now forms the core of the **Audubon Center and Sanctuary** at the Francis Beidler Forest. Today the Beidler Forest is managed by the society, but that management mostly means leaving the swamp alone and working to protect buffer areas from noise pollution and further development.

Within Francis Beidler's ancient forest of giant cypress, tupelo gum, water ash, and laurel oak live more than 300 species of birds, mammals, reptiles, amphibians, and fish. The plant life, too, grows in profligate variety and abundance—around the parking lot and boardwalk alone are 121 species of trees, shrubs, herbs, ferns, and vines. Among the 13 vine species you will see groping their way up trees or creeping along the ground are supplejack, trumpet vine, muscadine, and greenbrier, the last a prickly vine with green flowers. The largest bald cypress here measures 10 feet in diameter; the oldest is about 1,500 years old, nearly as old as the record holder in North Carolina.

What to See and Do

To reach Beidler Forest, take US 26 west 40 miles to S.C. 27 (exit 187). Head south to US 78, then follow the signs. At the visitor center, pick up a guide booklet and leaflets on the flora and fauna; then step out back and take the 1.75-mile **boardwalk** into the swamp. Rest stops and rain shelters are spaced to encourage you to take as much time as you'd like.

Skinks and green anole lizards slither over the boardwalk and the leaves along the ground; water striders dimple the surface of inky black pools. Moss-covered cypress knees rise from the water like miniature green volcanoes. In the spring, look among the trees for yellow flashes: The prothonotary warbler, or swamp canary, nests in tree cavities or hollow cypress knees, announcing spring's return with a "sweet sweet sweet" call.

Halfway along the boardwalk, the shallow river opens up to **Goodson Lake,** a serpentine channel overhung by limbs bearing Spanish moss and green-fly orchids. Yellow-bellied sliders may plop into the water at your approach, and a yellow-crowned night heron may flap to a new perch. At one point, if the water is low enough, you can walk down to the hollow trunk of a dead, but still standing, cypress; step inside it, and look up 100 feet to the sky.

Panels detail the loss of swampland over the years to draining, damming, and channelization; statistics cite the reduction of songbirds—blue jays by 50 percent between 1966 and 1993, and wood thrushes, the haunting melodists of the deep forest, by 73 percent.

To keep the swamp pristine, the boardwalk is the only access. Call the sanctuary to find out about special canoe trips and night walks. The latter are especially fun for children, who enjoy the eerie hoots, screeches, and trills of the swamp at its primordial best. ■

Big Hammock Natural Area

■ 801 acres ■ Southeast Georgia, about 10 miles southwest of Glenville off Ga. 121 ■ Year-round ■ Hiking, wildlife viewing ■ Contact Georgia Natural Heritage Program, 2117 US 278 S.E., Social Circle, GA 30025-4714; phone 770-918-6411

ONE OF THE LONGEST UNDAMMED RIVERS in the Southeast, the Altamaha begins in central Georgia and runs 137 miles out to the barrier islands near Darien. About 40 miles downstream from where the Oconee and Ocmulgee Rivers join to form the Altamaha is the 801-acre Big Hammock Natural Area, which preserves a tract of oak and scrub hammock on soil too sandy for farming.

Many of the wildlife species present when naturalist William Bartram journeyed through the area in the 1770s are still here, including alligators, wood storks, and herons. Some 50 rare or endangered species can be found, among them the gopher tortoise, eastern indigo snake, manatee, red-cockaded woodpecker, shortnose sturgeon, and Florida corkwood.

Trees have not fared as well. Beginning in the early 19th century, the tremendous old bald cypresses, tupelos, and pines that lined the Altamaha for much of its course were heavily cut and floated down-

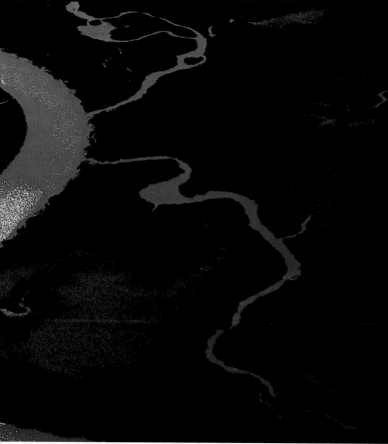

Tidal estuary, Altamaha River, Big Hammock Natural Area

stream to Darien's sawmills; ships then carried them to ports all over the world. Yet some bald cypresses still grace the riverbanks, as do wax myrtles, bays, pines, and hollies. In the Big Hammock Natural Area, a number of longleaf pines survived the logging. Rare species at this site include the state-protected Georgia plume, a flowering shrub that grows more extensively here than anywhere else in the state.

To reach the parking lot at Big Hammock, take Ga. 121 southwest from Glenville to Cty. Rd. 441. A 1.3-mile **nature trail** starts at the information kiosk and winds through the hammock by stands of Georgia plume and myrtle oak. Neotropical birds (which overwinter in South and Central America) include swallow-tailed kites and Swainson's warblers. You may see several other songbirds, as well as turkeys and deer. The river lies a little more than a mile southwest, through the **Big Hammock Wildlife Management Area** *(912-426-5267)*, a 7,015-acre parcel of swamps, fields, and oxbow lakes open for hunting, fishing, and wildlife viewing.

A bigger plot of managed land lies near the mouth of the river. The 29,000-acre **Altamaha Wildlife Management Area** *(912-262-3173)* is a haven for migratory birds from mid-October to mid-April. Within the Altamaha's boundaries, **Lewis Island Natural Area** contains groves of original-growth bald cypress and water tupelo. ■

Okefenokee Swamp

■ 438,000 acres ■ Southeast Georgia ■ Year-round ■ Camping, hiking, boating, fishing, bird-watching. ■ Adm. and user fees ■ Beware of biting insects, especially in summer ■ Contact Stephen C. Foster State Park, Rte. 1, Box 131, Fargo, GA 31631, phone 912-637-5274, www.gastateparks.org; Okefenokee National Wildlife Refuge, Rte. 2, Box 3330, Folkston, GA 31537, phone 912-496-7836, okefenokee.fws.gov; or Okefenokee Swamp Park, 5700 O.S.P. Rd., Waycross, GA 31501, phone 912-283-0583, www.okeswamp.com

A PEAT BOG SPANNING 38 MILES by 25 miles, the Okefenokee is the country's largest swamp; the **Okefenokee National Wildlife Refuge,** embracing 90 percent of the swamp, is the largest refuge in the East. About 90 percent of the refuge, in turn, is protected as a national wilderness area, which means a vast majority of the swamp has been returned to its original inhabitants—the sandhill cranes, herons, bears, alligators, and snakes that make the Okefenokee one of the great wildlife sanctuaries in the Southeast. Wet prairies, sandy pine islands, and cypress forests interweave to form a variegated landscape of greens, browns, and grays, stippled here and there with little fireworks of color—the purple of pickerelweed, the white and yellow of fragrant water lilies, the sunny gold of orange milkwort. In some places, the swamp resembles a primeval jungle, its trees tinseled with Spanish moss; elsewhere, long views open onto grassy lakes.

About 250,000 years ago, the Atlantic shoreline lay some 70 miles west of its current position. When the ocean retreated, it left an exposed sandbar 40 miles long (Trail Ridge, the eastern boundary of the swamp). Behind that wide sandbar, a shallow lagoon began to form. Over time, the lagoon drained, and on its sandy floor the swamp began taking shape. Fresh water filled in the lagoon, or basin, and piles of dead vegetation built up layers of peat over thousands of years. As seeds found their way onto these floating mats of peat, trees and shrubs took root and little islands formed. In some cases, the roots anchor the islands to the floor of the swamp; in other cases, the islands float free. The thinner, spongier ones jiggle when you walk on them—hence the Native American term "okefenokee," or "land of the trembling earth."

About 85 percent of the Okefenokee's water flows southwest to form the Suwannee River, which empties into the Gulf of Mexico; the rest flows eastward with the St. Marys River to the Atlantic. Tannic acid from decaying vegetation stains the slow-moving waters a dark tea color. In the early 1890s, Capt. Henry Jackson, an Atlanta lawyer, bought half of the swamp and tried to drain it via the St. Marys for logging and farming. After three years, Jackson's main line, the Suwannee Canal, stretched only 11.5 miles, and he realized that besting the Okefenokee was beyond the powers of his purse. Some 300 miles of canals, Jackson estimated, would be needed to drain the Okefenokee dry. His company soon went bankrupt and was sold to a lumber company, Hebard Cypress.

Water lilies in Okefenokee National Wildlife Refuge

On 20-foot pilings driven into the peat, Hebard Cypress laid 35 miles of railroad track from the west side of the swamp and harvested 431 million board feet of timber. To support operations, the company built a camp on Billy's Island. As many as 2,000 men labored in the swamp at one time, turning Billy's Island into a spirited community, complete with a hotel and theater.

By the time logging operations ended in the 1930s, most of the virgin cypress was gone, and trees that had grown in the swamp since before the time of Columbus were in use as rot-resistant ceilings and furniture. The Hebard property was sold to the U.S. government, and in 1937, the refuge was established. Today vines and thick growth entangle the rusting machinery and ruined buildings, as nature has reclaimed its turf.

Two recent issues facing the Okefenokee could have major impacts on its future. In the early 1960s, a 5-mile-long earthen sill was built on the west side to hold water in the swamp and keep its forests from burning. Many people now question the disruption of natural cycles of fire and flood, and as the time for repairing the sill draws near, some experts believe it should be removed. The long-term effects of such an action are unknown. Meanwhile, on the east side, the DuPont Company has bought 38,000 acres, where it plans to mine for titanium. Scientists are concerned that the 50-year project will contaminate the area's soil and water, add significant noise pollution, and jeopardize already troubled species.

What to See and Do

The three main visitor entrances to the swamp are on the west, east, and north sides; each is separately administered and has its own characteristics. On the west grow thick cypress forests; to the east lie open, soupy prairies fringed by pines; and the north is etched by dark, jungly corridors of glassy black water.

West Entrance

The west entrance, which leads to **Stephen C. Foster State Park** *(912-637-5274)*, is located well into the swamp, 17 miles east of Fargo via Ga. 177. The state park occupies 80-acre **Jones Island.** Because Jones is surrounded by swamp, you probably won't recognize it as an island even after you reach the narrow waterways that separate it from other pine islands and low-lying swampy areas.

If you want a 90-minute **boat tour,** it's a good idea to sign up at the boat basin when you arrive, especially during the busy spring and summer seasons. The tours travel along tannin-dark channels where alligators rouse for the occasional meal of fish or fowl and egrets stand hunch-shouldered.

Although this area was heavily logged, stands of pond and bald cypress have grown back. Florida cooters plop off snags as boats approach, but you may see them or other turtles splashing water upward from beneath the surface as they dive deeper. A single water lily or patch of rod-shaped golden club with their bright bands of color adds grace notes to an otherwise tree-shaded canal.

There are 25 miles of waterways within the park for day use, and you can rent a canoe or motorboat at the park's boat basin and explore on your own. The park store sells fishing and picnicking supplies. From the boat dock, head out on a narrow canal to long, thin **Billy's Lake,** at 3.5 miles in length the largest of the swamp's 60 named lakes.

Going east on Billy's Lake about 3 miles brings you to **Billy's Island,** where you can take a 1-mile walking trail and see the remains of the early 20th-century lumber camp. New growth has conquered most signs of civilization, but hidden among the tangled foliage are remains from three eras: Native American mounds, a pioneer cemetery, and a lumber company railroad bed.

North of Billy's Island lies narrow **Minnie's Lake** *(5 miles from boat basin);* another 7 miles beyond that is **Big Water Lake.**

Pitcher plants at Okefenokee Swamp

Along the way you'll see cypresses, a grassy prairie, egrets, and alligators. Vultures and hawks perch in tall trees or soar the updrafts.

Back at the boat basin, take a turn around the half-mile **Trembling Earth Nature Trail.** It offers informative panels on the logging era, bears, the swamp's carnivorous plants, prescribed fires, and the nation's vanishing wetlands. A 2,100-foot-long boardwalk extension pushes out into the swamp. You probably won't see any of the park's 500 black bears, since they often hide in dense thickets of titi ("tie-tie") trees, but you'll likely see a raccoon, an otter, or a deer.

East Entrance

If you enter on the east side of the Okefenokee *(11 miles SW of Folkston, via Ga. 23/121),* you'll find the **Suwannee Canal Recreation Area** *(921-496-7156).* It is administered by the U.S. Fish and Wildlife Service and has a **visitor center** to familiarize you with the natural and cultural history of the swamp. A concessionaire *(921-496-7156)* has **boat tours** and rental canoes.

One of the highlights of this area is the **Swamp Walk,** a 4,000-foot-long boardwalk that jogs out along the edge of a wet prairie. Lizards skitter along the boards; white ibises flap in the brush like fallen stars; and bullfrogs give voice to the swamp with their deep, plaintive "jug a rum." In fact, more than 20 species of frogs and toads, each with a distinct voice, inhabit the swamp. With a bit of guidance, you can easily distinguish the snore of the river frog from the snort of the pig frog and the banjo pluck of the bronze frog.

Look for steel-blue parula warblers nesting in the Spanish moss overhead. The plant, a symbol of the southern low country, is an epiphyte—that is, it takes all its nourishment from rain and sun and does not harm the tree.

The boardwalk takes you to a 50-foot-high **observation platform** festooned with the delicate tracery of big golden-silk spiders. From here you have a wondrous panorama of lily-spattered ponds,

Canoeing in Okefenokee Swamp

Alligator bellowing its mating call

Alligators

That 10-foot-long, 300-pound lizard you see sunning itself on a log or head-slapping the water during mating season looks much the way its ancestors did 160 million years ago, when dinosaurs ruled the Earth. Surviving into the 21st century as lords of the swamp and the largest reptiles on the continent, alligators continue to capture the imagination of the public for their ancient history, carnivorous habits, and fearsome appearance.

The Okefenokee holds 10,000 to 13,000 alligators, the majority of Georgia's alligator population. Situated at the top of the food chain, gators act as barometers of general health in the Okefenokee and other wetlands: A wildlife population large enough to support alligators is likely to be robust and varied.

Between 1870 and 1970, hunting alligators for their skins nearly extinguished the species as some 10 million gators were killed in Florida alone. Hunting regulations and restrictions on the hide trade have brought about a recovery, though habitat loss puts increasing pressure on the gators' numbers.

The main service alligators provide the swamp is to clear its channels and ponds of invading plants, creating pools that myriad animals depend on during droughts. Snakes, otters, fish, turtles, and other creatures take refuge in gator holes, willing to risk their host's sporadic appetite for a good place to stay.

When an alligator does get hungry, it will go after anything—insects, frogs, birds, turtles, other gators, deer, even a small bear if it can drown one. Shells and bones snap like dry twigs in the fierce vise of an alligator's jaws. Gators tend to avoid people, though small children could be mistaken for prey. It is always best to keep your distance.

If you think of alligators as cold-blooded killers, consider their maternal instincts. The mother painstakingly builds a mud-and-grass nest up to 3 feet high, then guards her eggs for three months. She helps the hatchlings emerge from the eggs, sometimes carrying them to the water in her mouth. The little ones often catch a ride on her back or head, and they stay with her for up to two years, until they are about 2 feet long.

pine islands, and wading birds. Golden yellow prothonotary warblers sometimes nest at the bottom of the tower in spring.

A resident colony of sandhill cranes is frequently seen nearby, particularly in winter—or just heard, like a renegade section of French horns, tuning up somewhere off in the swamp. The sounds that echo across the grassy ponds and the forms that shimmer uncertainly in the mist after a summer rain give you a glimpse of early life here.

Nearby, the **Swamp Island Drive** is a 9-mile driving or biking loop that includes a hardwood forest, meadows, a pond, a 1927 homestead, and a stand of slash pines. Gators and wildflowers can be spotted in ditches and along the edges of the pond, while wild turkeys and deer browse in the clearings. About halfway around the loop, a short foot trail into the woods offers an opportunity for seeing red-cockaded woodpeckers. Look high up in the pines for tree cavities stained white with sap.

Near the end of the loop, stop for a close look at the **Chesser Island Homestead,** a rustic building dating from 1927. Families such as the Chessers raised sugarcane and cattle, hunted, and kept beehives and gardens. They used palmetto leaves to weave hats and fans and palmetto stalks to make sturdy brooms. From slash pines, people could make turpentine, and after the resin ceased to flow, they cut the trees for lumber.

North Entrance

The north entrance to the swamp is through the privately run **Okefenokee Swamp Park,** 8 miles south of Waycross off US 1. Although this is the most commercial of the three entrances, the northern swamp's unique look

Francis Harper

When he first entered the swamp in 1912 with a biological team from Cornell University, 25-year-old naturalist Francis Harper began a love affair with the Okefenokee that would last more than half a century. Recording Cracker folklore and collecting specimens, Harper came to appreciate the fragile and primitive beauty of the swamp; he thereupon began working to protect it as a biological preserve.

Rejected by the U.S. Congress as a site for a migratory bird refuge, the Okefenokee fell in the path of a proposed Gulf-to-Atlantic canal in 1933. The next year, a plan for a highway through the swamp's heart galvanized Harper and others to intensify their efforts. Harper's wife, who had tutored Franklin D. Roosevelt's children, wrote the President for help. In 1937, an executive order created Okefenokee National Wildlife Refuge, protecting the area from any highways and canals.

Ironically, the establishment of the refuge hastened the decline of the swamp culture Harper had so lovingly documented. Most swampers moved out to small towns, but Harper's photographs and recordings of their way of life survive in *Okefenokee Album*, published in 1981 by Georgia professor Delma Presley.

Barred owl swooping through the cypress forest, Okefenokee National Wildlife Refuge

makes the park well worth a visit.

An **interpretive center** does a fine job of explaining the swamp's origins and topography; one diorama shows how peat mats release methane gas and float on the water to create the islands of "trembling earth." Boat and train **tours** explore the park's numerous lagoons and canals; boardwalks and an observation tower offer self-guided touring.

The one-hour railroad tour chugs around the edge of the wetlands, overlooking the swamp's waterways and its flora and fauna. Along the way, visitors will get a peek at a re-created Seminole village, a honeybee farm, and an old-fashioned swamper's moonshine still.

Although purists may be put off by both the animatronics bear show and the animal enclosures, a one- or two-hour excursion out into the real swamp is de rigueur. Whether you choose to rent a canoe or go on a tour, you'll thread close waterways overhung with mossy trees. The water is a black mirror that enfolds the prow of the boat, making stygian reflections of tree limbs and cypress knees. At times, the reflections are so vivid, and the water so still, that you have the illusion of floating through an airy canyon walled with trees and lily pads. ■

Providence Canyon
State Conservation Park

■ 1,109 acres ■ Southwest Georgia, 7 miles west of Lumpkin on Ga. 39C
■ Year-round ■ Hiking, backpacking, wildflower viewing ■ Parking fee ■ Contact the park, Rte. 1, Box 158, Lumpkin, GA 31815; phone 912-838-6202.
www.gastateparks.org

IF LOCAL SETTLERS HAD KNOWN and cared about the long-term effects of erosion, there might be no Providence Canyon today. Georgia's "little Grand Canyon" was not millions of years in the making, nor even hundreds. By 1850, area farmers had created erosion gullies 5 feet deep in the soft, clayish soil. With the soil depleted and washed away, the farmers moved on—but the erosion continued. Today the canyon is 150 feet deep. But instead of leaving an ugly ditch, the runoff exposed a series of

Colorful Providence Canyon

spectacularly colorful layers of sandy soil called the Providence Formation. The Ripley Formation, an erosion-resistant clay, gives way grudg-
ingly, while the canyon walls keep widening.

An **interpretive center** offers videos and exhibits to tell you more
about the canyon's geology and ecology. Outside, you can walk along the
rim, where overlooks provide jaw-dropping views of the rainbow of rich
colors on the canyon's walls and castlelike ridges and turrets. Bright
oranges, deep golds, russet reds, and creamy whites come into especially
sharp focus in the angled light of sunrise and sunset. The blooms of the
rare plumleaf azalea and other wildflowers heighten the effect from July
to September. The overlooks to the left of the picnic area are the most
thrilling. For a closer view, you can take the 3-mile **White Blaze Trail**
around and down into the canyon. Once at the bottom, you can explore
nine fingerlike side canyons, but be aware that the canyon floor can be
very muddy. The 7-mile **Red Blaze Trail** *(by permit only)* heads into the
canyon on the park's west side and offers campsites for backpackers. ■

White-tailed deer

Eufaula National Wildlife Refuge

■ 11,184 acres ■ Southeast Alabama, 6 miles north of Eufaula via US 431 and Ala. 165 ■ Year-round ■ Walking, wildlife viewing ■ Contact the refuge, 509 Old Hwy. 165, Eufaula, AL 36027; phone 334-687-4065. southeast.fws.gov/eufaula

THE EUFAULA NATIONAL WILDLIFE REFUGE straddles the Chattahoochee River, whose banks Creek Indians hunted and fished before the arrival of white settlers. The settlers cleared the land for farming; after World War II, pine plantations sprang up on former fields of cotton and grain. In 1964, officials established the Eufaula refuge and built the Walter F. George Dam, creating Walter F. George Reservoir, which lies at the heart of the refuge. The lake measures less than a mile wide here and features a number of small islands and feeder creeks.

The refuge sits on the eastern edge of the Mississippi flyway and offers critical habitat for migrating waterfowl, waterbirds, raptors, shorebirds, and songbirds. Its varied patchwork of wetlands, grasslands, woods, and old fields provides shelter for around 300 species of birds and 40 species of mammals. Alligators, wood storks, great blue herons, and anhingas are among those taking advantage of Eufaula's varied environment.

The **visitor station** offers mounted animals and information about the refuge. Outside, take the one-third-mile **nature trail** for a sampling of the kinds of scenery to be found here. Along the edges of woods and croplands, deer, rabbits, hawks, and owls find cover and food. The 7-mile

Wildlife Drive starts nearby. The drive takes you around dikes that hold impoundments where ducks, geese, little blue herons, great egrets, snowy egrets, and others dabble and stalk, swim and stand motionless. More than one-third of the refuge is open water; alligators are frequently seen in shallow water or sunning on banks during warm days. Wading birds step gingerly through the tall marsh grasses within the impoundments. An **observation tower** gives you a nice vantage point from which to view the wetlands.

Green tree frog

Farther along, another **viewing platform** overlooks the croplands covering roughly 10 percent of the refuge; farmers leave about a quarter of their crops—corn, peanuts, wheat, and soybeans—for wildlife. You can get out and walk along the dikes and roads. You may see armadillos, squirrels, raccoons, opossums, otters, coyotes, bobcats, beavers, and turkeys. Late fall through early spring is best for observing migratory waterfowl; southern bald eagles may be spotted during any season.

There are more nature trails, as well as a marina, a swimming pool, and other facilities, at the adjoining **Lakepoint Resort State Park** *(104 Lakepoint Dr., Eufaula, AL 36027. 334-687-6676).* ■

Dauphin Island

■ 7.5 sq. miles ■ Southern Alabama, Gulf of Mexico ■ Best seasons spring through fall ■ Fishing, bird-watching ■ Contact Dauphin Island Chamber of Commerce, P.O. Box 5, Dauphin Island, AL 36528; phone 334-861-5524 or 877-532-8744

IN THE SPRING, after a 500-mile flight across the Gulf of Mexico from Central and South America, many migratory birds make landfall on Dauphin Island, a 17-mile-long barrier island off the Gulf Coast of Alabama. Sometimes birds attempting to push on to the mainland meet with a rainy cold front, forcing a spectacular "fallout" of hundreds of birds. Exhausted, they rest. Come autumn, the island often sees the return of many migrants, as well as a healthy population of overwintering waterfowl, shorebirds, and seabirds.

The whole of Dauphin Island is a designated bird sanctuary, on which 345 species have been spotted—more than 85 percent of the state's total. Little wonder that it ranks high among birding locations in the Southeast.

A particularly rewarding place to bird-watch, the **Dauphin Island Audubon Bird Sanctuary** *(S side of Bienville St., E end of island. 334-861-2120)* covers 164 acres of maritime pine forests, marshes, and dunes.

A network of trails—about 1.5 miles of walking if you make a big loop—laces the sanctuary. Start out on the **Lake Loop Trail,** a boardwalk into a forest of loblolly and slash pine, southern magnolia, live oak, and tupelo gum. You can continue to the right on the yellow-blazed **Pond View Trail,** which has side trails to the left for a view of Gaillard Lake. In addition to wading birds, you might see turtles and alligators here.

Connect with the **Dune Edge Trail,** where you can take a boardwalk to the beach. This trail skirts a transition zone between the dunes and a tupelo swamp. Sea oats and goldenrod add strokes of texture to the dunes; warblers, vireos, tanagers, and painted buntings sing among the trees. The glassy tones you hear are the foghorns of natural gas rigs on

Hurricane Fury

When water temperatures in the Gulf of Mexico and the Caribbean rise in the summer, the energy released can fuel storms that pack a devastating wallop. If the storm turns into a cyclone with winds of 74 mph or greater, it's called a hurricane. Between 1986 and 1995, eight Gulf hurricanes—one severe —roared ashore. (That's actually a decline from the peak period, 1916-25, when 14 came ashore.)

When they do make landfall, the effects are striking. Hurricane Hugo, which hit the South Carolina coast in 1989 with 135 mph winds, destroyed more timber than any other natural disaster in the United States. Longleaf and loblolly pines 10 stories high snapped like sticks. Within hours, 100,000 acres of the luxuriant Francis Marion Forest had been turned into a battle zone of fallen giants, many of them leaning over as if they had not given up without a terrific struggle. Of the trees still standing, many later died because their cores had splintered as they twisted in the fierce winds. In all, enough trees were toppled to build 111,000 houses.

Heron resting in the aftermath of a hurricane

Pine seedling

the water. Fortunately, because natural gas is not soluble in water, its extraction has had a negligible effect on the local environment. In 30 years, the rigs will be removed or converted to fish farms.

Just east of the ferry dock, the **Dauphin Island Sea Lab's Estuarium** *(334-861-7500)* is an excellent place to learn about the surrounding coastal habitats. Using its 10,000 square feet of exhibit space, the facility outlines four systems: the delta, Mobile Bay, barrier islands, and the Gulf of Mexico. Highlights include a 9,000-gallon bay tank, an above-and-below display of freshwater marsh with turtles and gar, and a 16,000-gallon tank featuring amberjacks, sharks, rays, red snappers, and other denizens of the Gulf.

Outside, take the informative 2,000-foot-long **Living Marsh Board-walk** along the marsh at the edge of Mobile Bay. Fiddler crabs hide among long swatches of black needlerush and light green cordgrass, while pelicans hover overhead. Cordgrass stands farther out near the water, whereas needlerush usually grows above the high-tide line.

Egrets and herons comb the water's edge for crayfish, and gulls and terns congregate near the ferry docks. Watch for sharp-beaked terns that follow the ferries across to Fort Morgan on Mobile Point; many of them nest on this end of Dauphin Island. Laughing gulls can be identified by their black heads and raucous cries. If you see birds turning over oyster or clam shells, they are probably ruddy turnstones; their black-and-white heads, orange legs, and rust-striped wings give them a distinctive look.

As you look out onto the bay and Gulf, which are dotted with natural gas rigs, consider how critical the life in these bodies of water is to the United States. The waters out there produce 40 percent of the country's seafood, equaling about 100,000 annual tons. Shrimp leads the list of catches, while oysters, blue crabs, and mullet are also important. Further-more, the Gulf provides crucial habitat for an astonishing 75 percent of the migratory waterfowl in the nation. Water from two-thirds of the States funnels into the Gulf, and the waterbirds follow. ■

Bon Secour National Wildlife Refuge

■ 6,700 acres ■ Southern Alabama, about 9 miles west of Gulf Shores via Ala.
180 ■ Year-round. Spring and fall have smaller crowds and cooler temperatures
■ Hiking, fishing, wildlife viewing ■ Contact the refuge, 12295 Hwy. 180, Gulf
Shores, AL 36542; phone 334-540-7720. southeast.fws.gov/bonsecour

IN FOUR SECTIONS along the Fort Morgan Peninsula separating Mobile
Bay from the Gulf of Mexico, this refuge protects beach dunes and gently
rolling pine-oak woodlands, including 5 miles along the beach and more
than 12 miles along the bay. Though condominiums and beach houses
continue to sprout along this white-sand shore, Bon Secour provides safe
harbor for many native plants and animals, as well as undisturbed views
of wild dunes and pristine beach.

The **Pine Beach Trail** is the best place to explore the area's natural
heritage. Watch carefully for the single entrance sign on the south side
of Ala. 180. The 4-mile walk begins in a shady grove of live oaks and palmettos, the sandy path lined by feathery goldenrods and wax myrtles.
The trail skirts **Gator Lake** and **Little Lagoon,** where sand fringes a quiet,
shallow slip of water. Red basil, deer tongue, coral bean, and false fox-
glove are but a few of the many wildflowers you may see. On Gator
Lake, you can cast for bass, catfish, and bluegill; motorboats are not
allowed, so it stays peaceful. As you continue out through the loose sand
of the dunes, the going gets a little arduous. A hat and dark glasses are
essential to keep the intense glare from burning your eyes. Once on the
beach, you can see a few houses and high-rises, but you still have a clean
sweep of sand and surf shared mostly by birds.

Great blue herons, great egrets, tricolored herons, and snowy egrets
are commonly spotted in the refuge throughout the year, as are abundant
numbers of brown pelicans, swooping low along the coast and diving
for fish. Another fishing bird, the osprey, returns in the spring and remains through the fall; like eagles, ospreys catch fish in their long talons.
If you are fortunate, you may see them performing their amazing aerial
courtship displays, locking together and tumbling as if in unbound exal-
tation. In the springtime, the woods also resound with the twitter of
migratory songbirds.

In May, the wading birds begin their two-month nesting activities.
In breeding season, you can distinguish the snowies by the lovely white
plumes that stand up, punk-rock style, on their heads and necks. Cattle
egrets have similar plumes, but theirs are orange-brown.

Autumn, when temperatures are pleasant and crowds are nearly
nonexistent, makes for a delightful time to visit. The fall migration begins
in August and peaks by the middle of October. Hawks and sometimes

Palmettos in Bon Secour National Wildlife Refuge

Mole cricket burrows, Bon Secour NWR

falcons are to be seen riding thermals high up. October also brings hundreds of migrating monarch butterflies, adding dollops of saffron color to the plants on which the insects feed. Other refuge wildlife includes loggerhead sea turtles (in summer), alligators, gopher tortoises, bobcats, opossums, raccoons, squirrels, marsh and cottontail rabbits, and nine-banded armadillos.

About 3 miles east, pull to the right for the new **Jeff Friend Trail.** This pleasant 1-mile loop will take you through woods to a nice view of the saltwater Little Lagoon. ∎

Save the Mouse

Sometimes even the smallest creature requires special attention. The tiny Alabama beach mouse burrows in the dunes and lives off insects and seeds. But over the years, development, hurricanes, and heavy beach use have seriously reduced the creature's habitat, which is now limited to the strip of beach along the central and western portions of the Fort Morgan Peninsula. Current efforts to restore habitat focus on dune reconstruction through the use of drift fencing.

Why save these mice? They are a unique species and an important part of the food chain. And unlike other mice, this species is harmless: It does not invade buildings or dump sites. Furthermore, its existence is a good indicator that all is well on the dunes: Beach mice depend upon a healthy dune ecosystem to survive.

Weeks Bay National Estuarine Research Reserve

■ 6,000 acres ■ Southern Alabama, east shore of Mobile Bay, 10 miles west of Foley on Ala. 98 ■ Year-round, especially summer ■ Hiking, nature walks, bird-watching ■ Contact the reserve, 11300 Hwy. 98, Fairhope, AL 36532; phone 334-928-9792. www.ocrm.nos.noaa.gov/nerr/reserves/nerrweeks.html

BROWN PELICANS GLIDE over expanses of black needlerush, alligators and rare red-bellied turtles trundle across the sandy banks, and great blue herons pose in the backwaters of Weeks Bay, a fertile estuary of Mobile Bay. Blue crabs, shrimp, redfish, sea trout, and many other marine species find a vital refuge for breeding and feeding at this interface of salt water and fresh water. And within the reserve's extensive acreage of land and water are tidal flats, salt- and freshwater marshes, swamps, and upland forests that shelter nearly 350 species of resident and migratory birds.

Start at the **interpretive center,** which has several worthwhile hands-on and text exhibits about estuaries, Weeks Bay in particular. Then stroll out onto the 3,200-foot-long **boardwalk** behind the center. It begins in a low forested swamp of live oak and magnolia and continues out to a platform over a salt marsh, where rushes and grasses sigh in rhythmic cadence with the wind, and egrets flap along the meandering shoreline. In October and March, keep your eyes peeled for migratory white pelicans.

Another boardwalk trail heads out into a mossy, grassy **pitcher plant bog.** The bog has acidic, sandy soil low in nutrients, so plants have adapted ways of getting what they need in order to thrive. The carnivorous pitcher plants have hollow tubes that are lined with stiff hairs to trap insects, which fall to the bottom of the pitcher and are dissolved in an enzyme-rich liquid. The plants then absorb the insects' minerals. This is one of the few places in the wild where the queens of the bog, the scarlet-flowering white-topped pitchers, can be easily seen.

In the spring and the summer, the bog is transformed into an enchanted garden of miniature delights. You should look closely for pink and gold orchids, sunset-orange pine lilies, and black swallowtail butterflies. ■

Marsh at Weeks Bay

Gulf Islands National Seashore

■ 139,775 acres (includes Mississippi district; all but 19,000 acres are sub-merged lands) ■ Northwest Florida, in several sections, south of Pensacola; southern Mississippi ■ Year-round. Best in summer when the Gulf waters are warmest. Migratory birds pass through in spring and fall ■ Camping, hiking, boating, swimming, fishing, wildlife viewing ■ Adm. fees for some units ■ Contact the national seashore, 1801 Gulf Breeze Pkwy., Gulf Breeze, FL 32561; phone 850-934-2600. www.nps.gov/guis

BRILLIANT BLUE GULF WATERS. Dreamy mirror-smooth marshes. Sparkling sugar-white beaches, punctuated by 19th-century forts. Running along the coastal fringes of northwestern Florida, the eastern part of Gulf Islands National Seashore comprises six separate units that preserve the

Fisherman on Gulf Islands National Seashore

area's rich natural and cultural history (a western district lies about 75 miles away in Mississippi). Long, narrow barrier islands, the framework for the variety of habitats here, protect the mainland and the fertile salt marshes in between, forming a breeding ground for a host of marine life.

Serene slips of sand and sea oats, the barrier islands were formed over thousands of years by the constant forces of waves, winds, and currents. Possibly they were a dune system built up during the last ice age, when the sea level was much lower. In any event, they are still forming and changing. If you could see a time-lapse film of the past thousand years, the islands would appear to be slowly migrating west. The santa ends of the islands gradually erode, while the western ends build up. Big storms sometimes accelerate the process, dramatically altering the landscape. Hurricane Frederic in 1979 shoved dunes all over Santa Rosa Island, and Hurricane Opal in 1995 demolished the picnic pavilions and boardwalks on the same island. Sea oats and other plants with extensive root systems can help to anchor the dunes, but even they are powerless in the face of brutal storms.

Finding niches among the sandy dunes, pine woods, grassy bayous, and warm waters are an abundance of animals, from hermit crabs and loggerheads to pelicans and pompano. Behind the dunes, scrubby growth gradually builds to stands of slash pines and live oaks where reptiles, birds, and mammals find homes away from the salt spray of the ocean. Interlacing the islands and the mainland are lovely grass-edged lagoons and bays that harbor egrets, herons, alligators, and thousands of migratory birds in the spring and the fall.

What to See and Do

Naval Live Oaks Area

The main **visitor center** is located at the Naval Live Oaks Area (*2 miles E of Gulf Breeze via US 98*), where you can get information and view a 12-minute slide show. There are several trails near here. Out back, a three-quarter-mile **nature trail** twists through a forest of pine and moss-draped live oak, red cedar, and spiky saw palmetto.

In 1829, John Quincy Adams established the first federal tree farm here to secure a supply of timber for building warships. The heavy, disease-resistant live oaks were perfect. As you walk the trail you can see, with the help of interpretive panels, how a V-shaped crook or a curved limb could have been used for a ship's keel or rib.

The trail ends at an observation deck overlooking Santa Rosa Sound, especially peaceful at sunset. Or you can take a beach trail to the water's edge to watch long-legged birds and barges. In the sound, sea grasses tremble in gentle currents, acting as nurseries for redfish, striped mullet, crabs, oysters, and shrimp. Noise from the nearby highway is slight, although jets from nearby Pensacola Naval Air Station do occasionally rip the silence.

Across the highway, more than 3 miles of trails lace another section of oak-and-pine forest. Look for sand pines (short needles), longleaf pines, pignut hickories, and magnolias. Spanish moss curtains the green windows of this

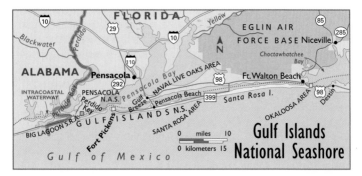

Arsenal, Santa Rosa Island

haunting southern forest, where solitary and unseen clapper rails make staccato calls at dusk and great blue herons wade the edges of Pensacola Bay just beyond the stillness of the trees.

Fort Pickens Area

Drive out to **Santa Rosa Island** and head west on Fort Pickens Road from Fla. 399 to reach the Fort Pickens Area. The national seashore scrolls out to the end of the peninsula—8 beautiful miles all told. In some places, you have breathtaking views of Pensacola Bay to the right as well as the wide sun-spanked Gulf to the left.

After about 6 miles, pull over for the **Dune Nature Trail,** a 1,600-foot-long boardwalk through primary and secondary dunes. You walk over a rolling terrain of scrubby growth—Florida rosemary, yaupon holly, and little sand live oaks that grow smaller as you head toward the beach. The farther out you go, the fewer species you find; not many can take the environment. Vegetation near the last dunes is gnarled and twisted by wind and salt spray.

Bird tracks litter the sand above the wrack line amid polished driftwood and other flotsam. Look for ghost crabs sidling like tiny wind-blown skeletons toward their holes, while along the surf sanderlings skitter about in search of small crustaceans.

On the opposite side of the road, off the campground, **Blackbird Marsh Nature Trail** makes a half-mile loop around an open marsh. The lower limbs of one old live oak lean like elbows on the sandy ground. Slash pines reach skyward, needles scenting the air. The bark of the trees is patterned with large scales that peel like paper. Panels explain historical uses of local plants. The caffeinated leaves of yaupon holly, for example, were used to make coffee during the Civil War, but too much could cause vomiting—hence the Latin name *Ilex vomitoria*.

A few feet difference in elevation in this maritime forest can result in a completely different plant community. Water drains and evaporates quickly from higher areas, making them less suitable for moisture-loving plants.

Down at the west end of the island, you can poke around the ruins of **Fort Pickens,** a colossal bastion completed in 1834 to defend Pensacola Bay in concert with forts on the mainland and Perdido Key. From atop some of the batteries, there are fine views of the blue-green Gulf and the bay.

Perdido Key

Across the channel lies the wild eastern end of Perdido Key, a separate unit of Gulf Islands National Seashore. Access is by Fla. 292 southwest from Pensacola. You can park at the Rosamond Johnson Beach swimming area or continue a couple of miles to road's end, then get out and walk. Ahead lies a strand of untouched beach and dunes more than 5 miles long. Among anglers' prizes are whiting, red drum, bluefish, and sea trout.

Herons and egrets, also hunting seafood, frequent the estuaries along Big Lagoon on the left, while to the right pelicans plane the waters of the Gulf and terns hang like paper kites above the foam. In the summer, scan for the treadmark tracks of sea turtles leading from the beach to the dunes.

Big Lagoon State Recreation Area

Across the Intracoastal Waterway from Perdido Key, the Big Lagoon State Recreation Area *(12 miles W of Pensacola, on Fla. 292A. 904-492-1595. Adm. fee)* is worth a stop. The road curves through a pine forest and coastal dunes. Trails explore marshes and woods, as well as the lagoon area. Foxes and raccoons find cover in the slash pine woods, and songbirds such as cardinals and towhees fill the uplands with music. Scrub vegetation grows on the rises of ancient dunes, while in the swales between the dune ridges, a dense, moisture-loving thicket makes travel nearly impossible.

Don't neglect to take the **East Beach Boardwalk** at the end of the road. It leads across a tidal marsh, where a 40-foot observation tower offers a choice perch for spying on fish, wading birds, and other wildlife sheltering among the sun-struck shallows and high grasses. From here you can see the curves of the lagoon and Perdido Key.

Finally, two parcels of shore on the east end of Santa Rosa Island complete the national seashore mosaic. The **Santa Rosa Area** contains a long sliver of dazzling white beach topped with waving fronds of sea oats. About 13 miles to the east, the **Okaloosa Area** occupies a gentle curve of beach on the sound side. In addition to swimming and other recreation, these areas offer opportunities for sighting wildlife, finding shells, and walking along undeveloped coastal margins. ∎

Live oaks at Gulf Islands National Seashore

Wisteria, Conecuh National Forest

Blackwater River State Forest and Conecuh National Forest

■ 274,000 acres combined ■ Northwest Florida and south Alabama ■ Year-round. Spring and early autumn good for quiet visit ■ Camping, hiking, canoe-ing, fishing, horseback riding ■ Use caution during late fall and winter hunting season—wearing hunter orange advised. During summer, wear insect repellent against mosquitoes, chiggers, and ticks. Carry your own water, or boil what you find ■ Contact Blackwater River State Forest, 11650 Munson Hwy., Milton, FL 32570, phone 850-957-6140. www.fl-dof.com/Fm/stforest/blackwater/; or Cone-cuh National Forest, Rte. 5, Box 157, Andalusia, AL 36420, phone 334-222-2555

AN IMMENSE, UNPUBLICIZED TRACT of hilly woodlands, Blackwater River State Forest and Conecuh National Forest together encompass the largest unbroken expanse of longleaf woodland in existence. With the spread of urban and agricultural areas throughout the Southeast Coastal Plain and the replacement of longleaf with competing species, longleaf pines have been reduced to less than 4 percent of their original 90 million acres.

In order to maintain the area's historical, parklike openness—tall pines floored by grasses—the Forest Service burns several thousand acres in a controlled way each year. The prescribed fires do a number of other things as well. By cleaning up the pine needles, branches, and vines that litter the forest floor, the burns reduce the chances of a catastrophic forest fire. They also stimulate seed production, control needle blight on pine seedlings, and stem the advance of hardwoods and other competing species—all of which helps to protect the travel and feeding niches of the local wildlife. What's at stake here is one of the most biodiverse of all forest ecosystems, suited to the particular needs of hundreds of kinds of animals.

Still preserved within these forests is a wealth of plant and animal life, including numerous threatened and endangered species. Wild turkeys, bears, and bobcats track along the many lakes and streams; elusive red-cockaded woodpeckers make homes in tall pines; and carnivorous pitcher plants grow in bogs, unseen by humans until the growing-season fires opened the area up.

Over the eons, sand and gravel and other sediments from southward-flowing streams gradually built up the area's ridges with sandy, clayish soil. Elevations now range from 10 feet in the Florida bottomlands to about 335 feet in the Alabama uplands. Admittedly not a strikingly diverse terrain, it still creates a variety of forest niches. Cypresses, slash pines, and assorted bottomland hardwoods thrive in the moist bottomlands and bogs. Once you leave the bottoms, wire grass occupies the entire forest floor, except on the highest, driest ridges, where bluestem becomes the primary ground cover. Above the bottomlands, longleaf pines are the dominant species, with mixtures of slash pines, oaks, and loblolly pines on the lower slopes.

It's not easy to tell these three kinds of southern pines apart: All have long needles; tall, straight trunks; and an orange-brown bark divided into plates covered by papery scales. The longleaf has lower limbs that tend to droop a little more than do those of the other two pines and a wilder, less rounded crown. The longleaf can reach 120 feet in height; its needles can grow to 18 inches long and its cones up to 12 inches. The needles and cones of the loblolly are usually less than half the size of the longleaf's. All three pines produce seeds that are eaten by wild turkeys, fox squirrels, and some songbirds. Out in the forest, these pines give off a delightfully resinous smell and provide hikers with a soft carpet of needles.

What to See and Do

Blackwater River State Forest

Etched with roads both paved and unpaved, this 189,594-acre state forest offers plenty of opportunity for exploring the natural history of a longleaf pine community. Bear in mind that this is a multiuse forest, so people are here for a number of reasons: hiking, birding, fishing, canoeing, swimming, horseback riding, and hunting. If you plan to do any extensive walking, check on when and where the hunting occurs. Logging continues here, though clear-cutting has for the most part been phased out, resulting in a forest that still feels primeval.

For maps and information, stop by the **Forestry Center** (*Just S of the junction of Fla. 4 and 191*). From here, it's less than a mile east to the turnoff (*left*) for **Krul Recreation Area,** where you can swim in a cold, clear, spring-fed lake. Lofty pines preside over the scene, and dogwoods wear snowy blossoms in spring.

Just past the campground, pick up the 4.5-mile **Sweetwater Hiking Trail,** which crosses Sweetwater Creek on a swinging bridge, goes over a dam, and winds

around manmade **Bear Lake.** About a mile from one end to the other, Bear Lake is an exceptional place to cast for largemouth bass, bluegill, and channel catfish.

At the lake, Sweetwater Hiking Trail joins up with the 21-mile **Jackson Trail,** part of the Florida National Scenic Trail (see pp. 244-45). The Jackson Trail heads southwest and northeast. If you walk northeast, you'll cross the Blackwater River in about 5 miles, then intersect with the Wiregrass Trail a few miles later. You can take the **Wiregrass Trail** several miles northwest to the **Hurricane Lake area** or southeast to **Karick Lake.**

The Jackson Trail crosses various roads, so you can figure out a loop or arrange a pickup spot. Wildlife you may see includes deer,

Blackwater River State Forest & Conecuh National Forest

Canoeists rounding a bend in Blackwater River State Forest

armadillos, hogs, red and gray foxes, quail, and endangered red-cockaded woodpeckers.

In the extreme southwest pocket of the forest, **Blackwater River State Park** *(3 miles N of US 90 on Deaton Bridge Rd. 850-983-5363. Adm. fee)* is situated on a scenic 2-mile stretch of the Blackwater River, a sand-bottom river with lovely white sandbars. The water's dark tea color comes from tannins in local plants. The Blackwater River forms part of the designated **Florida Canoe Trail;** nearby outfitters can set you up with a canoe.

Canoeing on the river, you will glide past inviting wire grass and gallberry meadows and beneath the shade of oaks, tupelos, sweet bays, and red maples. If you prefer land travel, the 9-mile **Chain of Lakes Nature Trail** follows the river's edge through a swampy area and a forest of longleaf pine and turkey oak. By foot or canoe, you'll find the views of white sand undulating beneath currents of black water captivating and timeless.

Several horse trails in the western part of the forest start from the **Coldwater Recreation Area.** The Atlantic white cedar and titi (an evergreen shrub) line the banks of Coldwater Creek. Look for tracks of snakes and bobcats on quiet slips of sand beach, and green herons fishing in oxbow lakes.

Conecuh National Forest

Like the Blackwater River to the south, the Conecuh (kuh-NAY-kuh) is known as a longleaf pine forest. Spliced among stands of pines are cypress ponds, pitcher plant bogs, and purling creeks lined by scrub oaks and flowering dogwoods. Canebrakes scattered throughout the forest are remnants of once prominent patches of native switch cane that grew along the rivers; Native Americans used the cane in baskets, weapons, and dwellings. In fact, the name *Conecuh* reputedly derives from the Muskogee Indian words for "land of cane." Pick up brochures

Hiking trail marker

and trail information at the
Conecuh Ranger Station *(US 29,
3.3 miles S of US 84 Andalusia
bypass, on right).*

A good place to get a taste for
the forest, the **Open Pond Recreation Area** *(5.2 miles S of US 29
on Fla. 137, then left on Cty. Rd. 24
and follow signs)* boasts a 30-acre
sinkhole lake for fishing and boating *(electric trolling motors only)*
and a 1938 heartwood-pine picnic
shelter.

Largemouth bass, bream, and
catfish glide beneath the opaque
waters of the lake, and you can
stretch your legs with a picturesque 1.5-mile stroll through the
woods around its perimeter. Pied-
billed grebes float with the herons
and egrets that wade along the
reedy shore, sometimes sinking
until only their heads are above
water. Alligators bask in pools of
sunlight, while snaky anhingas and
beautiful purple gallinules with
parrotlike red-and-yellow beaks

contribute a hint of the tropics in
summertime.

The lake loop is part of the
20-mile **Conecuh Trail,** which explores several of the forest's ecosystems, from river bottoms and
bay swamps to pine uplands and
hardwood habitats. A lovely 5-mile
loop for hikers leads from Open
Pond to the crystalline cold waters
of Blue Spring near Five Runs
Creek. The hiking is slightly hilly.
Along the way, you pass Buck and
Ditch ponds—water-filled sinkholes formed when porous underground limestone caved in.

The call of the bobwhite rings
in the shadowy, open woods, and
the mourning dove sighs its unre-
solvable, infinitely sad tritone in
the late afternoon. Look for common nighthawks soaring the
heights, great crested flycatchers
with bright yellow bellies working
the upper forest canopy, and warblers and vireos spangling the
mid-story with sudden riffs of
color and song. If you want to
wake up to the sounds and sights
of this forest, you can pitch your
tent near the trail *(except during
the mid-November to January
hunting season).*

The trail has a branch leading
in about 3 miles to the **Blue Lake
Recreation Area** *(April-Oct.; adm.
fee),* or you can drive up *(1.5 miles
N on Fla. 137, then right 2 miles).*
You can swim here, then investigate more of the Conecuh Trail.
It's about another 1.5 miles to the
big 13.5-mile **North Loop,** which
passes ponds and swamps aquiver
with myriad forms of life.

Tree frogs blat in cool bogs, and
gopher turtles trundle among the
underbrush. To find red-cockaded

Old cabin in Conecuh National Forest

woodpeckers, look for pines with white smears of resin high up, like dripping candles. Woodpeckers create this resin flow to deter snakes and other predators from climbing into the tree cavities and taking the eggs. During nesting season (March-July) at sunrise or sunset, you can see adults flying and hear nestlings calling from within the trees.

Keep on the lookout in the boggy areas for rare plants designated "sensitive" because of their declining populations: The rose orchid droops its pastel head beneath a crown of three red petals; the panhandle lily, with its freckled yellow blooms, has a stem up to 6 feet tall; the delicate white arum opens like a candle flame from a straight green shoot; yel-low-eyed grass stipples a green marsh like a field of pulsing stars.

Perhaps the most fascinating plants growing here are the various pitchers and other carnivorous plants. These plants capture insects to supply themselves with nutrients lacking in the soil. Pitcher plants have tall vaselike stems with nectar and flowers to attract bugs, which become entangled in the long hairs. During love bug season, white-topped pitchers can fill with more than 2,000 insects. The sundews and butterworts trap insects in a mucousy dab that glistens like dew; hairs enfold prey and release digestive juices. The bladderwort is covered with tiny bladders that flash open in .002 seconds to capture mosquito larvae and other insects. ■

Torreya State Park

■ 2,600 acres ■ Northwest Florida, east side of Apalachicola River, south of I-10 via Cty. Rd. 1641 ■ Year-round ■ Edge of Eastern Time Zone runs along the park's western border ■ Camping, hiking ■ Adm. fee ■ Contact the park, HC 2, Box 70, Bristol, FL 32321; phone 850-643-2674. www.dep.state.fl.us/parks/District_1/Torreya

SPREAD ALONG THE HIGH BLUFFS of the Apalachicola River, this out-of-the-way state park in the Florida Panhandle holds many natural features worth seeing. The views, first of all, are quite lovely, especially from the 150-foot-high bluffs in the late afternoon, when golden light turns the lazy river and its forested banks into a luminous landscape. You also have the rare opportunity to see torreya trees, which the park was established to preserve. The 30-foot-tall conifers have become endangered because of a fungus that attacks their stems, and they exist now only along the river here and just over the Georgia border. These trees are beautiful to behold.

The 15-mile **Torreya Trail,** accessible from several points on the park

Gregory House, 19th-century plantation house in Torreya State Park

road, loops through a forest of hardwoods, shrubs, and wildflowers, passing cypress swamps, pine uplands, and hardwood hammocks. Deer and bobcats forage far back in these woods, and some 20 kinds of birds live here or pass through regularly. The best part of the trail is along the river bluffs; in autumn, the wooded ravines blaze with the kind of color you don't expect to find in Florida.

Up here you'll also pass the remains of a Confederate gun pit, installed to protect this important water route from federal warships. It's hard to imagine the peaceful, winding river down there as a key highway, but until about 1910, steamboats loaded with trade goods paraded up and down the **Apalachicola River.** While standing here, you can also try to picture cotton fields spreading along the other side of the river, where bottomland hardwoods now stand.

Before the Civil War, the plantation of Jason Gregory operated just downriver. In 1935, his Georgian-style house was dismantled, floated across the river, and reassembled over a three-year period by the Civilian Conservation Corps, which developed the park. The structure was painstakingly restored and now commands a prime spot at the end of the park road. A rolling lawn in back leads to a fine river view. ∎

Apalachicola Bluffs and Ravines Preserve

■ 6,248 acres ■ Northwest Florida, north of Bristol ■ Year-round ■ Hiking, wildlife viewing ■ Contact the Nature Conservancy, NW Florida Program, P.O. Box 393, Bristol, FL 32321; phone 850-643-2756. www.tncflorida.org/pages/apalachicola_preserve.html

A RIBBON OF WOODED RAVINES running north from Bristol for about 20 miles, this Nature Conservancy site protects rare biota on the east side of the Apalachicola River. The preserve's property includes pine uplands and sand hills, spring-fed creeks, river bluffs, and ravines holding a consortium of plants and animals that has remained practically unchanged for millennia. Cold air masses funneled from rivers during the ice ages met with warm Gulf air and produced a foggy climate favorable for the penetration of northern plant species this far south. Isolated by new mountain ranges, relict species held on here. The presence of steep bluffs, shade, and seepage from creeks has helped this microclimate persist. The area continues to support such rare species as the Florida yew and the torreya. When a power company targeted one of the bluffs for a coal-burning plant in 1981, scientists convinced the company that building the plant elsewhere would save a unique piece of the Southeast's natural history. To preserve the local ecology, the Conservancy has planted more than 1.5 million longleaf pine seedlings and is presently restoring the richly diverse ground cover. Prescribed burns have helped control invading hardwoods and maintain the open upland vistas.

The easiest place to learn about the bluffs and ravines is the 3.5-mile **Garden of Eden Trail** (*Just N of Bristol, W off Fla. 12*). Traversing a lost remnant of the Miocene epoch, the trail takes its name from local lore claiming that Adam and Eve were buried near Bristol, not far from the original Paradise. Though you'd hardly call it a garden stroll, the trail does give you a feel for one of Florida's most topographically interesting areas. Cut by underground streams, steep ravines are forested with beech and dogwood, holly and mountain laurel, and sweet-smelling magnolia. You'll also find steephead ravines—natural amphitheaters 50 yards wide, where the terrain suddenly slopes away and you are at eye level with treetops 100 feet above the ground.

The trail leads to a bluff overlooking the Apalachicola. The steep, exposed bluff was formed by a steady eastward migration of the river, which continues to cut away the bank while leaving a flat floodplain opposite. Bald eagles and swallow-tailed kites soar here. ■

Blooming cactus

Wire grass and longleaf pines

Hiking through the dunes, Topsail Hill State Preserve

Topsail Hill State Preserve

■ 1,639 acres ■ Northwest Florida, Santa Rosa Beach, 1 mile west of US 98 and Cty. Hwy. 30A intersection, then south ■ Year-round. Swimming best in summer ■ Hiking, swimming, fishing, bird-watching ■ Contact the preserve, c/o Gregory E. Moore RV Resort, 7525 W. Cty. Hwy. 30A, Santa Rosa Beach, FL 32459; phone 850-267-0299. www.topsailhill.com

TO EXPERIENCE THE GULF COAST the way it was before development, drive out to this unheralded coastal wilderness. The park's 1,639 acres include 3.5 miles of pristine, white-sand beach, 25-foot-tall dunes, and freshwater lakes. You'll find nothing man-made except the 0.7-mile dirt road to the beach, a picnic shelter, kiosk, portable restroom, and a trail. The lack of civilization is precisely what makes this place so appealing.

Park your car and traipse over the fine quartz sand to the beach, where you'll have acres of shoreline and limitless vistas of sun-bright Gulf waters to admire. Pale gray sanderlings scoot along the apron of surf, brown pelicans glide beyond the breakers, and laughing gulls chuckle overhead. Watch for black skimmers dipping their distinctive black-and-red bills, plowing for fish as they skim right above the water's surface.

Just north of the parking area, pass the "Road Closed" sign on the left to access the 2.5-mile **Maritime Nature Trail.** Starting out in a forest of slash pines and saw palmettos, the trail curls to the right, beside lovely Morris Lake. Bird and mammal tracks dot the sandy shore. Great blue herons can often be spotted along here, as can common loons during winter migrations. A boardwalk picks up the trail for a while, threading between the lake and a line of tall dunes, though you do have many views of the Gulf in the swales. Saltwater intrusion from Hurricane Opal in 1995 killed a lot of the slash pines, giving the marsh a war zone look in places. But it's far from dead. Here and there grow little clumps of feathery conradina, and vines of morning glory trail in the sand like purple bows on a long ponytail. Far to the west you can see a high-rise hotel or condominium, and the occasional Air Force jet rends the blue vault; otherwise you're wrapped in a cocoon of prehistoric peace and quiet. ■

St. Joseph Peninsula State Park

■ 2,516 acres ■ Northwest Florida, 20 miles southwest of Port St. Joe ■ Year-round, especially spring through fall ■ Camping, hiking, boating, swimming, fishing, bird-watching ■ Adm. fee ■ Contact the park, 8899 Cape San Blas Rd., Port St. Joe, FL 32456; phone 850-227-1327. www.dep.state.fl.us/parks/District_1/StJoseph

OCCUPYING A SLENDER FINGER of land hooking into the Gulf of Mexico, this gorgeous 2,516-acre park presents a 9-mile-long ocean beach of white sand, mirrored by a slightly longer bay shore on lovely St. Joseph Bay. Among the natural highlights are giant dunes, 209 bird species, and annual migrations of hawks and monarch butterflies. With 70 percent of it—the north end of the peninsula—a designated wilderness zone and with a lovely, quiet beach for shelling and strolling, this park ranks as one of the top nature venues on the Gulf Coast.

Raccoon among the grasses

From the warm, shallow waters of St. Joseph Bay, Native Americans once reaped a rich harvest of shellfish. Bay scallops, fiddler crabs, horseshoe crabs, hermit crabs, octopuses, and many other marine animals are still prevalent. In the 1600s, a Spanish fort presided over the peninsula; in the 20th century, the peninsula served as a training facility for the Army during World War II. The park was established in 1964.

Boardwalks from the campgrounds lead past dunes more than 55 feet tall and out to a wide beach on the gentle Gulf Coast. Black-necked stilts, sandpipers, and other shorebirds skim the sandbars and patrol along the surf. You can fish Gulfside for pompano, bluefish, sea trout, and flounder, to name a few, or just walk or swim and enjoy the tranquillity. From May to August, sea turtles heave themselves up on the shore to dig nests.

It's a trek of 7 to 9 miles from the boardwalks to the solitary end of the peninsula. Primitive camping is allowed in the wilderness *(permit required),* or you can book a remote cabin for comfortable bay views. Just off the first campground, the quarter-mile **Barrier Dune Trail** *(no parking for day-use visitors)* loops through a sandy maze of Florida rosemary, scrub pines, yaupon, and Spanish bayonet. Mammals here include raccoons, skunks, and cotton mice, though they are primarily nocturnal.

Summer draws the most people, but fall and spring have the best weather and the fewest insects. If you're here in fall, you may witness the hawk migration, which can—especially after a cold front—be spectacular: Hundreds of sharp-shinned, broad-winged, and other hawks funnel through here on good days. Because broad-winged, red-tailed, and red-winged hawks are high soarers, binoculars are helpful. Other birds of prey you may see include swallow-tailed kites, kestrels, merlins, ospreys, and peregrine falcons. Also in autumn come hosts of monarch butterflies, spilling through like floating orange flowers on their way to Mexico.

To explore the bay side, take the half-mile **Maritime Hammock Trail,** which starts not far from the park entrance. An arch of pines and muscadine grapes leads into a palm hammock anchored by old live oaks. Red cedars and shady magnolias consort with wax myrtles and red-berried yaupons. Out in the high-grass marshes, time ceases to matter: Herons pose like statues, fiddler crabs scurry to bubbling holes, and bay scallops and shrimp live by the rise and fall of the tides. ∎

Soaring

Slowly circling hundreds of feet up, hawks use their sharp eyes to spot fellow birds, mice, and other prey. How do they stay up there with hardly a flap? They ride columns of hot air called thermals, which rise over sun-warmed water or ground. The hot air fountains from the top of the column and curls back around, forming a doughnut-shaped bubble. The hawks gyre in this bubble until they reach its base, then use gravity to glide until they hit another thermal. Fluffy, flat-bottomed cumulus clouds are an indication of thermals directly beneath.

Turtles queuing on the safe side of an alligator, Wakulla Springs

Wakulla Springs State Park

■ 4,743 acres ■ Northwest Florida, 16 miles south of Tallahassee on Fla. 267
■ Year-round, primarily summer ■ Hiking, swimming, wildlife viewing, boat
tours ■ Adm. fee ■ Contact the park, 550 Wakulla Park Dr., Wakulla Springs,
FL 32305; phone 850-224-5950. www.dep.state.fl.us/parks/District_1/Wakulla

A GRACIOUS SWEEP OF LAWN overhung by mossy live oaks leads from
a 1937 Mediterranean Revival-style lodge down to a spring-fed lake
where glass-bottom boat tours transport visitors on a river filled with
natural wonders. Yes, Wakulla Springs State Park is an old-fashioned
tourist attraction, but it eschews commercial hype. Instead, this low-
key site gets by on its well-deserved reputation as a wildlife sanctuary
of great beauty and richness. The park's parcel of longleaf pine forest
and old-growth floodplain swamp centers on a crystal-clear, first-
magnitude spring that forms the headwaters of the 9-mile Wakulla
River. In and around the spring waters live alligators, turtles, deer, and
thousands of birds.

Though no one knows the origins of Wakulla's water, scientists esti-
mate that the source of the springs covers more than 600 square miles of
caverns and tortuous tunnels forming one of north Florida's key aquifers.
Wherever the springs arise, their output is tremendous—more than 200
million gallons of pure cold water a day, or enough to fill a 3-square-mile
lake to 12 feet. Using underwater scooters, divers have explored more
than 3 miles of the vast cave system, reaching depths of 300 feet.

The unfathomable nature of the springs remains part of their allure.
Though many area springs (including Wakulla) claim they were visited in
the early 1500s by Ponce de Leon in his search for the legendary fountain
of youth, Wakulla has a tangible link to an even longer lineage: The bones
of a mastodon which probably fell through the ice during the last ice age
lie about 85 feet down. They are visible on a clear, sunny day.

Following pages: Moss-draped cypress trees, Wakulla Springs

What to See and Do

Proceed to the dock and sign up for a river tour. Summer can draw a crowd, but the wait is not bad. Guides narrate the 30-minute glass-bottom boat tours *(fee)*, which give you a chance to see above and below the surface. (The see-through wells are a great improvement over the glass-bot-tomed buckets handed to visitors on tours long ago.) If the water is murky, as happens after heavy rains, you'll have to settle for a 40-minute, narrated river wildlife cruise—still a wonderful chance to study the extensive life above the surface.

The tours travel about a mile downstream, through a shadowy waterway overhung by ancient buzzard-haunted cypresses, live oaks, water oaks, black willows, and vine-wrapped palms. It's not surprising to learn that the early Tarzan movies and the 1954 *Creature from the Black Lagoon* were filmed here; you can almost imagine a fin-faced monster crawling into the boat.

What's actually here is breathtaking enough. Alligators loll on murky banks, and scores of herons and egrets flutter about. Perched on a low branch, an anhinga spreads its graceful wings to dry, while emerald green turtles splash one by one from a sunny log and a rare limpkin—a chocolate brown wading bird named for its unusual, limping gait—hides behind a fan of wild rice. Red-beaked moorhens cackle like monkeys among the lily pads. Other migratory species include coots, wigeons, and hooded mergansers.

Fall and spring see lots of migratory waterbirds.

You might think the boats would scare the birds, but much of the resident wildlife has grown up accepting the low, slow rumble of tour boats as background noise. If you're not on a glass-bottom tour, take a look over the edge of the boat for close-up views of hydrilla; the kudzu of the underwater world, this exotic green weed native to Sri Lanka has been taking over the region's eelgrass.

The river continues another 2 miles within the park, then 6 more down to the **St. Marks River.** The 2-mile section beyond the tour is a wildlife sanctuary, part of the park but off-limits to the public.

On land, you can head out from the lodge's west side on the 2-mile, wood-chip-strewn **Sally Ward Nature Trail.** It winds through a hardwood forest of ash, beech, magnolia, and red maple along **Sally Ward Creek,** ending at a spring near the park entrance. Part of the trail passes through a slough that may be muddy, but you can detour around it.

Exciting plans are afoot at Wakulla. In 1999, the park acquired some 2,800 acres of property, nearly doubling its size. In addition to protecting the watershed on Wakulla's northwest and southwest sides, the extra acreage will be managed in part for recreation. Trails will explore the old-growth floodplain swamps, longleaf pine forests, and other communities, and local wildlife will have that much more room to live in peace. ∎

Wax myrtle berries in longleaf pine forest, St. Marks NWR

St. Marks National Wildlife Refuge

■ 67,000 acres ■ Northwest Florida, 23 miles south of Tallahassee via Lighthouse Rd. ■ Year-round. Bird-watching best fall through spring ■ Hiking, fishing, bird-watching, auto tour ■ Adm. fee ■ Contact the refuge, P.O. Box 68, St. Marks, FL 32355; phone 850-925-6121. saintmarks.fws.gov

ONE OF FLORIDA'S BEST KEPT SECRETS, this spacious refuge on Apalachee Bay offers long sweeping views of salt marshes and tree islands that rival the Everglades in beauty. Created in 1931 as one of the first national wildlife refuges, St. Marks now spans 26 pristine miles of the Gulf Coast. Prodigious numbers of animals favor this enormous property: 274 species of birds (migratory and year-round), 52 species of mammals, 40 species of amphibians, and 66 species of reptiles. Rare and endangered animals include the least tern, red-cockaded woodpecker, wood stork, and Florida black bear.

In the layered canopy of the pine-palmetto flatwoods, songbirds flash through shafts of sunlight and the scent of pine and fresh earth fills the air. Alligators and bobcats take to the moist recesses of the cypress swamps and hardwood hammocks, where purple pickerelweed and other wildflowers add accents to little ponds and sloughs.

Out on the needlerush marshes, single wading birds make lovely sun-burnished silhouettes, and crowds of waterfowl rise in raucous accord at daybreak. Among the most easily spotted birds that nest here are great blue herons, great egrets, little blue herons, tricolored herons, cattle egrets, white ibises, pied-billed grebes, and anhingas. Look for belted kingfishers hovering like hummingbirds and diving for fish and pairs of bald eagles chasing flocks of ducks. Eagles usually lay their eggs at St. Marks during December. In 1979, the wildlife refuge had only one known eagle nest. Two decades later, more than a dozen of them were spotted.

What to See and Do

The **visitor center** has several fine dioramas of mounted animals in their habitats, as well as a good selection of books and free literature. The short (one-third mile) **Plum Orchard Pond Trail** teaches you about the native flora as the path winds past a pond and dips into a palm-and-hardwood forest. The star-shaped leaves of sweet gums sprinkle coins of sunlight on the forest floor; southern magnolias provide shady hideaways for lizards and small birds. You can recognize the prevalent cabbage palm (palmetto) by its cross-hatched trunk of thick fibers.

Next, take the 7-mile **Lighthouse Road,** surely one of the highlights of ecotouring in the Southeast. A beautiful way to spend a morning is to arrive at dawn with your bicycle and take your time riding quietly down the road, stopping at viewing areas or wherever you want. A car is not a bad alternative. The road is straight, uncrowded, and you can take as much time as you like.

There are several places, keyed to an interpretive brochure, where you can stop and get out for a quick look or a long walk. Fall through spring are the best times of the year—waterfowl tend to amass here mid-November through December, shorebirds in late spring and early fall. Early morning and late afternoon hours are great for wildlife viewing.

As you head out through a slash-pine woodland and a cypress swamp, look for osprey nests in the treetops. If you want a real taste of this environment, try one of the primitive trails. They eventually hook up with the **Florida National Scenic Trail** (see pp. 244-45), which runs for some 41 miles through the refuge (including the two units to the west).

As you continue on Lighthouse Road, views begin to open up on both sides. The culverts and dikes you see off the roadsides were built by the Civilian Conservation Corps to hold water for wildlife. The water level is raised in winter to provide for migratory waterfowl; in spring and summer, the lower level benefits herons, egrets, and other resident waders.

By all means pull to the left for a 1-mile trek by foot on **Mounds Trail,** which goes through various habitats as it circles an impoundment pond. Near the start of the trail, the large midden mound topped by a fire tower is an Indian dump site dating from around 300 B.C. The parklike pinewoods fade as you come to an observation deck, where you can watch anhingas, cormorants, and other birds in the pond. Out on the dike are heart-filling views of tidal creeks and marshes—splayed to the edges of the world, it seems, with breezes whispering in the cordgrass like waves washing on the shore.

Back in the car, continue to the end of the road, dominated by a lighthouse built in 1831. You can walk along the levee here, observing the alligators and birds in the managed pool. Out on the bay, pelicans skim along the surface, and loons and horned grebes dive for fish and crustaceans. ∎

Great egret in the marsh at St. Marks NWR

Canoeing Ichetucknee Springs

Ichetucknee Springs State Park

■ 2,276 acres ■ North-central Florida, 20 miles west of US 75 via Fla. 27
■ Year-round. Tubing best in summer ■ Hiking, canoeing, swimming, snorkeling,
tubing, cave diving (Oct.-March) ■ Adm. fee ■ Contact the park, Rte. 2, Box
5355, Fort White, FL 32038; phone 904-497-2511. www.dep.state.fl.us/
parks/District_2/Ichetucknee

GUSHING AN AVERAGE OF 233 million gallons of clear water a day, the
springs at Ichetucknee form a short 6-mile river that joins the Santa Fe
River before feeding into the Suwannee. This park around the springs
preserves a riparian habitat of cypress swampland and hardwood hammock, inhabited by turtles, wading birds, and fish. Owls, wood ducks,
river otters, and beavers are sometimes spotted. Oaks, maples, and other
hardwoods have moved into formerly open, grassy areas left over from
logging and phosphate mining in the past. If you see smoke, it likely
comes from controlled fires, an attempt to restore the longleaf pine community on the dry uplands. On the park's sand hills can be found gopher
tortoises, fox squirrels, wild turkeys, deer, and bobcats.

Tubing is the activity of choice at Ichetucknee Springs. You can rent
inner tubes at several places outside the park and then drive to the north
entrance *(summer only)* for a three-hour float downriver. Starting at the
south entrance gives you options for shorter trips (a tram is available to
take you back to your car). With the water at a pleasant 72°F, you swirl
through a wooded haven, the knees and limbs of cypresses making reflections on the flat water and wild rice festooning the shore. Fish swim over
the sandy bottom, and a limpkin stalks crayfish along the banks.

Other possibilities for exploring the Ichetucknee River include canoeing and snorkeling; from October through March, certified divers can
go cave diving in **Blue Hole Spring.** There and at **Head Springs,** you
also will find good summer swimming holes, with pools that vary in
depth from 1 to 30 feet. About 5 miles of **trails** wind through the park's
various environments. ■

Sinkholes

Along with springs, ponds, and lakes, the north Florida landscape is known for its ubiquitous sinkholes. Hundreds of new sinkholes develop in Florida every year. Though most of them are less than 20 feet wide, a record-breaking 300-footer swallowed six vehicles and a house in Winter Park in 1981.

These depressions in the ground form when the underlying limestone foundation weakens and gives way, allowing the topsoil above to fall. A solution sinkhole occurs slowly over time, while a collapse sinkhole happens when a cavern suddenly caves in. Both types are the result of rainwater trickling down into the soil and becoming more acidic as it passes through decaying vegetation. The acid then begins dissolving the calcium in the limestone, making the bedrock vulnerable to collapse. Periods of heavy rain often precede the formation of a sinkhole, which can then become the basin for a pond, a lake, or a swamp.

Just outside Gainesville, **Devil's Millhopper State Geological Site** (*4732 Millhopper Rd., Gainesville, FL 32653. 352-955-2008. Adm. fee*) preserves a 500-foot-wide, 120-foot-deep sinkhole that opened up around 14,000 years ago. Fossilized sharks' teeth, shells, and prehistoric animal bones found here led to the local legend that the devil threw people into his mill hopper (a funnel-shaped device for feeding grain into a mill). Marine fossils in the lower layers suggest that the sea once covered this area, then receded around the time of the land-animal fossils.

Water now trickles down the walls of Devil's Millhopper, and ferns, mosses, and other plants grow in lush profusion. You can take a 236-step wooden stairway to the dank, shady bottom. Why doesn't the water pool down here? Because it runs into several fissures in the limestone, then drains out into a dozen nearby springs; from there the water eventually makes its way to the Gulf. Suburban joggers and walkers make serious use of the half-mile trail that loops the sinkhole and gives a taste of the surrounding woodlands. The informational gazebo offers exhibits and a short video.

Devil's Millhopper State Geological Site

Lower Suwannee National Wildlife Refuge

■ 52,935 acres ■ West-central Florida, along mouth of Suwannee River ■ Year-round ■ Hiking, biking, wildlife viewing ■ Take precautions against insects in summer ■ Contact the refuge, 16450 Northwest 31 Pl., Chiefland, FL 32626; phone 352-493-0238. www.fws.gov/r4swe

LOCATED ALONG THE LOWER END of the Suwannee River in Florida's Big Bend area, this out-of-the-way refuge—one of the country's largest undeveloped river-delta estuary systems—encompasses a tremendous spread of prime Coastal Plain wilderness that few people know about. Within the refuge's boundaries are found cypress swamps, scrub oak habitats, and pine plantations on both banks of the Suwannee River and among its tributary creeks.

The most scenic area lies along the Gulf Coast, where the river flows into the sea. These 26 miles of pristine coast encompass tidal flats and marshes, tiny islands and broad sweeps of water, where majestic birds have free rein over land and sky.

What to See and Do

Lower Suwannee NWR offers 40-some miles of unpaved roads and 50 miles of hiking or biking trails for exploring. The refuge spans the river and its wide delta, with no easy way to get from one side to the other unless you have a boat. If your time is limited, the eastern

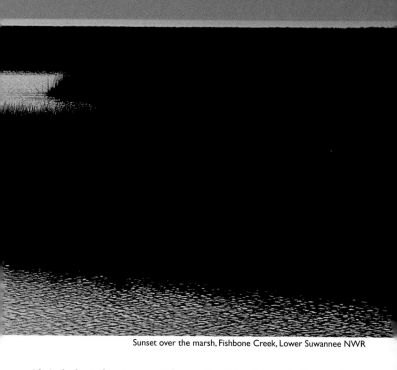
Sunset over the marsh, Fishbone Creek, Lower Suwannee NWR

side is the best place to start. Take County Roads 345 and 347 southwest of Chiefland for 17 miles, following the signs, and turn right at the sign for refuge headquarters. On the right, just before headquarters, is the 0.6-mile **River Trail.** You can pick up brochures here and at other trailhead kiosks. This pleasant little floodplain ramble takes you through a thick forest of cypress, oak, elm, ash, hickory, and other hardwoods over a soft carpet of cypress needles. Sun dapples the ground through high branches where barred owls and various warblers nest.

Near the end of the trail, a raised boardwalk keeps you above the mucky swamp, and an observation platform on the water provides nice views of Florida's second largest river. Much of the Suwannee's flow comes from the 50 or so springs scattered along its course. An occasional motorboat punctuates the beatific silence, and

the distant blast of a shotgun in winter is a reminder of the many uses made of the refuge.

The river and its floodplain provide habitat for 232 species of birds, 42 species of mammals, 72 species of reptiles, and 39 species of amphibians. Ninety kinds of birds nest here, including bald eagles, swallow-tailed kites, and ospreys. Among the more impressive animals are manatees, which swim through in summer. The estuary also supports the last viable breeding population of Gulf sturgeon, as well as thousands of overwintering waterfowl.

In any season, look for great blue herons, great egrets, little blue herons, tricolored herons, black-crowned night herons, and white ibises. One year-round resident, the wood duck, is recognizable by his bright head and swept-back crest or by her tear-shaped eye patch. The ducks nest in tree cavities and artificial nesting boxes.

Continuing south on County Road 347, you can take the 9-mile loop at the North Entrance sign. There are countless opportunities to hike on unmarked trails, or you can drive south on County Road 347 a few more miles to County Road 326 and turn right. Drive 4 miles to the **Shell Mound area.**

Get out and stretch your legs over the short (one-third mile) **Shell Mound Trail,** which circles a 28-foot-tall Indian shell midden now overgrown with vegetation. Within the 5-acre mound are oyster and clam shells, fish bones, and pottery shards from Timucuan ancestors living here from around 2500 B.C. to A.D. 1000. At the top, there are gorgeous views of grassy mudflats and marshes, with the sun casting sparkling gold doubloons on the water.

Adjacent to the mound, the **Dennis Creek Trail** makes a lovely 1-mile loop over a coastal island. You start out on a boardwalk above a wire grass and needlerush marsh that varies from soupy in summer to parched in winter. The expansive views here hold a special luminance at sunup and sundown. You then reenter a pine and palmetto woodland and return to the denser woods, where swags of moss from live oaks look like tangled shadows cast by sunlight as it falls through the trees.

To reach the west side of the refuge, take US 19/98 north from Chiefland to County Road 349 and head south. On this side of the river, a **canoe trail** *(ask for directions in Suwannee, on Cty. Rd. 349, 23 miles SW of the intersection of 349 and US 19/98)* winds among brackish and freshwater creeks. Paddling the wetlands will give you an opportunity to study the feeding and nesting habits of ospreys, ibises, herons, and egrets, as well as alligators, frogs, and other animals. You may even spot an endangered wood stork in the summer or fall. Depending on the route you take, you can make a loop that varies from about 75 minutes to 3 hours. Fish you can catch include largemouth bass, catfish, bluegill, and panfish. ■

Boating in the marsh on the Lower Suwannee

Paynes Prairie State Preserve

■ 21,000 acres ■ Central Florida, south of Gainesville, via Fla. 441 ■ Year-round ■ Camping, hiking, fishing, horseback riding, bird-watching ■ Adm. fee ■ Contact the preserve, 100 Savannah Blvd., Micanopy, FL 32667-9702; phone 352-466-3397. www.dep.state.fl.us/parks/District_2/PaynesPrairie

JUST SOUTH OF THE BUSY TANGLE of Gainesville, this huge sprawl of marsh and wet prairie comes as a welcome surprise. Extending 8.5 miles at its widest, Paynes Prairie still has much the same look and diversity of animal life witnessed in 1774 by naturalist William Bartram. He dubbed the area the "great Allatchua savanah" and described "a vast plain of water in the middle of a pine forest 15 miles in extent & near 50 miles in circumference, verged green with level meadows. . . . [T]he prospect is greatly beautiful by the prodigious numbers of wild fowl of various kinds, such as cranes, herons, biterns, pluvers, coots & vast herds of cattle, horses, & deer which, we see far distant."

Bartram's vast plain is actually a basin formed over a concave bed of limestone. In wet times, the basin fills with water—enough in the late 1800s to create a lake that was navigable by steamboat. Two centuries earlier the basin had been dry enough to support the largest cattle ranch in Spanish Florida. The presence of humans in the area goes back about 12,000 years; its present name was likely taken from Seminole chief King Payne.

Today it is the lack of human activity that is most obvious—and most valuable—at Paynes Prairie. On the prairie and in the surrounding swamps, hammocks, ponds, and pine flatwoods live most of the animal species cited by Bartram—though not in the same prodigious numbers. Some of the more notable residents include wintering bald eagles and sandhill cranes, alligators, otters, wild horses, and bison. The latter two species were reintroduced in the 1970s and '80s to help restore the prairie ecosystem to its pre-European state. Spanish horses

18th-century Ecotourism

Like his father John Bartram, top botanist of the American colonies, William Bartram (1739-1823) developed a passion for botanical exploration. His journey in the early 1770s was the first botanical expedition through the Carolinas, Georgia, and Florida, and one can only imagine his excitement at discovering new flora and fauna. *Travels through North and South Carolina, Georgia, East and West Florida* (1791), his rhapsodic account and skilled drawings of the region's Indians and wildlife, gained a large audience in Europe. Among the Romantic writers he influenced were William Wordsworth and François Chateaubriand. Not until 1928, when a new edition came out, did the book receive widespread recognition in the United States.

Red-winged blackbird, Paynes Prairie State Preserve

have lived in the Southeast since the 16th century. Bison, of course, roamed here long before, though in much sparser numbers than in the West, and most of them had disappeared by the end of the 1700s. A herd of ten bison acquired from Oklahoma tripled in size before being nearly wiped out by a disease called brucellosis. Currently the herd comprises about a dozen animals, and you may spot them grazing in the distance.

What to See and Do

If you approach through the south entrance, you'll drive a little more than 2 miles through a tunnel of sweet gum, maple, and live oak, and you may see charred trunks from a prescribed burn that keeps large trees from taking over the prairie. At the end of the road, the **visitor center** has exhibits and a 20-minute film that provides a good introduction to the area.

Take the quarter-mile **Waca-hoota Trail** out back to a 50-foot-high **observation tower** at the edge of the prairie and prepare yourself for a breathtaking vista of land tumbling away in waves of green and brown. Birds twitter among tawny grasses and sedges, or soar high into the blue sky above the basin. The sounds of civilization are almost absent here;

the faint rumble of a jet melds into the low background buzz of insects and the cacophony of birds. From a similar vantage, Bartram wrote that "sonorous stork & whooping crains proclaim[ing] the near approaches of the summers heat, decend from the skies in musical squadrons."

The trail loops back through a hammock to the visitor center, where you can pick up the 1.3-mile **Jackson's Gap Trail** to the east. Follow this trail north through hardwoods and slash pines until you arrive at the dike on the edge of the prairie. (The term "slash" derives from "plash" —an antique word for wetlands. Hence, you'll likely find slash pines growing near wetlands.) In summer, the prairie is usually wet or flooded, but the dike system will keep you high and dry.

If you walk the full length of the system, called **Cone's Dike Trail,** you'll have more than 8 miles (round-trip) for observing herons, egrets, ducks, and more. Red-tailed hawks spiral high up, scanning for marsh rabbits, and flocks of red-winged blackbirds swoop like nets cast among the shrubby trees. The sandy grooves you see on the dike are places where wild horses roll to rid themselves of ticks and fleas. For dike hikers, insect repellent comes in handy in the summer, as does a bottle of water.

To the south of the dike trail, the **Chacala Trail** offers various loop options (totaling about 6 miles) through a shady hammock and pinewoods. You can walk all the way to **Lake Wauberg** or drive down. The most developed area of the preserve, the lake offers a boat ramp and playground. A short trail here leads through a picnic area under humongous live oaks and sabal palms. From the bridge over the marsh, look for wading birds focused on prey in the water. The motionless heron is a study in concentration.

From the south entrance, travel about 3.5 miles north on Fla. 441 to the **Bolen Bluff Trail,** which will take you to a wildlife viewing deck for sweeping prairie views. The trail makes a nice 3-mile loop east of the highway. The preserve actually sprawls across Fla. 441 and US 75 along here, making this section of highway one of the deadliest in Florida for wildlife. In the past decade alone, more than 35,000 animals, representing 82 species, have been killed on this stretch. Barriers and underpasses for wildlife have been built to deal with the problem.

Another 3-mile hike is available from the **North Rim Interpretive Building** (*accessible from S.E. 15th St. in Gainesville*). Called **La Chua Trail,** it wends through marsh and prairie habitats to views of Alachua Sink and Alachua Lake.

Listen for the loud chortles of the sandhill cranes in fall and winter. These large birds migrate in by the thousands starting in mid-October, and you have especially good odds of seeing them on the trail. They have long necks and legs and a 6-foot wingspan. You can distinguish them from great blue herons by their "bustles"— rump feathers—and, in adults, by their bald red foreheads.

Though not commonly seen on the prairie—and never in fall or winter—one of the most curious things about the cranes is their mating dance. Wings out, they face each other and jump excitedly into the air with their feet forward, making noisy croaks. Then they bow to each other and do it again.

Alligators frequent this area, though in fewer numbers than in 1774, when Bartram observed that he could walk across the basin on their heads "if permitted by them." Still, there are hundreds of gators present, adding the flavor of the dinosaur age to the preserve. (*Warning: Keep your distance when photographing them.*) From this trail you can pick up the 15-mile **Gainesville-Hawthorne State Trail,** a greenway along a former rail line now open to hikers, bikers, skaters, and equestrians. ∎

Ocala National Forest

■ 383,000 acres ■ Central Florida ■ Year-round ■ Camping, hiking, canoeing, swimming, fishing, biking ■ Contact Seminole Ranger District, 40929 Hwy. 19, Umatilla, FL 32784, phone 352-669-3153; or Lake George Ranger District, 17147 E. Hwy. 40, Silver Springs, FL 34488, phone 352-625-2520

A VAST SOCK-SHAPED WILDERNESS in the middle of Florida's lake district, the Ocala National Forest extends some 40 miles from Lake Oklawaha to the south border of Marion County and about another 40 miles from the Oklawaha River east to Lake Woodruff. Within its boundaries are hiking trails, canoe runs, glassy springs, lakes, and creeks edged by lofty palms and ancient live oaks. Set aside in 1908, the Ocala is the oldest national forest in the East and holds the largest sand pine scrub ecosystem in the world.

The Ocala's wetland habitats are home to scores of easily observed animal species. Great and little blue herons regularly stalk the shallows, while anhingas (locally called water turkeys) dive and spear fish, then spread their wings to dry in the sun. You can also see yellow- and black-crowned night herons, tricolored herons, green herons, and snowy egrets. Wood storks, gallinules, limpkins, and glossy and white ibises are other possibilities. The herons (including the egrets) tend to nest in colonies, or heronries. Look for the stick nests of these long-legged birds in bushes or trees near the water. You can often see or hear them squawking over territorial rights; these squabbles can take the better part of an hour to work out, rendering observers transfixed. You'll also have no trouble spotting alligators, trolling like submarines with their eyes above water or stretched out like logs on the banks.

What to See and Do

The forest has three visitor centers. The main one is located about 6 miles east of Silver Springs on Fla. 40. Stop in for maps and exhibits and for trip-planning help. This western area of the forest contains several sites worthy of a visit. Continue east on Fla. 40 about 11 miles to the turnoff *(left)* for **Mill Dam Lake,** which has a 300-foot sandy beach. Swimming, fishing, and bird-watching are the basic bill of fare here.

For hiking in this part of the forest, drive 6.5 miles north on Forest Road 79 *(or 10 miles NE via Cty. Rd. 314 from US 40)* to **Lake Eaton.** The 1-mile **Lake Eaton Sinkhole Trail** leads to an 80-foot-deep sinkhole, created about 100 years ago by the collapse of underlying limestone layers. Wider than a football field, the hole has not filled with water because in this relatively high, ridgy area of the Coastal Plain the bottom of the hole lies above the water table. A boardwalk and a stairway lead to the cool bottom, where trees such as magnolia and dogwood flourish out

Alexander Springs Creek, Ocala National Forest

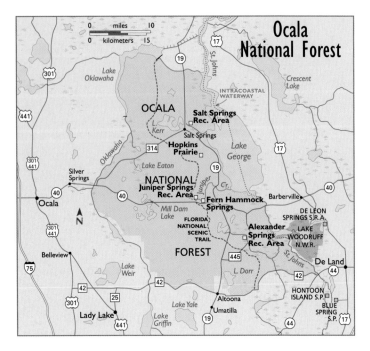

Ocala
National Forest

of reach of fire and constant sun.

There's also a 1.2-mile extension of the trail through a forest of sand pine and scrub oak. Be on the lookout for wild turkeys, woodpeckers, and rare scrub jays. To determine whether it has rained recently, examine the small resurrection ferns—brown after a dry spell, lush green after a soaking.

Across the road, the 2.1-mile **Lake Eaton Loop Trail** meanders through a dry hammock of palm, pine, and live oak, and along the edge of the lake. Ospreys nest in the tops of dead trees, while songbirds flutter and fuss in an understory of wax myrtle, scrub oak, and aromatic silk bay. Prickly pear cactus and scrub morning glory color the forest floor, and pink-flowering calamintha mint contributes a spring-clean scent.

In the north part of the forest,

the **Salt Springs Recreation Area** *(352-685-2048)* has a visitor center on Fla. 19 *(just N of Fla. 314)*. From here, it's 0.2 mile south to the springs, where aquifer water percolates up from the riddled limestone underlayers. Nine vertical fissures within the ground gush 52 million gallons of water a day. Swimming and snorkeling are popular in these pellucid green waters, where fresh and salt water at varying depths can create interesting underwater distortions. The salinity comes from the presence of sodium, potassium, silica, and magnesium salts.

The 2-mile **Salt Springs Trail** wanders out to Salt Springs Run, where an observation platform lets you watch herons, alligators, and sometimes ospreys and eagles. Black bears carry on secluded lives deep within the forest; you're more

Palmettos and live oaks

Canoeing Wekiwa Springs

Finding yourself in the Orlando area and needing a dose of the real Florida, head north to Wekiwa Springs State Park (we-KI-wa, from the Creek for "spring of water"), located between Ocala National Forest and Orlando, just north of Apopka *(follow Fla. 438 to Wekiwa Springs Rd. 407-884-2008)*. A good day trip starts about 15 minutes north of the park at King's Landing (407-886-0859), where you can rent a canoe for the 8.5-mile paddle south along Rock Springs Run to the park.

You paddle through a canopy-enclosed channel about 30 feet wide, lined with water oak, swamp bay, dahoon holly, and loblolly pine. Gators float among cypress knees, and white ibises and little blue herons fish along the banks, heedless of passersby. Lilies brighten the cool, clear water, and in summer hummingbirds pivot around red-blooming cardinal flowers, a threatened species. In fall, birds go crazy for the feathery wild rice that

grows on the mossy banks.

Several sunny places beckon you to stop for a picnic and a swim. The river bottom is hard and sandy, and the fishing is good for bream. You can lie out, even pull up your canoe, on one of the tremendous cypress stumps left by loggers who cleaned out the area in the 1920s and '30s. From these perches, you can watch for turtles and fish, or you can look up to spot a wood stork or a red-shouldered hawk. In the spring and the summer, prothonotary warblers (swamp canaries) whistle for mates and flash by like sparks of golden sunlight.

The run ends at the park, which has a 3-acre swimming hole and several miles of hiking trails. The King's Landing concessionaire will pick you up at the Wekiva Marina *(located just outside the park)* and drive you back to your car. Other possibilities for canoeing include the **Wekiva River** (we-KI-va, from the Creek for "flowing water"), a wider channel than Rock Springs Run that flows out from the park.

Swimming in Alexander Springs

likely to see a few of the nearly 9,000 resident deer. The run flows about 5 miles east to **Lake George,** a 12-mile-long oval in the St. Johns River and Florida's second largest lake. To travel this waterway, rent a canoe or fishing boat at Salt Springs Run Marina *(352-685-2255).*

Take Fla. 19 about 15 miles south, then Fla. 40 west 5 miles to the **Juniper Springs Recreation Area** *(352-625-3147),* a somewhat smaller facility than Salt Springs but with similarly dense subtropical scenery. You can swim in a spring-fed pool and take a three-quarter-mile nature trail along graceful fans of saw palmettos and overhanging live oaks. The 7-mile Juniper Creek makes a fine canoe run to Lake George. The **Florida National Scenic Trail** (see pp. 244-45), which carves 66 miles through Ocala, passes right through this area; there are several other access points within the forest.

To the south, the **Alexander**

Springs Recreation Area *(352-669-3522)* is the focal point of the third section of the forest, which is served by a visitor center on Fla. 19, 4 miles north of Fla. 42. Alexander Springs is located on Fla. 445 about 7 miles north of the visitor center. The first-magnitude springs that rise here leak about 70 million gallons of water a day into a good-size pool surrounded by a swamp of cypress, sabal palm, live oak, and maple. You can swim, snorkel, or scuba dive with fish and turtles amid an underwater garden of waving vegetation.

Providing an excellent cross section of subtropical wilderness, the 1.1-mile **Timucuan Indian Nature Trail** leads you through the woods and around to a couple of wooden observation decks on the pool. One primitive plant that you will see in the forest is the fernlike coontie, now a protected species, whose starchy roots were a staple in the diets of Indians and settlers. ■

Coast

Sea oats beneath the rising moon on South Carolina's coast

From Myrtle Beach down to Cape Canaveral, the South-east coast is a long, gentle curve of sandy beaches, sea oat-topped dunes, and grassy marshes. Some of the country's most beautiful scenery lies here among the low sweeps of marsh, threaded with tidal creeks and dotted with white-plumed wading birds, the water bruised a deep crimson in the half-light of dusk. The big concave shoreline, the Georgia Embayment, makes for a shallow shelf that channels water into the shore with great force.

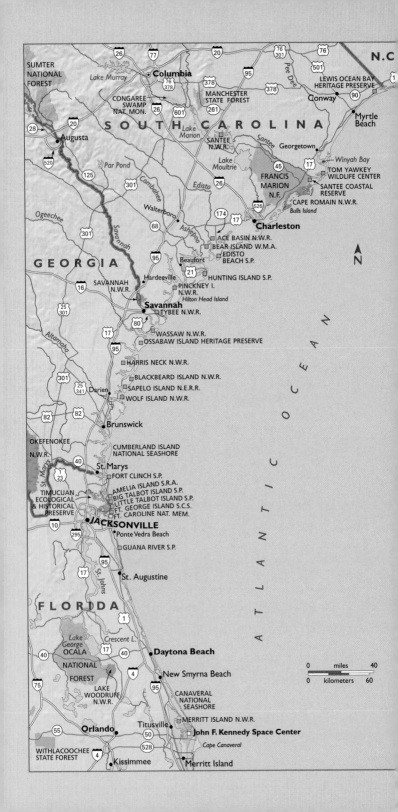

Over the millennia, waves and tides meeting with sea-running rivers from the mountains have created a hemline of inlets and barrier islands. From central South Carolina to north Florida, barrier islands are the rule, the shoreline broken up into a complicated pattern that makes "driving the coast" impossible. Roads snake down through soft and sinuous wetlands, cross spectacular bridges, and dead-end on remote islands,  many still remarkably undeveloped. Other islands, even large ones, remain unconnected by road and thus even more adrift in time.

Along the coast run three main ecozones in north-south stripes: salt marsh, maritime forest, and beach. The salt marshes, often considered the world's most productive acreage, are the rich breeding and feeding grounds of a litany of wildlife from crabs and shrimp to fish, dolphins, and herons. An acre of marsh is 10 times more fertile than an acre of Iowa farmland. The stillness of the marsh belies the vigorous teeming of life beneath the surface—a world of crustaceans and other mud dwellers, revealed only when the sea holds its breath at low tide to expose the mudflats where birds come to hunt for treasure. Georgia alone boasts 25 percent of all the salt marsh on the eastern seaboard; add to this the considerable amount in South Carolina and northeast Florida, and you have a region like no other in the country.

Between the salt marsh and the beach, the maritime forest provides a cool, green sanctuary for deer, raccoons, amphibians, and songbirds. Live oaks, the dominant trees on the south Atlantic coast, extend their brawny boughs out and up, making huge evergreen umbrellas that shade the sandy forest floor. Yaupon hollies, wax myrtles, and saw and cabbage palmettos find niches and in turn provide homes and food to birds and other wildlife. Out near the dunes, the salty spume and relentless wind-blown sand prune back trees and shrubs to dwarf sizes.

The beach rolls out a blinding-white carpet of sand to a hazel-green sea. On Cumberland Island and Canaveral National Seashores and other beaches of the region, there are breathtakingly untouched views. Pelicans dive for fish, sandpipers scurry away on spindly legs, gulls screech, and the dramas of sea and sky play out again and again. Late summer often brings storms, which smash against the barrier islands, reshaping the shoreline. In fall and winter, thousands of migratory waterfowl return from northern climes on the Atlantic flyway. In spring, songbirds journey back from the distant south as the air warms. The seaside heats to a sleepy torpor by July, but the pulse of wildlife stays strong. Endangered and threatened wood storks, bald eagles, alligators, loggerhead sea turtles, and other species all find refuge on these inviting southern shores. ∎

Lewis Ocean Bay Heritage Preserve

■ 9,383 acres ■ Northeast South Carolina, north of Myrtle Beach, 6 miles
east of Conway ■ Year-round ■ Wildlife viewing ■ Contact Wildlife Diversity
Section, S.C. Dept. of Natural Resources, 420 Dirleton Rd., Georgetown, SC
29440; phone 843-546-3226

CLOSE TO THE INTRACOASTAL WATERWAY, this unusual preserve protects
a geological feature not noticed by the casual observer: Carolina bays.
The Atlantic coastal plain is pitted with these large elliptical depressions,
possibly formed by meteorite impacts, ocean currents, or sinkholes. In
winter and spring, the bays fill with rainwater; in summer, they dry up.
More than 20 of the bays, some of them overlapping, are found in this
15-square-mile preserve.

Visitor access to the preserve is limited. Only a network of dirt roads
penetrates the jungly vegetation (four-wheel drive or high-clearance
vehicles are recommended), and some roads go into private inholdings.
Still, you can drive as far as you feel comfortable and get a sense of the
area. To reach the preserve, take S.C. 90 east from Conway, turn right on
International Road for 1.5 miles, then left on Old Kingston Road.

The size of Carolina bays can range from 1 to 1,000 acres. They lie
mostly hidden beneath thickets of shrubby gallberry, titi, sweet bay, red
bay, and catbrier, above which grow thin canopies of pond pines and
loblolly bays. These evergreen shrub bogs grow in peat, which sits on a
layer of hard-packed sand that tends to keep water from seeping through.
The result is a peaty wetland that supports acid-tolerant plants such as
blueberry bushes and other heath-family members. Deer and bears
browse and hide in these thickets, while a number of bird species
nest in the trees above.

Sand rims outlining the bays hold a desert-type plant community—prickly pear cactus and
dwarf live oak thrive on these higher and drier edges. Blueberries grow in the transition zone
between rim and bay, as do insect-loving Venus's-flytraps, sundews,
and pitcher plants.

The sweet bays give off a fresh, spicy odor, and the large white
flowers of the loblolly bay waft a heady perfume through the air. ■

Pitcher plant, Lewis Ocean Bay
Heritage Preserve

Shorebirds winging over tidal wetlands

Tom Yawkey Wildlife Center

■ 20,000 acres ■ Coastal South Carolina, 10 miles south of Georgetown
■ Accessible by tour, once a week ■ Year-round ■ Wildlife viewing is available
by reservation ■ Contact the center, One Yawkey Way South, Georgetown, SC
29440; phone 843-546-6814

THE TOM YAWKEY WILDLIFE CENTER anchors the north end of a 66-mile
strip of protected, publicly owned shore and maritime forest extending
southward from Georgetown to just north of Charleston. It encompasses
three large islands around the mouth of Winyah Bay: North Island, Cat
Island, and South Island. To reach the center, take US 17 south from
Georgetown to South Island Rd. (S.C. 18). Follow the signs to the ferry.

In 1919, 16-year-old Tom Yawkey inherited part of the current property from his uncle, William Yawkey, owner of the Detroit Tigers. The
newly made teenage millionaire had already developed a love for the Low
Country, and bit by bit he increased his holdings. He later bought the

Boston Red Sox and spent his summers in Boston, reserving his winters for the South Carolina plantation and game preserve.

In his will, Yawkey left the property to the state to be managed as a wildlife preserve and research area, funded by a perpetual trust—the Yawkey Foundation. Since Yawkey's death in 1976, the vast stretch of tidal marsh, longleaf pine forest, and pristine beach has been turned over to local and migratory wildlife. Here they come first and foremost.

Because Yawkey believed wildlife flourished best when left alone, visitation is kept to a minimum: Half-day visits and tours are offered once a week by reservation. But it's worth the trouble to see a place on the Atlantic Coast left so supremely intact. Tens of thousands of ducks still come each winter, hundreds of sea turtles build nests every summer, thousands of shorebirds from 25 species live or visit, and rare species such as red-cockaded woodpeckers and bald eagles nest here.

Two-mile-wide **Mosquito Creek** and two canals separate Cat from the seaward South Island. Site of the Tom Yawkey headquarters, **South Island** features 2,000 acres of wetlands. Perimeter dikes overlooking sheets of water studded with salt marsh bulrush, wigeongrass, and sea purslane provide prime viewing of gadwalls, wigeons, coots, mallards, shovelers, and other species. Geese are not as numerous here as they once were because many of them now winter farther north. In addition to the standard shorebirds, South Island attracts a number of rare visitors, including black-necked stilts, wood storks, sandhill cranes, glossy ibises, and up to 1,000 avocets.

The wild sweep of **North Island** has one of the East Coast's most unspoiled shorelines. A field of sea oat-crowned dunes, rising to 50 feet, backs 9 miles of beach; behind the dunes is a maritime forest of live oak, red cedar, palmetto, and loblolly, frequented by bobcats, deer, and raccoons; and behind the forest spreads a broad salt marsh of pine, magnolia, smooth cordgrass, and needlerush. Even if you see it only from South Island, the untouched look of such a large island is impressive. ■

Santee Coastal Reserve

■ 24,000 acres ■ Coastal South Carolina, south of Georgetown off US 17, south of South Santee River ■ Year-round ■ Hiking, fishing, wildlife viewing ■ Portions closed during hunting season ■ Contact the reserve, P.O. Box 37, McClellanville, SC 29458; phone 843-546-8665

SPREAD ALONG THE SINUOUS SLIDE of the Santee River delta, this wildfowl management area embraces tidal marshes, woodlands, and impoundments (enclosed pools of water) on old rice fields. To reach the reserve, drive south on US 17 from Georgetown, crossing the North and South Santee Rivers, then turn east on the first paved road (you'll see a reserve sign). Go 2 miles, then bear left on Santee Club Rd. to the entrance of the reserve. A road, tunneling through old live oaks, ends at a grassy spread.

Giant longleaf pine cones, Santee Coastal Reserve

Park at the kiosk outside the gate, and study the information-board map.

The best way to see the area is to take the 2.9-mile **Marshland Nature Trail.** It starts on a pine-needle track under massive live oaks and pines that splinter the sunlight and shelter a host of tuneful songbirds and drumming woodpeckers. The trail follows an old road, along which stand bald cypresses strung with gauzy moss. Take the 800-foot boardwalk out along the **Washo Reserve** watercourse; bright green duckweed stipples the water and Baton Rouge lichen makes red stripes on the trees. At the end of the walkway lies a deck for viewing the cormorants and wading birds that flap from lagoon to tree with throaty complaint at the intrusion of humans into this primitive landscape. In the spring, cypresses and other trees display their colorful tassels. Though a few of the trees, such as the cypress, drop their leaves in fall, for the most part the swamp and forest stay green throughout the year.

You can shortcut over to the marshes or continue around by the impoundments. In either event, you'll likely see egrets and herons, breezes toying with their plumes as they focus on their jobs. Alligators lumber out to warm themselves in the heat of the day. Stand still and listen to the marsh grass crackling and popping with slight shifts in temperature and breeze. Some reeds, brown and dry by winter, stand more than 6 feet tall. To get to the river, walk about half a mile along the dike.

For more exercise and a more in-depth look at this appealing wilderness, try the 7.2-mile bike/hike trail or the 4.25-mile canoe trail (bring your own bike or canoe). A short way back up the road, the 1.1-mile **Woodland Trail** loops into a forest of pine, holly, magnolia, and live oak bearded like patriarchs. Deer bound off, their white flags up, blending into the scenery. Keep on the lookout for the unusual fox squirrel, the largest of the tree squirrels, with its black face and white ears. ■

Wood duck

Cape Romain National Wildlife Refuge

■ 64,000 acres ■ Coastal South Carolina, north of Charleston on US 17
■ Year-round ■ Hiking, fishing, crabbing, clamming, oystering, wildlife viewing
■ Biting insects and high temperatures in summer ■ Contact Sewee Visitor
and Environmental Education Center, 5821 Hwy. 17N, Awendaw, SC 29429;
phone 843-928-3368

A GENEROUS SPREAD OF COASTAL WATERWAYS, sandy beaches, and maritime
forests, Cape Romain covers 22 heavenly miles of South Carolina coastline, including a 30,000-acre designated wilderness. The wilderness centers on Bulls Bay and its mosaic of marshy islands, separated by creeks
that reputedly harbored 18th-century pirates.

In the salt marsh estuaries, where fresh water meets salt, a long and
healthy chain of life thrives, from plankton to shrimp, crabs, clams, fish,
and bottle-nosed dolphins. Ospreys dive for mullet, great blue herons fish
in the shallows, and the dance of life goes on as it has for centuries. Out
on the long sandy beaches, loggerhead sea turtles dig nests in the summer; refuge workers often rebury the eggs under meshes or enclosures to
protect them from erosion as well as from raccoons and other predators.

Because most of the refuge is open water, it's accessible primarily by
boat. But there are several places worth exploring along the mainland as
well, some of them in the adjoining **Francis Marion National Forest,**
which encompasses 250,000 acres.

What to See and Do

A good place to start is the new **Sewee Visitor and Environmental Education Center** *(20 miles N of Charleston)*. Worthy exhibits and an orientation film give you some background on the ecology. Then take the 1.1-mile **Nebo Nature Trail**—a boardwalk through a pine-and-hardwood forest—to the observation ponds and the red wolf enclosure. In 1978, the refuge became the first site of a red wolf reintroduction experiment (see sidebar p. 178).

You can spend a relaxing day or half day on **Bulls Island** by taking a 30-minute ferry from Moore's Landing *(20 miles N of Charleston on US 17. Call 843-881-4582 for schedule and fare)*. The ferry travels across Sewee Bay, then threads the system of small keys behind Bulls Island. In addition to sea turtles and red wolves, the island protects bald eagles and other pressured species.

There is a designated 2-mile **nature trail** through a live oak and palmetto forest. Cedar, bay, and wax myrtle scrub the air with freshness, and in spring the sound of warblers fills the woods. Black fox squirrels gather nuts and seeds; the tracks of raccoons tell secrets in the daylight.

To see alligators, walk by the freshwater ponds. Refuge workers have replaced invasive cattails with banana water lilies, causing ducks to return in numbers to the ponds here. The trail continues out over the dunes, mantled with sea oats and lavender.

But perhaps the most appealing

sight for first-time visitors is the 6-mile stretch of unspoiled beach. Terns, laughing gulls, and plovers sail overhead; pelicans cruise low beyond the breakers. Because few people visit the island on any particular day, you're apt to find a wealth of lovely shells. For more walking, head out on the island's 16 miles of dirt-and-sand road.

Spring and fall are the migratory bird seasons. But in summer, you may see wood storks in the mainland swamps and brilliantly colored wood ducks feeding in freshwater ponds and nesting in trees. Late winter and early spring offer a chance to view the oyster-catcher, distinguished by a long orange bill, black head, and white underparts. This bird pries open mollusk shells with its flat bill.

Just south of the visitor center on the mainland, turn west on Swamp Road and drive 2 miles to the head (on the left) of the **I'on Swamp Interpretive Trail** (named after a local Revolutionary War hero), a 2-mile loop around embankments built in the 1700s for rice production. Along the trail, panels limn the cultural and natural history.

Here ducks and herons take readily to the watery impound-ments, while alligators and yellow-bellied turtles are seen along the edges, the latter sometimes lying one atop another on logs. Otters slink across the path from time to time, and in the spring, beautiful yellow prothonotary warblers bejewel the trees.

For another short trail, turn

Following pages: Gulls alighting on a dock near the Cape Romain National Wildlife Refuge

Saving the Wolf

By the late 1960s, the red wolf population in the United States numbered fewer than 100. Habitat loss, hunting by humans, and interbreeding with coyotes had devastated the once wide-ranging Southeast predators and reduced their territory to a sliver of coastal Texas and Louisiana. In 1967, the red wolf was placed on the federal endangered species list.

Three years later, the U.S. Fish and Wildlife Service began an attempt to rescue the species from extinction. The agency captured as many wolves as it could, then sent the 14 believed to be pure red wolves to a zoo in Tacoma, Washington, to begin captive breeding.

In 1978, the first red wolves were released on Bulls Island in South Carolina, where they could adjust to the wild before being recaptured and moved to mainland sites. Since that time, wolves have been released and monitored on refuges and parks in North Carolina, Tennessee, Mississippi, and Florida. Bulls Island remains one of the agency's propagation sites for temporary release and acclimation.

Currently there are believed to be between 50 and 130 red wolves living in the wild and about 175 living in captivity. The goal of the program is to have 220 wild and 330 captive wolves.

About the size of German shepherds, red wolves stay together in mated pairs or family packs of five to eight members. They eat mostly deer, if available; otherwise, they catch raccoons, rabbits, and other small mammals.

The wolves rarely go after farm animals and pets. If they do, however, the offending wolves can be killed legally by the landowners, or the landowners can choose to receive compensation for their dead animals. For their part, the red wolves help rid farms of pest animals and help maintain a vibrant, well-balanced ecosystem.

Although there have been no documented cases of healthy red wolves attacking humans, the historical fear of wolves continues to jeopardize their survival.

right north of the visitor center onto Doar Road (S.C. 432) and go 2.5 miles to Salt Pond Road; turn right and drive half a mile to the parking area on the right, just beyond the powerline. The 1-mile **Sewee Shell Mound Interpretive Trail** courses through woods to an oyster-shell ring that was built nearly 5,000 years ago and a clamshell mound that dates back about 2,500 years.

From the trail you have views of the marsh, a tidal creek, and the Intracoastal Waterway. You'll also see a forest still recovering from the devastation caused by Hurricane Hugo in 1989.

Just 4.5 miles north of the visitor center, you can pick up a 42-mile section of the **Palmetto Trail,** which eventually will cross the entire state. Starting on the left side of the highway, the trail passes through an early successional forest, a shrubby Carolina bay habitat, and a longleaf pine forest in the first 6 miles. ∎

Fishing for shrimp at sunset in Hunting Island State Park's salt marsh

ACE Basin

■ 350,000 acres ■ Coastal South Carolina, between Charleston and Beaufort
■ Donnelley and Bear Island Wildlife Management Areas are closed periodically
during public hunts ■ Hiking, canoeing, kayaking, fishing, wildlife viewing, auto
tour ■ Contact ACE Basin National Wildlife Refuge, P.O. Box 848, Hollywood,
SC 29449, phone 843-889-3084; or S.C. Dept. of Natural Resources, 585 Donnelley Dr., Green Pond, SC 29446, phone 843-844-8957

THE ASHEPOO, COMBAHEE, AND EDISTO RIVERS meander through old rice
plantation country to mingle in St. Helena Sound. Encompassing an
area of startling beauty, their lower drainages combine to form one of the
East's largest estuaries, giving a home to myriad birds, fish, shellfish, and
other wildlife. The basin's wetlands, pine and hardwood uplands, tidal
marshes, and barrier islands host such endangered and threatened species
as bald eagles, ospreys, wood storks, and loggerhead sea turtles. Although
most of this acreage is still in private hands, the ACE Basin holds six separate public areas: two state parks, two state wildlife management areas, a
national wildlife refuge, and a national estuarine research reserve. More
than one-third of the ACE's 350,000 acres are protected either as public
property or through conservation easements permanently restricting
commercial and industrial development.

In 1988, the ACE Basin Project was born. A cooperative arrangement
among Ducks Unlimited, the Nature Conservancy, the South Carolina
Department of Natural Resources, the U.S. Fish and Wildlife Service, and
private landowners, the project was created to protect the area's natural

heritage, as well as the fishing, hunting, forestry, and farming activities that have been a way of life here for generations. That same year, media mogul Ted Turner became one of the basin's first plantation owners to voluntarily place easements on his property, inspiring neighbors to do the same. The project also has helped private landowners create better wildlife habitats on their properties. Its success in stemming the kind of resort development characterizing much of South Carolina's coast has made the project a model for other conservation-minded groups.

Hunters, too, have played a part in the area's conservation. In the mid-18th century, tidal swamps were cleared and diked for rice fields. With the collapse of the rice culture in the late 19th century, northern sportsmen began buying up the plantations for use as hunting preserves, managing them to attract wildlife. Here as elsewhere, the ironic cooperation between nature observer and hunter, between camera and gun, has helped keep a large and varied ecosystem intact.

As a result, you can still drive narrow, empty backroads across endless marshes and out to hidden boat docks and, from land or water, behold a timeless landscape of curving waterways and bird-filled skies. Migratory waterfowl continue to flock here in the winter, and neotropical songbirds travel thousands of miles from Central America and the Caribbean to spend spring through fall in the safe forests and wetlands of the ACE. Even peregrine falcons make occasional visits.

What to See and Do

Some of the basin's public areas are easily accessible by car; others can be reached only by boat.

The 1,255-acre **Edisto Beach State Park** (*S end of S.C. 174. 843-869-2756. Adm. fee*) has a lovely 1.5-mile sweep of sand, sea oats, and sparkling water, backed by a grove of tall palmettos. Willets and sandpipers shrill and scurry along the shoreline. Loggerhead sea turtles and Wilson's plovers make nests in the sand, though their numbers have declined because of beach development. Least terns have also declined somewhat, in part because of Hurricane Hugo, and are now on the state's threatened species list.

A mile north of the park on S.C. 174, turn left for the **Spanish Mount Nature Trail,** an easy walk of about 4 miles through a forest of live oak maned with lush ferns. Arm-thick vines of wisteria and muscadine insinuate themselves around the trunks of trees, and fans of saw palmetto catch fleeting scraps of paisley sunlight. Yellow jasmine, the state flower, wafts its honey-sweet scent in spring, while scarlet buckeye and bluets contribute to the spectrum of understory color. Halfway along the trail, a catwalk crosses a fertile, bubbling marsh covered in salt-tolerant cordgrass (*Spartina*). At the end of the walk, a bench overlooks Scott Creek. You may see ospreys diving for mullet and herons standing on reedy legs near the shore.

A bit farther inland, the **ACE Basin National Wildlife Refuge** (*From US 17 take S.C. 174 to*

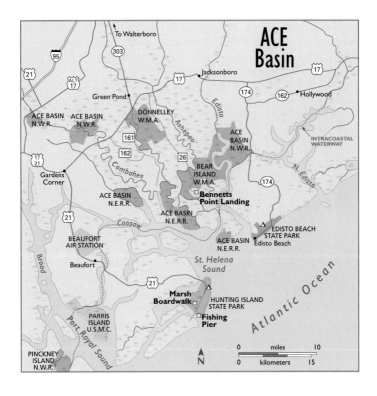

*Willtown Rd; turn right and con-
tinue 2 miles to refuge sign; office
is 2.2 miles down dirt road)* holds a
number of different habitats along
the **Edisto,** the ACE's largest river,
and the **Combahee,** the second
largest. The refuge is divided into
two units, appropriately named
the Edisto and the Combahee.
The former, the larger unit, nestles
along the Edisto River's east bank
and encompasses **Jehossee Island;**
the refuge office is located on the
Edisto in one of the basin's few
surviving antebellum mansions.

Tidal marshes and hammocks
(little islands) cover about 40 percent of the refuge. The twice-daily
7-foot tides bring in fish, crabs,
and a variety of birds. During low
tide, look for otters and mink, as

well as wading birds that feed
on fiddler crabs and other crustaceans on the exposed mudflats.
The refuge's lack of development
makes it an adventure for those
who journey in. Anglers are
rewarded with largemouth bass,
bluegill sunfish, and huge channel
catfish, though fishing is restricted
during some months.

The **Donnelley Wildlife Management Area** *(843-844-8957.
Mon.-Sat.)* comprises some 8,000
acres of rice fields, farmlands,
forested wetlands, and longleaf-
pine forests. Positioned on the
northwest edge of the tidal marsh,
the area maintains a well-balanced
roster of plant and animal species.
The refuge entrance is located
just north of the junction of US 17

Marsh on ACE Basin's Bear Island

and S.C. 303, near Green Pond.

Almost immediately on your left is a sign for the 1.5-mile **Backwater Trail,** a little-used woodland romp. About a mile down the trail on the left is the Department of Natural Resources office. Go another mile and pull left for the 2.3-mile **Boynton Trail,** which ventures into a wetland forest.

Not far to the southeast, the 12,000-acre **Bear Island Wildlife Management Area** *(mid-Jan.–Oct. Mon.-Sat.)* lies closer to the sound than Donnelley and thus has more tidal marsh—about 42 percent of

its acreage. Impoundments cover another 45 percent, and woodlands and agricultural lands the rest. The tidal marsh extends along about 20 miles of river beyond the sound, tapering off north of Bear Island in a complicated fashion dictated by the height of the tides and the amount of rainfall. For many miles, fresh and salt water can mingle, with the lighter fresh water floating on the top. Fish and other animals that can tolerate high levels of salinity are found near the saltwater sources.

Both driving and walking on

the dike roads of the **Bear Island area** are excellent ways to see a number of the basin's 265 species of waterfowl, wading birds, shore-birds, and birds of prey. In warm months, you'll probably see alligators and other animals as well. The roseate light that seeps across the marshes at sunrise and sunset is itself worth the visit.

Primarily accessible by boat, the **ACE Basin National Estuarine Research Reserve** *(843-762-5062)* harbors large expanses of open water and salt marsh, crucial to nesting and wintering birds, as well as the marine species that use the calm estuary as a nursery and feeding area. The core research area comprises more than 12,000 acres. A 15-mile **boat trail** (boats should be no longer than 20 feet) explores some of the reserve's waterways near **St. Helena Sound.** Commercial tours out of Charleston and Beaufort travel much of the same territory *(call Charleston's Visitors Bureau 800-868-8118 or the Walterboro Chamber of Commerce 843-549-9595).*

The three rivers of the ACE also make for some fine canoeing and

Beach erosion, Big Talbot Island State Park

Shearing the Shore

Bearing the brunt of tides and waves, barrier islands shield the marshes and mainlands from rough seas and create ideal nurseries for marine life. But what protects the islands? Until recent times, nothing. The islands shifted at nature's whim, changing shape dramatically when hurricane-driven waters transported tons of sand.

People have sought to change all that, erecting jetties, seawalls, and groins to stabilize the beach and protect the cottages and light-houses built there. But those structures also cause problems. While they hold sand on the north side, the south side—the direction of current flow—gets robbed. To the sea, jetties are merely speed bumps.

The problem for beaches from Cape Lookout, North Carolina, down into Florida is the Georgia Embayment, a scooped-out shore-line that gives the region a shallow continental shelf. The flow of water over this shelf often produces tides twice as high as those at either end of the embayment. The higher tides have created numerous inlets and sandbars, which complicate the flow of water around barrier islands such as Big Talbot Island in Florida (see p. 204) and Hunting Island, one of South Carolina's most popular parks. For instance, shoals to Hunting's north and south bend incoming waves so sand is carried away from the island's middle.

One response is to replenish the eroded beaches with new sand. Pipelines carry the sand from 2 miles out, then bulldozers push it around the beach. In 1991, a renourishment project on Hunting Island put 700,000 cubic yards of sand back on the beach.

In eight years that imported sand was all gone—one-third of it in the first few months, when it had yet to cement itself to the existing shore. In the 1990s, Beaufort County spent more than 30 million dollars putting sand on beaches. Yet cost-benefit analyses in areas of high tourism have shown that, financially, it may be worth the expense.

There may be other costs: Pumping massive amounts of sand onto a beach, some experts claim, can bury crustaceans that shorebirds eat and thus disrupt the ecosystem. But other experts counter that nature quickly bounces back and new beaches create new niches.

All experts agree on one thing, however: Beach erosion is a problem that will not go away. And locals still fear the kind of storms that howl in from the ocean and alter the shoreline in a single day.

kayaking excursions. Bald eagles, ospreys, Mississippi and swallow-tailed kites, and alligators are common sights as you paddle along. Scenes from *Forrest Gump* were filmed along the Combahee. Boat ramps on all three rivers make it easy to plan a half- or full-day trip. About 10 miles southwest of Edisto Beach State Park, across St. Helena Sound, **Hunting Island State Park** *(16 miles E of Beaufort on US 21. 843-838-2011. Adm. fee)* holds 5,000 acres of beach, maritime forest, and salt marsh. A 3-mile beach is just right for strolling, shelling, and swimming, and a 135-foot-tall lighthouse provides matchless views of the Atlantic, the sound, and the way the island fits in like a puzzle piece.

Because erosion is so rapid on this island (see sidebar opposite), the forest sits right at the edge of the beach. Huge tree trunks and giant driftwood sculpture littering the beach give it the rugged look of the Northwest coast, but the warm waters speak with a Southern accent. The skeletons of trees far out in the surf mark where the forest stood a few generations ago.

A 4.5-mile **nature trail** takes you through the subtropical forest of cabbage palmetto, loblolly, live oak, and slash pine. You can take the trail or drive to the **marsh boardwalk,** a lovely stroll out to a little pine island and a viewing platform where you can watch herons and egrets flying with folded necks or standing in low water. Peer out to miles of cordgrass and silky slips of water, which in the morning mist look like something out of a dream.

About a mile down the road is a fishing pier where you can cast for sea trout, whiting, and spot.

ACE Basin Driving Tour

Well off the beaten path, this 60-mile drive takes you through some of the most scenic areas of the ACE. Roads into the low-lying tidal marshes generally dead-end at a creek or river, so you'll have to do some backtracking, but the effort is well worth it. You pass former rice plantations, the Donnelley and Bear Island management areas, and miles of achingly beautiful wetlands, alive with the sounds of bird wings and calls.

All but about 12 miles of the tour are on paved roads, but plan to spend half a day to get the most out of the trip. Starting 7 miles west of Jacksonboro on US 17, turn left (south) onto S.C. 26 (Bennett's Point Road), which tunnels through a pine and live oak forest. To the left, behind closed gates, are long avenues leading to private plantations. In the rice-production days, plantations used the **Ashepoo** (1 to 2 miles from the road) as a highway for floating bags of rice to St. Helena Sound. There they were transported to Charleston for distribution.

After about 11 miles, the road crosses a bend in the river, and the bridge offers a slightly elevated view of the marshes. A little more than a mile farther along, pull to the right at an observation deck for more fine views of rustling cordgrass and white egrets. A feeling of infinite time permeates this wide, prehuman scene.

A bit farther down on the left is

Following pages: Sunset over Bear Island's marsh

Black-and-yellow argiope

a kiosk for the Bear Island Wildlife Management Area. You can, if you wish, travel for several miles through here on dike roads and almost certainly add to your bird list. Snowy egrets, cormorants, coots, wood storks, mottled ducks, yellowlegs, gulls, and many others visit this open wetland.

It's another 3 miles to road's end at Bennett's Point Landing. Here you'll find an ACE Basin National Estuarine Research Reserve field station for research and education. There is also a small marina, a seafood company, and a little store. You're likely to see shorebirds such as terns, gulls, and brown pelicans, as well as such marsh dwellers as horned grebes, double-crested cormorants, and red-breasted mergansers.

Return to US 17 and turn left; in 3.7 miles turn left onto S.C. 161 (Stocks Creek Road), a good dirt road through a forest of oak, hickory, and spruce pine. Look for indigo buntings and deer, as well as wildflowers such as phlox and orange milkwort. Roll your window down to listen for the flutey measures of the hermit thrush.

In 5 miles, the road joins paved S.C. 162; head south (straight)

about 2 miles until the pavement ends. Keep going and bear right at the boat landing sign. You travel now through a longleaf pine forest that is periodically burned to maintain the ecosystem. After a total of 3.2 miles, the dirt road ends at a shady, isolated grove of big live oaks. There are tables and a boat ramp, but no other facilities.

Get out and enjoy the rich, fresh smell of the marsh and the view over the lazy lower Combahee. Here and Bennett's Point are as far seaward as you can drive into the basin. Woodpeckers tap in live oaks behind, while clapper rails and laughing gulls call out over the water. Mats of decaying *Spartina* fringe the muddy edge of the river, starting anew the chain that nourishes life from plankton to dolphins. New shoots of pale green *Spartina* wave like shoals of prairie grass.

Whereas the marshes by the boat landing at the junction of S.C. 161 and 162 are carpeted with black needlerush, it is salt-tolerant *Spartina* that grows here, closer to the sea. This tough grass absorbs the shock of storm waves and excretes salt through its leaves; during floods, air gets to the roots through tubes in the leaves. The dense roots hold the marsh mud as sea oats hold the sand and protect mussels and other creatures.

To finish the tour, motor back up S.C. 162 to US 17; staying with S.C. 162 instead of S.C.161 offers fresh scenery and a paved exit. The west side of US 17 is worth seeing, though roads are busier. Traveling through bottomland swamps and plantation lands, you'll see plenty of songbirds and wildflowers. ■

Cycling through Pinckney Island National Wildlife Refuge

Savannah Coastal Refuges

■ 55,483 acres ■ 7 refuges from Hilton Head, South Carolina, to Darien, Georgia ■ Year-round ■ Hiking, fishing, wildlife viewing, auto tours ■ Contact Parkway Business Center, Suite 10, 1000 Business Center Dr., Savannah, GA 31405; phone 912-652-4415

EVERY WINTER, THOUSANDS OF SCAUP, teal, and other ducks descend upon the warm and welcoming salt marshes and freshwater ponds of the Savannah Coastal Refuges, a chain of Low Country sanctuaries on the barrier islands and adjoining wetlands from near Hilton Head to near Darien—about 70 flight miles. In spring and fall, songbirds and shorebirds pass through on their way to or from nesting grounds in the north, joining a host of resident species from wood ducks and wading birds to bald eagles and gulls. Of the seven refuges here, three—Pinckney Island, Savannah, and Harris Neck (described on the following pages)—are accessible by car. Two others, **Tybee Island** and **Wolf Island,** are closed to the public except for saltwater fishing by boat. Secluded **Wassaw Island** and **Blackbeard Island** are accessible only by boat, but making the effort practically guarantees you an unforgettable wilderness experience.

Wassaw National Wildlife Refuge's 10,070 acres include a live oak and slash pine forest, ample marshes, and an extensive field of rolling dunes. There are 20 miles of dirt roads and about 7 miles of beach for secluded walking, bird-watching, and nature study. In the humid days of summer, look on the beach for the tractorlike tracks of threatened loggerheads—turtles that emerge from the sea at night to nest, then return to

Blooming crimson clover

the depths for three more years. You can arrange a trip to Wassaw at the marinas on Skidaway Island and the Isle of Hope, near Savannah. Even more remote than Wassaw, Blackbeard lies more than 50 miles south of Savannah. Its 5,618 acres encompass habitats similar to Wassaw's, and it holds several miles of trails and roads. Arrange excursions at Shellman Bluff, on the mainland.

Pinckney Island National Wildlife Refuge

Maj. Gen. Charles Cotesworth Pinckney, a signer of the U.S. Constitution, once owned the land that makes up Pinckney Island National Wildlife Refuge *(N off US 278, just E of Hilton Head Island)*. From 1937 to 1954, the island and its associated islets and hammocks served as a private hunting retreat. Declared a refuge in 1975, the land has been returning to a natural state ever since, providing a haven for wildlife and Hilton Head visitors. About two-thirds of its 4,053 acres are swathed in salt marshes and tidal creeks; the rest consists of forests, grasslands, and freshwater ponds. A 3-mile gravel road extends most of Pinckney's length, with grassy trails branching off to various points overlooking the Intracoastal Waterway and the small islands in the lee of Pinckney.

There are 14 miles of trails for hiking and biking. Because the main road offers little shade, it's a good idea to bring a hat and sunblock. From the parking lot to the tip of White Point and back is an 8-mile walk, but you can see a lot in that first mile. White and glossy ibises, recognizable by their long, curved beaks, feed in the exposed mud at low tide. Great and snowy egrets work the edges of the marsh grass. Black-crowned night herons, tricolored herons, and great blue herons—the largest of the herons—are also fairly common. You may even see a rare wood stork; look for a long, dark, pelican-like beak and black-fringed white wings

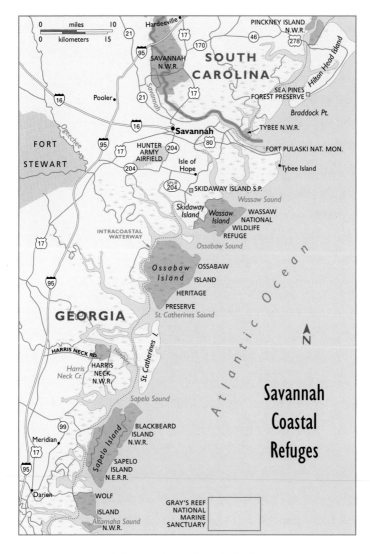

that make slow, steady beats as the stork circles high up. With such a variety of friendly habitats, it's little wonder that more than 250 species of birds live or call in on Pinckney.

Savannah National Wildlife Refuge

The largest of the seven refuges, 27,771-acre Savannah National Wildlife Refuge *(6 miles S of Hardeeville, SC, off S.C. 170)* lies north of Savannah on the east side of the Savannah River. Its migratory waterfowl and other animals depend on the freshwater marshes that the refuge maintains. With a slew of smoke-belching factories just across the river, the refuge

Shell seeker's bounty

Shells by the Shore

South Carolina's and Georgia's protected and deserted beaches make for fine hunting of shells—the discarded calcium exoskeletons of mollusks. One of the prettiest and most common of shells is the knobbed whelk shell, shaped in a spiral and measuring as long as 10 inches. The whelk, a type of snail, lives in shallow water along the seashore or in tidal creeks. It feeds on clams by opening their shells with its muscular foot, then springing open the prizes with the edge of its own shell and sucking out the meat with its proboscis.

The smaller but equally beautiful channeled whelk shell has a groove around its top instead of knobs. Another snail, the lettered olive, has an oblong shell with a pointed end; its distinctive, sandy-colored, lacquer-smooth exterior makes it a favorite for collectors.

Among noticeable bivalves are the various angelwings—long white shellfish that filter food from water in tidal creeks. Brown and translucent as mica, fan-shaped pen clams also live in the mudflats of the marshes. Found just offshore, giant Atlantic cockles grow to 4 inches long and possess a rounded, ribbed outside and nacreous inside.

One popular find, the sand dollar, belongs to a different phylum altogether—the echinoderms. A kind of sea urchin, the sand dollar burrows into sand beneath shallow water and feeds on organic particles. The flat, bleached object you find on the beach is actually the internal skeleton. The notches and inscribed floral pattern add to the sand dollar's beauty. Your chances of finding whole sand dollars and shells are best in the early morning or right after a storm.

Shelling can give purpose to a walk, as well as increase appreciation for the resourceful architecture of the natural world. If not collected, shells eventually break down into tiny pieces on the seafloor, ready for recycling.

is vulnerable to oil and chemicals that can flow into its tidal creeks, and managers are at great pains to monitor the composition of the water. But wildlife persists here in abundance.

The easiest way to see this refuge is to take the 4.8-mile **Laurel Hill Wildlife Drive,** which traverses earthen dikes erected in the late 18th and early 19th centuries to contain rice fields. Through hardwood hammocks and freshwater pools, this drive gives you a chance to slow down and observe waterfowl, wading birds, and alligators. Fall, winter, and spring see thousands of migratory birds. White-beaked coots whinny and chuckle among the duckweed, then tip headfirst, tail feathers up, bicycling their green feet to stay down. In spring and summer, you'll see common moorhens and purple gallinules—the latter with blue heads—walking over the lily pads. Gators cruise the canals, preferring the cool water on the hottest days. Ibises, egrets, and herons often fish together. Ibises have curved bills and fly, gooselike, with outstretched necks. Snowy egrets are sometimes confused with immature little blue herons because of the latter's nearly all-white plumage. Snowies—the smallest egrets—have darker legs and a black, stiletto bill. Adults sport a fluffy crown. Pull out your binoculars to get a look at their huge, cartoon-yellow feet. Great egrets are distinguished by their size, yellow bills, and black legs.

Harris Neck National Wildlife Refuge

About 40 miles south, the Harris Neck National Wildlife Refuge *(South Newport River exit off I-95, then S on US 17 for a mile and E on Harris Neck Rd. 7 miles)* resides on 2,762 acres surrounded by marshes, woods, and farmlands. The only reminder of the modern world, the interstate, is 7 miles away. At the refuge entrance, you can view birds from a boardwalk on the marshes of Harris Neck Creek. Many birds build nests in the Spanish moss that hangs in copious swags from live oaks and other trees.

Covering wetlands and woods once occupied by a World War II army airfield, the refuge attracts large flocks of mallards, gadwalls, wigeon, and teal in the fall and winter, who wing across overgrown runways where fighter planes once rose into the skies. In summer a host of egrets and herons make snow-white blips across the landscape, busy with annual nesting rituals. Neotropical songbirds such as the black-throated blue warbler pass through in spring and fall, resting and feeding.

Take the 4.5-mile **auto tour route** around the refuge. One of the most interesting places is the abandoned airfield. Traveling directly down a paved runway, the route shows you how in just a few decades nature begins to regain control: Grass and prickly pear have sprung through cracks in the concrete, as have tall thickets of titi and wax myrtle. There are places to get out and walk along freshwater ponds and see white ibises, wood storks, and white-tailed deer. You can pull off the road about halfway around and walk down to the **South Newport River** for long, lovely views across the marsh grass and the water. Sweet-smelling magnolias and other flowering trees bloom in a forest of live oak and pine, and in the long summer the drone of cicadas rises and falls incessantly. ■

Sapelo Island National Estuarine Research Reserve

■ 6,110 acres ■ Coastal Georgia ■ Ferry dock and visitor center in Meridian, 8 miles northeast of Darien, off Ga. 99 ■ Year-round ■ Marsh and beach walks, bird-watching, wildlife viewing, guided van tours ■ Four-hour tours Wed. and Sat. mornings (also Fri. June–Labor Day); fee ■ Contact Sapelo Island Visitors Center, Rte. 1, Box 1500, Darien GA 31305; phone 912-437-3224. inlet.geol.sc.edu/SAP/home.html

ONE OF GEORGIA'S many protected barrier islands, Sapelo anchors a vast estuary that nurtures a rich and complex system of marine life. Carbon dating of shells shows that the bulk of the island formed 25,000 to 36,000 years ago, whereas the more mutable seaward side dates back no more than 5,000 years. Guale Indians began living here some 3,400 years ago. After passing through the hands of various nations, the island became a plantation and later the property of tobacco heir Richard J. Reynolds, Jr., who donated much of the land to the University of Georgia. In 1976, a portion of Sapelo was set aside as the nation's second estuarine research reserve. Today, the reserve covers more than one-third of the island; the rest belongs to a state wildlife refuge, a University of Georgia marine institute, and the private owners of Hog Hammock—a 434-acre community of about 85 people, most of them descendants of island slaves.

About two-thirds of the reserve is salt marsh, visited twice daily by the tides that stream around from the sea. Most of the marsh—some 90 percent—lies under a healthy cover of golden green smooth cordgrass. On hammocks of high ground within the marsh grow junipers and pal-

Dolphins gliding through Georgia waters

mettos. Alligators and wading birds are often found in freshwater sloughs between the marsh and the forest. The largest of the herons, the great blue, nests in high pines or oaks—preferably away from eagles, which prey on the herons' young. During early spring mating season, the great blues swoop over the trees and water, with unearthly squawks, on wings that span 6 feet. You often see them posing like statues, which they can do for hours while waiting for fish large enough to satisfy them.

The reserve's other third, the maritime forest, is a dark, humid zone of live oaks and mixed pines—mostly slash, longleaf, and loblolly. On the forest floor and around its edges grows a botanical garden of coastal species—saw palmetto, yaupon holly, red cedar, dog fennel, smilax, wax myrtle, sweet grass, Spanish bayonet, broomsedge, bayberry, and more.

The reserve also holds a small sliver of the island's 5-mile shoreline. This pristine beach and dune habitat is home to nesting loggerheads, mollusks, sea oats, and wax myrtle. Out on the water, trawlers haul in shellfish, while back in the dunes, hawks and snakes keep populations of mice and marsh rabbits in trim.

The research reserve's guided tours (starting from the mainland visitor center)—currently the only way to visit the island—offer a good overview of the island and its history. The four-hour tours begin and end with a 30-minute non-narrated ride aboard the commuter ferry. Vans, which hold up to 36 people, carry you around the island. You learn a good deal about the island's cultural history, and you see the Reynolds mansion and some of the plantation ruins, but there's not a lot of opportunity for wandering about on the island's trails. The tours do take you to **Nanny Goat Beach** for about a half-hour's worth of beachcombing, or to an 1820 **lighthouse,** which provides good views of the island, marshes, and ocean. The reserve also offers some guided walks *(call ahead).* ∎

Cumberland Island National Seashore

■ 37,000 acres ■ Southeast Georgia, 8 miles east of St. Marys by ferry ■ Year-round ■ Camping, hiking, beachcombing, swimming, wildlife viewing ■ Ferries twice a day March-Sept, Thurs.-Mon. rest of year ■ Rest rooms and water at the docks ■ Contact the national seashore, P.O. Box 806, St. Marys, GA 31558; phone 912-882-4336 (info) or 912-882-4335 (reservations). www.nps.gov/cuis

AN 18-MILE-LONG FIN of sparkling sand and surf, live oak forests, and winding marshes, Cumberland Island is Georgia's largest and southern-most barrier island. Within its quiet woods and productive wetlands a vast array of wildlife lives unmolested. Pelicans dive for mullet out beyond the breakers; feral horses graze between the dunes; armadillos, deer, and bobcats find shelter in the dense forest; fiddler crabs scuttle across mudflats; raccoons and dowitchers make quick work of the crabs and shellfish; and ospreys and vultures soar above it all, eyes alert.

Separated from the mainland by a 10,000-acre thumbprint of mean-dering waterways and marshes, the island's soft western side is character-ized by miles of cordgrass rippling in gentle breezes. High tide brings in salt water and an organic soup that nourishes a budding chain of life; outgoing tides carry away debris from inland rivers. Thus the marsh is renourished and flushed clean twice a day—a perpetually recycling sys-tem that has never been improved upon. The green-tipped cordgrass has the unusual ability to secrete salt from its pores, the mineral crystallizing on the leaves (rub your fingers along a blade for a taste of sea salt). One of the more prevalent creatures out on the marsh, the fiddler crab, lives in burrows several feet down in the mud. A male waves his big right-hand claw to attract a mate into his burrow. Why do some crabs have a large left claw? Because if a crab loses his right claw, his left will continue grow-ing while a new right one forms. The result is a larger left claw.

Cumberland's maritime forest is the next ecosystem you encounter as you cross to the island's beach side. The island's thick green midriff, the live oak forest, accounts for about 60 percent of the acreage on the island. Most of the old oaks were logged, many of them in the late 1700s for building ships. The wood's heaviness, hardness, tensile strength, and adaptability to sea spray and air made it the preferred choice, and the large curved boughs were easily shaped into ship ribs. Still, the live oaks remaining have created a healthy canopy. The Spanish moss hanging from the limbs makes good nesting sites for warblers.

Woodpeckers knock persistently on tree limbs for insects. Great horned owls and hawks are especially prevalent in the woods in fall and winter. During colder weather, you also have a good chance of seeing an armadillo, which is diurnal (active by day) then. These well-armored little mammals snuffle about on the forest floor in search of insects, amphib-ians, and carrion. Over the past few decades, the island's armadillo popu-lation has been expanding slowly northward.

Rippling sand dunes, Cumberland Island National Seashore

Wildlife concentrates in and along the forest's numerous ponds and sloughs—some 1,000 acres in all. Alligators and about 18 kinds of amphibians that somehow made it to the island keep the ponds alive with their bellowing and croaking. Herons and other birds often make rookeries near these freshwater sources of life.

From the forest you reach the dunes and the beach. A line of older rear dunes protecting the forest rises about 45 feet; between the rear and fore dunes lies a shrubby meadow of grasses and sedges.

Out on the beach, ghost crabs move as if on rollers. Their gray sand color makes them almost invisible. They sidle out from their holes several times a day to moisten their gills in the swash and pick up a meal of carrion or turtle eggs.

Loggerheads, the only sea turtles that regularly nest here, lay a clutch of about 100 leathery eggs the size of Ping-Pong balls. Once a mother has laid the eggs in a hole and covered them with sand—a job of up to three hours—she trundles back into the sea, returning in two weeks to lay another clutch. After creating several of these nests, she goes back out to places unknown, not to return for another three years. Many of the nests are robbed by raccoons, ghost crabs, and hogs, but in recent years researchers have given the turtles an advantage by relocating and protecting some nests. Of the hatchlings that emerge in about 60 days and scurry to the water, only 2 percent will survive to maturity—an incredible 25 to 30 years—at which time the females will return to lay their own eggs. The males never return.

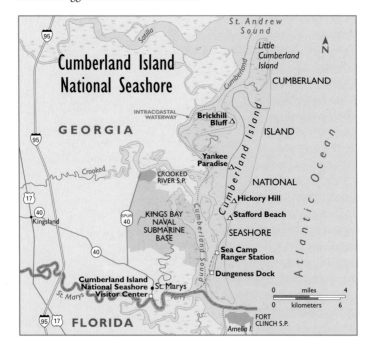

Calla lilies in Plum Orchard, Cumberland Island

Although the various ecosystems have their own distinct identities, plants and animals don't necessarily recognize the boundaries. While you certainly won't find sea oats on the marsh or cordgrass on the beach, you will see wax myrtle and other plants growing near the marshes, in the forest, and out near the dunes. Raccoons and bobcats wander wherever they might find a meal. The bobcats were reintroduced several years ago, and while one swam all the way back across the soggy marshes to the mainland, the population as a whole has done quite well for itself and Cumberland. The cats help keep the deer from overpopulating the island.

Other animals have proved more problematic. Over the years, free-ranging livestock have caused considerable damage to the dunes. Most of the rear dunes are bare of vegetation and are eroding badly. Formerly free cattle are now penned on private land; some 1,300 feral hogs have been trapped and removed since 1975, though several hundred remain; and an annual hunt helps keep the deer population in check.

But you can still see feral horses on the island. Though horses first arrived here with Spanish missionaries around 1560, the 200 grazing the dunes today are mostly descendants of animals released by the Carnegie family, who owned 90 percent of the island in the late 1800s.

What to See and Do

You can book passage on the ferry at the **visitor center** in St. Marys, though it's safest to call ahead. Ferries leave at 9 a.m. and 11:45 a.m. and return to St. Marys at 5:30 p.m. The ride out takes 45 minutes, so whether you plan to spend the day lounging on the beach or exploring the trails, you will have several hours at your disposal. On some days there's an earlier return ferry, but it's best to go for the full day if you can—the price is the same, after all, and there's a lot of ground to cover.

An alternative is to camp, which you can do for up to seven days at developed or backcountry

Deer on Cumberland Island

sites. Day and overnight visitors should remember to bring food, drinks, sunscreen, hats, sunglasses, and sturdy walking shoes.

From the ferry, many people head directly over to the beach. The shortest trail is from the **Sea Camp Ranger Station** *(second ferry stop)*. This route gives you a nice half-mile walk through a sun-dappled maritime forest of live oak dripping with Spanish moss.

Out on the beach, you'll see how quickly a ferry-load of people disperses. With an 18-mile-long strand that can measure 1,000 feet wide at low tide, the island offers plenty of wilderness and solitude. Almost all of the island is open to the public for walking, shelling, and swimming (a small portion remains in private ownership).

Abandoned chicken coop at Dungeness

The farther you walk north or south, the better the beachcombing. Perfect whelks, cockles, and sand dollars lie untouched along the wrack line (see p. 192). Bring a small bucket for your treasures, and take only empty shells.

If you would like to do some fresh- or saltwater fishing, you will need a Georgia license. Cast in the surf or sound for red bass and sea trout.

A number of trails crisscross the island, especially in the designated wilderness in the island's middle. Those that you're most likely to reach on a day trip are located on the island's south end and are described below.

Cumberland Loop

By connecting trails that start at the island's ferry docks, you can make a loop of about 4 miles and visit Cumberland's various ecosystems. Start at Sea Camp and take the half-mile trail through a lush forest of live oak and saw palmetto, spicy bayberry, and aromatic wax myrtle. Crush a fallen wax myrtle leaf between your fingers to release the fragrance. A boardwalk then leads over the dune fields, where you are likely to see feral horses grazing.

Out on the sun-bright beach least terns hold conventions, a couple of hundred birds strong, that scatter and regroup at your intrusion. Some hop along on one leg, ruffling feathers in the sun; others look for coquinas and similar treats. Black skimmers graze the water's surface, their long lower bills open for small fish. A bit farther out, pelicans fold their wings halfway—leaving enough wing out for last-second adjustments—and dive onto fish with great splashes. Look for dolphins rolling just beyond the waves, partaking of the same banquet.

One of the prettiest birds on the island, the American oystercatcher, has a long, carrot orange bill and contrasting black head and white underparts. Look for these birds starting in spring, huddled on the beach or feeding in noisy flocks. Way out on the southern horizon, trawlers work the Atlantic from March to December, part of a multimillion-dollar shrimp industry.

Walk south along the beach a little over a mile to the trail for the Dungeness dock. At this point, you have the option of adding up to 6 more miles to the walk by continuing south along the beach. It's a good idea to sample at least some of the remote south end. In about 1.5 miles, you come to the jetty and the island's rounded southern tip. Across the inlet lies **Fort Clinch State Park** and a paper mill on Amelia Island, Florida. A track behind the dunes leads past some freshwater ponds to the marshes.

Heading toward the Dungeness dock, you will pass the crumbling, vine-choked ruins of the Carnegie mansion, which is surrounded by oleander and stately royal palms. Called **Dungeness,** the mansion was built in 1884 by Andrew

Carnegie's brother Thomas, but then burned down in the 1950s.

Continue down to the dock and around the small historical museum to the **River Trail,** which wends its way along the **Cumberland Sound** for a mile back to the Sea Camp dock. The wooded trail offers more opportunities for spotting wildlife and views over the gentle marshes. The **Sea Camp ranger station** presents natural-history films and programs for those waiting for the afternoon ferry back to St. Marys. ■

From Rubbish to Relics

Though it is hoped that no visitor to any ecosystem will leave trash behind, some, unfortunately, do. Rates for the decomposition vary widely, depending upon soil conditions and the amount of moisture available.

Paper and cotton cloth can decay within a month or two. Rope and painted wood, on the other hand, may take anywhere from 1 to 10 years. These organic products are dispatched relatively quickly by bacteria, fungi, molds, and protozoa, then mites, millipedes, centipedes, beetles, and earthworms.

But what about inorganic trash such as cans and bottles? If you toss an aluminum can or plastic soda bottle, your descendants 200 to 500 years from now could find vestiges of it. And if you leave a glass container in the woods, you may as well put in a message to the next millennium—no one knows exactly how long glass will last.

Talbot Islands

■ 5,049 acres ■ Northeast Florida, Fla. A1A ■ Year-round ■ Camping, hiking, swimming, fishing, bird-watching ■ Adm. fees ■ Contact Talbot Island State Parks, 12157 Heckscher Dr., Jacksonville, FL 32226; phone 904-251-2320. www.dep.state.fl.us/parks/District_2/LittleTalbot

COMPRISING FORT GEORGE ISLAND, Little Talbot Island, and parts of Big Talbot and Amelia islands, this barrier-island park system offers a rich tapestry of unaltered beaches and dunes, coastal hammocks, and tidal marshes. The low sweep of maritime landscape, fractured from the mainland by the convoluted creeks and rivers of the Intracoastal Waterway, provides refuge to hundreds of species of shorebirds, wading birds, songbirds, and other animals just beyond the urban corridors of Jacksonville and its developed beaches.

At the south end, Fort George Island is an open catalog of the history of the region. Tremendous shell mounds indicate that Native Americans occupied the area for more than 7,000 years, their piles of discarded oyster shells proof of the area's continuous, fruitful harvest of seafood. Gen. James Oglethorpe, the founder of Georgia, reputedly established a fort here to launch attacks against the Spanish, though no traces of such a structure have been uncovered.

Elsewhere on Fort George Island, a cotton plantation that flourished in the 19th century is today a part of the 46,000-acre **Timucuan Ecological and Historical Preserve.** The preserve includes Fort Caroline, which is located on the south bank of the St. Johns River. Although many of the coastal acres in the area have been converted to golf courses, the reverse has happened here. Where the fairways of an elite 1920s golf club once rolled, tall pampas grass now grows, edged about with ever advancing pines and other plants.

Little Talbot Island, just to the north, has stayed wild throughout the years. The entire 2,500-acre island is now the protected property of Little Talbot Island State Park. Five miles of sandy beach offer a welcome landing strip for shorebirds and nesting sea turtles, while up among the cabbage palms and slash pines of the dune swales, reptiles and small mammals make their homes. A variety of wading birds and invertebrate marine life prefer the quiet nursery waters of the estuaries.

Fla. A1A crosses knife-thin Long Island before arriving on the island of Big Talbot, the northern part of which is occupied by Big Talbot Island State Park. The park is a relatively undeveloped swath of shore and forest. The highway then curves north and over Nassau Sound, offering dramatic views of the coastline and the tumult of ocean waves meeting the outpouring Nassau River. Across the sound, the 200-acre Amelia Island State Recreation Area covers the southern tip of Amelia Island. In all, the Talbot Islands state parks preserve more than 5,000 acres of maritime ecosystems.

Hiking through Timucuan Ecological and Historical Preserve

What to See and Do

If you are coming up from the south, take the ferry from Mayport across the St. Johns River, and within a few minutes you'll arrive at the **Fort George Island State Cultural Site.** Orchid-sleeved live oaks and laurels frame the drive to the site. At the former Ribault Club, you can start a 4.4-mile driving or walking tour around ponds, woodlands, and overgrown fairways, marveling at the power of nature to reclaim land.

Where a yacht basin once thrived, otters and herons now hunt for fish. Putting greens in use until 1991 harbor wild grasses and flowers, and rare eagles are now of the winged variety. Hawks and ospreys also soar in the area and nest in nearby trees. In spring and fall, warblers migrate through, brightening the underbrush with their songs. Ruins from Spanish, French, and English occupations abound. On the island's northwest corner, a visit to the well-preserved **Kingsley Plantation** will add dimension to your awareness of the changes the island has seen.

Just north, **Little Talbot Island State Park** is the best place locally to surround yourself with miles of precivilized seascapes. To get a feel for the diversity of habitats here, take the 4-mile **hiking trail** that starts out through the coastal hammock on the island's north end. American holly, live oak, and magnolia compose a lush setting for warblers and owls, bobcats and marsh rabbits. The trail continues

Fishermen on Big Talbot Island's Sawpit Creek at sunset

through a series of dunes—the older, more vegetated ones farther back from the shore. Red cedars and cabbage palms have moved onto the old dune ridges, while the newer dunes sport a coat of sea oats and morning glories. Willow thickets and sedges fill the troughs between dunes, providing cover for gopher tortoises and skinks.

The trail ends out on the beach, where black skimmers glide open-beaked in the lanes between breakers and royal terns fight their way through northerly breezes, whistling to each other as they fly. A 1.7-mile walk brings you back to the park's northernmost boardwalk, where you can cross the dunes to the parking lot.

To explore the marsh side in more depth, take the 1-mile **nature trail** off the campground across the road. Out on the mudflats, male fiddler crabs wave their massive claws to attract mates and intimidate rivals; herons and egrets stalk the high grasses; and scores of mergansers and other migratory waterfowl billow up off sun-polished planes of water. Back in the hardwood hammock, needles of slash pine carpet the trail and the berries of American and yaupon holly contribute color.

For more trails, stop at **Big Talbot Island State Park,** which also features a marsh-side canoe trail and a primitive beach. Fishing on **Nassau Sound** is good for flounder, mullet, speckled and striped bass, and bluefish. On the sound's north side, the **Amelia Island State Recreation Area** offers hiking, shelling, bird-watching, fishing, and horseback riding. ■

Laughing gull

Guana River State Park

■ 2,489 acres ■ Northeast Florida, south of Ponte Vedra Beach, Fla. A I A
■ Year-round ■ Hiking, boating, swimming, biking, bird-watching ■ Adm. fee
■ Contact the park, 2690 S. Ponte Vedra Blvd., Ponte Vedra Beach, FL 32082;
phone 904-825-5071. www.dep.state.fl.us/parks/District_3/ GuanaRiver

THIS GENEROUS TRACT OF beachfront, salt marsh, and pine flatwoods
protects a lovely stretch of barrier island where wildlife and photogenic
beauty abound. The Tolomato River to the west (a labyrinthine stretch
of the Intracoastal Waterway) and the Guana River to the east create a
peninsula where hardwoods and pines shelter deer, foxes, bobcats, and
other animals. Along the coastal strand, a relict dune system wears a thick
layer of vegetation. But flanking this system, an active dune ridge rises up
to 40 feet, anchored by sea oats, railroad vine, and panic grass.

Among the more common of the 226 bird species found in the park
are brown pelicans, great and little blue herons, wood storks, roseate
spoonbills, black-crowned night herons, and great egrets. More than a
dozen kinds of terns and gulls have been seen out on the beach, including
ring-billed gulls, herring gulls, laughing gulls, and royal terns. Look for
sanderlings skittering along the surf and ruddy turnstones wheeling
overhead or flipping shells with their beaks. In spring and summer, two
threatened species, least terns and loggerhead sea turtles, and two endangered species, green turtles and leatherbacks, make nests on the beach.

More than 9 miles of dirt tracks crisscross the southern part of the
wooded peninsula, accessible over the dam separating Guana River
(south) from Guana Lake (north). The dam lies about 3.5 miles south of
the South Beach area. The north part of the peninsula is occupied by the
9,800-acre **Guana River Wildlife Management Area** *(904-825-6877)*—
more walking and wildlife viewing *(except hunting season, Nov.-Feb.)*. ■

Canaveral and Merritt Island

■ 140,000 acres ■ East central Florida, 45 miles east of Orlando ■ Year-round
■ Camping, hiking, swimming, fishing, auto tour ■ Adm. fee for the national
seashore ■ Contact Canaveral National Seashore, 308 Julia St., Titusville, FL
32796-3521, phone 321-267-1110. www.nps.gov/cana; or Merritt Island
National Wildlife Refuge, P.O. Box 6504, Titusville, FL 32782-6504, phone 321-
861-0667. merrittisland.fws.gov

SITUATED ON A BARRIER ISLAND 35 miles long, the interwoven boundaries
of Canaveral National Seashore and Merritt Island National Wildlife
Refuge encompass some of the Southeast's most important coastal habitats. Twenty-one state and federal threatened and endangered species live
here, the most at any U.S. refuge. Among the species are manatees, wood
storks, southern bald eagles, Florida scrub jays, Atlantic loggerhead sea
turtles, Atlantic green turtles, and leatherback turtles. More than 500
species of animals and 1,000 species of plants living on the refuge repre-
sent biota from subtropical and temperate climates. Tens of thousands
of birds take advantage of the refuge's position on the Atlantic flyway
for the winter months.

The refuge and seashore share a common boundary with the Kennedy
Space Center, but only 5 percent of the land is used for the space program.
The rest is reserved for wildlife. People are not allowed, except on tours.
One of the most unforgettable images here is the sight of hundreds of
shorebirds flushed into flight by the awe-inspiring rumble and fire of a
shuttle launch. Even when the
launchpads are empty, you can see
them from the refuge and get a sense
of that ironic coexistence of human
aspirations and nature's feather-
and-bone technology.

Humanity's historic presence
in the area is also recognized in
the maintenance of 1,500 acres of
citrus groves, about 1 percent of the
refuge's total area. An early 19th-cen-
tury pioneer named Douglas Dum-
mitt established an orange grove on
Merritt Island. Located between the
temperate waters of Mosquito
Lagoon and the Indian River, the
grove emerged from winters frost-
free and became the forerunner of
the Indian River fruit industry.

On the wildlife refuge, scrub
habitat intermingles with pine flatwoods, merging into hardwood

Otters

You may have the good for-
tune to see river otters, which
frequent freshwater ponds and
marshes along the coast and
coastal plain. Look for them
loping along the ground or
swimming gracefully through
the water. They measure 3 to
4 feet in length, and their fur
looks black when wet.

Otters are intelligent and
playful, sometimes fishing in
pairs, sometimes sliding and
frolicking along riverbanks.
Among their amazing attrib-
utes is the ability to dive as
deep as 55 feet and swim a
quarter mile underwater.

hammocks in which pileated woodpeckers and warblers light up an understory of tropical trees and air plants. Hammocks give way to open marshes and saltwater estuaries thrumming with life. Sheets of water in the form of freshwater impoundments and brackish marshes play host every year to 23 species of visiting waterfowl, as well as the home-team herons, egrets, spoonbills, pelicans, and wood storks. Out on the gorgeous and unspoiled shoreline, sanderlings and herring gulls surf air currents, and sea turtles lumber in the summer toward protective dunes.

What to See and Do

Plan to spend the better part of a day if you want to see the refuge and seashore in detail. From Titusville, take the Fla. 406 bridge over the Intracoastal Waterway (Indian River), bear right on Fla. 402, and drive to the **Refuge Visitor Information Center.** A half-mile **boardwalk trail** out back loops through a quiet wetland jeweled with orb weaver spider webs and inconspicuous marsh blooms.

From here, continue east on Fla. 402 a mile, then turn left for the **Oak** and **Palm Hammock trails.** These two concentric loops offer half-mile and 2-mile walks through a dense subtropical hammock of oak, elm, and maple.

Down one trail, a feral hog noses the ground, then, startled, runs snorting into the forest; a pileated woodpecker thunks a cabbage palm high up for beetles. Dragonflies and butterflies maneuver among gaily flowering lantana shrubs and massive ferns. Here and there, an orange tree, possibly descended from sour oranges brought by the Spanish in the 1500s, seeks the light among taller hardwoods. In the summertime, the hammock edges become soaked, and a large population of mosquitoes and other biting insects moves in.

About 5 miles farther east, you enter **Canaveral National Seashore** (*closed three days before shuttle launches; fee*). It's another 7 miles out to **Playalinda Beach,** the southern portion of a 24-mile-long strand of untouched coastline. Backed by a meditative mosaic of marshes and lagooned islets and crowned by a grass-soft dune ridge, this is southern coastal wilderness at its best. Leading out to the beach are boardwalks framed by saw palmettos, leafy sea grapes, and feathery sea oats.

In the south parking lot you can see the shuttle launchpads and the blocky Vehicle Assembly Building rising several miles away, but from this distance they are dwarfed into insignificance by the natural beauty all around. Gulls and terns cruise the foamy margin, tilting in the downdrafts. With strong prevailing northeast or east winds, look for pelagic birds (seabirds) blown shoreward from far out over the ocean; boobies, shearwaters, and storm petrels are a few of the long-range fliers you might see.

Fishermen surf cast along the beach or find sheltered coves in Mosquito Lagoon. From the far north parking lot, it is 15 roadless miles along the beach to the north

section of the national seashore. The only way to reach this unpeopled midsection of the seashore, known as **Klondike Beach,** is on foot or by bike or horse.

You can take hikes along this pristine strand in the company of willets and little sanderlings. Pelicans swoop overhead in low formations. In the lagoon, wading birds are more common. Some of the shells you may find include lightning whelks, spiral moon shells, angelwings, and Atlantic augers. Up in the dunes, gopher tortoises feed on prickly pear cactuses, and small rodents hide amid wild gardens of beach sunflowers and Spanish bayonets (yuccas).

From Playalinda Beach, return to the Kennedy Parkway (Fla. 3) and turn right (north). Go 3.5

miles, then left on Fla. 406 for about another 3.5 miles to the entrance of the **Black Point Wildlife Drive,** a 7-mile loop across open expanses of salt- and freshwater marshlands *(leaflets available at trailhead and refuge visitor center).* You should allow at least 30 minutes to an hour—more if you plan to do any walking.

The drive courses over impoundment dikes, built for mosquito control in the 1950s, and offers front-row viewing of birds and other wildlife. Visitors are encouraged to drive as slowly as they wish and to pull over frequently. Look for eagle nests in pine trees near the beginning of the drive. Farther along, great blue herons—at 4 feet, the tallest of the herons—step gingerly among

Wildlife drive, Merritt Island National Wildlife Refuge

the mudflats, looking for meals. Long assembly lines of white-beaked coots paddle across a pond, otters play along the reedy edges, and alligators lurk on the banks.

The winter waterfowl population of the refuge can swell to 100,000. Sunsets and sunrises are especially active times, as masses of chattering, honking ducks, marsh birds, and songbirds settle in or take off like swirls of windblown leaves. Birds such as dunlin, ruddy turnstone, and northern pintail travel all the way from Alaska—6,000 miles—many in just a week.

About halfway around the drive, hop out for the **Cruikshank Trail,** a 6-mile circuit of a shallow marsh. Even if you don't do the whole loop, you'll see plenty of wildlife, especially from the observation tower about 5 minutes from the parking lot.

Back on Fla. 406, turn left on Kennedy Parkway and head north about 8 miles to Haulover Canal, where you should haul over for the manatee observation deck. Manatee sightings are not guaranteed, but you do have a good chance of spotting one of these rare mammals surfacing near the deck or a short distance out in the inland waterway. Spring and fall are when they usually visit.

From Haulover Canal, it's about 33 miles north and around

through New Smyrna Beach to the **Apollo Beach** area of the national seashore. Pick up brochures at the well-stocked information center. Just north of here you can take a short boardwalk trail up the back of **Turtle Mound,** a huge shell midden built up by Timucuan Indians from A.D. 800 to 1400.

The rhythmic buzz of cicadas vibrates lethargically in an understory trellised with lavender morning glories. Views from the top take in the Atlantic, the peaceful island-dotted lagoon, and the strip of barrier island in between.

Another worthwhile walk, the mile (round-trip) **Castle Windy Trail,** named for another mound,

leads through a tunnel of massive live oaks, stunted and twisted by salt air into the shapes of prehistoric beasts. Air plants such as golden serpent fern and resurrection fern coat the branches of large trees, while redbay and eastern red cedar lend a fresh-scrubbed scent to the air. The trail ends on the shores of the lagoon, where you can scan for a variety of wading and migratory birds.

The road extends some 5 miles south from the entrance station. Beyond the end lies a long empty stretch of unadulterated national seashore, yours to enjoy. You can walk the 15 miles from here to Playalinda Beach. ■

South Florida

Bahia Honda State Park

BELOVED AROUND THE WORLD, sunny South Florida unrolls
gently from the Lake Okeechobee basin, tilting slightly
to spill the region's water off the tip of the continent. Its
famous sandy beaches are but the margins, framing a lush
and varied landscape of wet prairies, freshwater sloughs,
pine flatwoods, ancient cypress swamps, and vast saw-
grass marshes. Though part of the coastal plain, the
region is like no other in the Southeast. The flora, the
fauna, and the landscape itself are all different from

anything that lies above. One hundred miles separate most of South Florida from the Tropic of Cancer, yet as environmentalist Marjory Stoneman Douglas wrote, "the laws of the rain and of the seasons here are tropic laws." Most people describe the region as subtropical or "semitropical," but everyone agrees that the biota to a large extent derives from that steamy belt that girdles the Equator. Much of the vegetation, in fact, migrated as seeds from the Caribbean, borne either by birds or the wind.

South Florida is alternately considered the beginning or the end of the continent. It is at any rate the newest region, emerging from a warm sea between 10 and 15 million years ago. During the ice ages and warm periods that followed, the flat, low-lying land typical of today's South Florida was exposed and submerged time and again as sea levels dropped and rose. At present, the land exists somewhere in between—neither as dry nor as wet as it has ever been. An annual 55 inches of rain keeps the region well watered. Most falls during the April to September wet season, turning much of the region into a humid, buggy jungle. Yet even in the dry season the sloughs ("sloos") and short rivers that slash the land contain some water.

Water, in fact, is the principal element dictating South Florida's interdependent ecosystems. From the renowned Everglades and the keys' coral reefs to the lesser known wildlife sanctuaries and state parks, water determines where animals will feed, when they will breed, what plants will grow, and how many people a given area

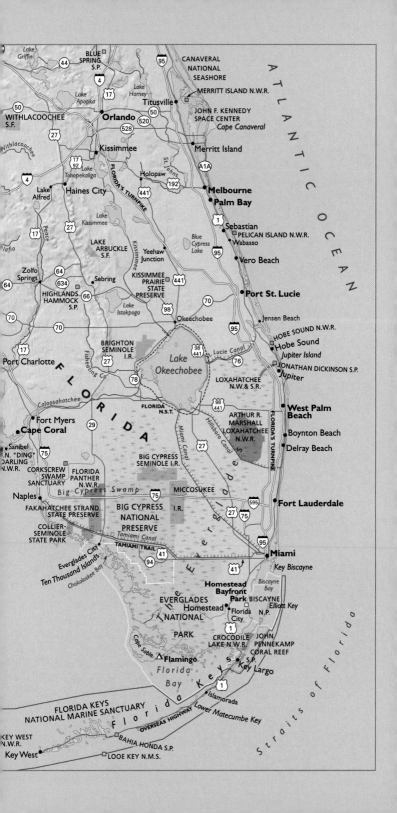

can support. The complex hydrology of South Florida, coupled with the warm climate, nurtures a profusion of life as wildly different as panthers and parrotfish, anhingas and alligators, palm trees and pickerelweed.

No matter what time of year you plan to visit, a cornucopia of wildlife awaits you. The dry season, though, provides somewhat easier viewing—migratory birds are abundant then, and animals tend to concentrate at water sources. In the north part of the region, the dry prairies spreading east of the Kissimmee River hold the first glimmerings of the landscapes to come. Low scrubby vegetation hosts innumerable rare birds and other wildlife. The Kissimmee and other streams empty into Lake Okeechobee, fount of the huge Lake Okeechobee-Everglades Basin—the largest in the state. Its 17,000-square-mile drainage area covers the whole sweep of South Florida, cities, suburbs, and natural areas alike.

Along the west coast, state parks beside the Myakka River and on sun-baked Caladesi Island stand opposite Atlantic coast havens such as Hobe Sound National Wildlife Refuge and Jonathan Dickinson State Park. Palm and oak hammocks are common in the west, while the vanishing sand-pine scrub community makes a last-ditch stand in the east. Throughout the region—but in ever greater quantities as you head south—you're sure to see herons, egrets, woodpeckers, alligators, turtles, lizards, and huge golden orb weaver spiders. Time and diligence will almost certainly repay you with sightings of other wild creatures, including raccoons, otters, deer, feral pigs, and manatees, as well as anhingas and other wading birds. Then there are the rare, but not unheard of, sightings of bobcats, endangered wood storks, and limpkins. And you'll hear many creatures that you don't see—the unforgettable bellow of the alligator, the thrumming bass of the bullfrog, the reedy call of the bittern.

Farther south, in Corkscrew Swamp Sanctuary, you can immerse yourself in a primeval retreat where moss-swagged cypresses, huge ferns, and rare orchids compete for attention with wading birds and secretive reptiles. Big Cypress National Preserve and adjoining Everglades National Park form the last great wilderness in the East. Thick swampland gives way to a miles-wide river of tall grass shining and waving like tresses of hair in the sun. Down here, the Florida panther and the American crocodile have made their final retreat. Survivors of a long-vanished world without man-made boundaries, they—along with the Cape Sable sparrow and the snail kite—have nowhere left to go.

Finally, in the coral reefs of the Florida Keys comes the kind of topographical relief missing from the pan-flat surface of South Florida. This sunken world offers high and low terrain where gold-striped angelfish and supple-winged rays fly like birds over a multicolored garden landscaped by tiny nocturnal polyps. From Biscayne National Park out to the Dry Tortugas National Park, the Keys themselves harbor wildlife in tropical hardwood hammocks, mangrove-belted shores, and beds of sea grass. Wildlife, then, comes first and last in South Florida's natural world. If the geography is too young and unvarying to put you on the edge of your seat, the profusion of flora and fauna will more than compensate. ■

Honeymoon Island near Caladesi Island State Park

Strolling the boardwalk, Caladesi Island State Park

Caladesi Island State Park

■ 2,450 acres ■ 15-minute ferry ride (fare) from Honeymoon Island State Recreation Area, off Fla. 586 northwest of Dunedin ■ Best season fall ■ Four-hour maximum stay ■ Hiking, walking, guided walks, boating, canoeing, swimming, bird-watching, wildlife viewing ■ Adm. fee ■ Contact the park, Gulf Islands GEOpark, #1 Causeway Blvd., Dunedin, FL 34698; phone 727-469-5918 or 727-469-5942; 727-734-5263 (ferry information). www.dep.state.fl.us/parks/District_4/Caladesi/index.html

ONE OF PRECIOUS FEW unspoiled barrier islands in the state, this 3-mile-long strand of mangroves, maritime forest, and pristine beach ranks as one of the Gulf Coast's greatest natural treasures. Boaters may dock overnight; hikers can take on an extensive nature trail; and beachcombers have a long stretch of sand practically to themselves.

Approaching Caladesi over St. Joseph Sound, you can see where a brutal storm in 1921 opened up Hurricane Pass, separating Caladesi from Honeymoon Island. The buzz of personal watercraft dies away as you push farther into the sound, headed for the more primitive pleasures of this unsullied preserve. Red mangroves line the east side of the island. The mangroves thrive in salt water; their spreading roots build up the shoreline and provide sanctuary for a variety of young fish. Dolphins and manatees frequent these calm backwaters.

What to See and Do

Most people head immediately over to the beach. That leaves the three-mile **Island Trail** open for those who want to see what coastal Florida looked like before development. Walk at least some of this interpretive trail (brochures at trailhead) to immerse yourself in a tropical paradise of green palms edging a brilliant cerulean sky, underlain by a gaudy white-sand floor. With imagination you can visualize shipwrecked castaways emerging from the palmettos.

Pink mallows and yellow-eyed grass bloom beside the trail. Breezes ruffle the honey-colored hairgrass. A great egret stands tethered to its shadow in a tidal pond, making the quietness of the day almost palpable.

About halfway along you can cut over to the beach or continue, looping through a lovely live-oak hammock to a virgin stand of slash pine. Slow down and look for snake tracks in the sand and prickly pear cactus flourishing in the island's sun and salt spray.

Among the semitropical species at their northern limit are small trees such as the white stopper, whose leaves were once brewed as a diarrhea remedy. In addition to the numerous native species, you'll also certainly see some exotics.

The Brazilian pepper is a particularly noticeable exotic that thrives in South Florida. Its showy red berries in fall and winter illustrate why the shrub was prized by many late 19th- and early 20th-century gardeners. Unfortunately, it soon escaped its confines, turning into a rampant pest that choked out local species. Florida's parks wage an ongoing war on the Brazilian pepper, spraying, digging, and burning this interloper so that natives can survive.

At the beach, look for a bird with brown wings, a white underbelly, and a dark stripe across the eye. You can also recognize the osprey by its loud whistle. Once in decline because of the pesticide DDT, ospreys are making a comeback. You might glimpse one in flight diving for fish from a height of 150 feet or spot a nest atop wooden pilings or in a dead tree.

Waving sea oats herald the edge of land, where vines of morning glory trail through the sand, then give way to beach. Sandpipers skitter in the surf, terns wheel overhead, and the shallow aqua waters of the Gulf of Mexico lap gently against the shore. As you walk keep your eyes peeled for conchs, whelks, scallops, and other shells.

If you travel by ferry, you'll start and end at **Honeymoon Island State Recreation Area** (727-469-5942), which, though more developed, has its own charms. This former stomping ground of Indians, pirates, hog farmers, and honeymooners has been allowed to revert to a more or less natural state. The **Osprey Trail** on its northern end meanders through virgin slash-pine forest, mangrove swamps, and tidal flats. In the past eight years more than 130 osprey have fledged from nests located near the trail. A fine beach is good for swimming, sunning, and casting for flounder, trout, and snook.

At the top of this barrier island chain, slender **Anclote Key State Preserve,** lying three miles off Tarpon Springs, is well worth a visit if you have access to a private boat. Because there are no trails, you'll have the responsibility of avoiding fragile dune vegetation. Plant and animal life exist here in a precarious balance, dependent largely on the lack of human visitation. Among the bird species that frequent this island are bald eagles, American oystercatchers, piping plovers, and ospreys; green turtles and endangered loggerheads are sometimes seen. A decommissioned lighthouse, built in 1886, rises on the island's southern tip. ∎

Marvelous Manatees

RIPPLES APPEAR AT THE SURFACE of the water, followed by a whiskered snout, a tremendous round gray head, and the wrinkled hump of a neck. The fantastic creature snorts and gives you a brief, incurious glance, then gracefully turns and disappears back into the still waters of the lagoon.

The sighting of a manatee is a rare and wonderful treat. Though occasionally straying into other states during warm weather, the Florida manatee, a subspecies of the West Indian manatee (*Trichechus manatus*), generally confines itself to the coastal waters of Florida and south Georgia. It can survive in fresh, brackish, or salt water, and its preferred habitat includes estuaries, bays, canals, and lazy rivers.

Feeding on sea grasses, manatees especially like water that's only 3 to 7 feet deep—and this has been their undoing. Most of the deaths among manatees are caused by collisions with boats. Propellers rake their backs and slow-moving barges crush them against the seafloor. It is an amazing fact that the majority of Florida manatees have had a run-in with a boat at some point; the lucky survivors are left with scars and deformities.

Even though manatees are seriously endangered, there is no evidence that, in Florida at least, their population was ever much larger. The 2,000 or so manatees known to exist in Florida may be the largest number that ever lived at this northern extreme of their range. If boaters observe the no-wake zones and other regulations, manatees have a fighting chance for survival.

Why should we care about the continued existence of these odd-looking creatures? They have no direct economic value. Indians hunted them for food and leather, but they probably cannot be raised commercially because of their low reproductive rate—one calf every two to five years. One proposal considered using them to control aquatic weeds, but it would take 3,000 manatees just to graze the 400-acre headwaters of the Crystal River. So these "sea cows" are not of much use. But to see them swimming up from the murky depths is to feel a surge of gratitude—that nature still has secrets, that animals this large and strange can still emerge from rivers right off highways. Besides, their value to the state as a tourist attraction is incalculable.

A few facts: Manatees average about 9 feet and 1,000 pounds, though they can weigh up to 3,000 pounds, or about as much as a car. They use their forelimbs to maneuver and feed; the body tapers back like a seal to a flat tail. They are harmless and unaggressive, have acute hearing, and sometimes make squeals to communicate. One observer noted that a mother and her calf, separated by a floodgate, vocalized for three straight hours until the gate was opened. They also like to play. Five manatees were seen bodysurfing the flumes at Blue Lagoon Lake for over an hour, vocalizing and nuzzling each other between rides.

Several places in Florida offer good chances for you to see manatees, sometimes at close range. **Merritt Island National Wildlife Refuge** (see pp. 209-213) has a manatee observation deck. Other good possibilities include **Homosassa State Wildlife Park** *(352-628-2311)*, and **Everglades National Park** (see pp. 250-261), as well as **Bahia Honda State Park** (see p. 274) in the Keys. ■

Manatee, Homosassa State Wildlife Park

Myakka River State Park

■ 28,850 acres ■ 9 miles east of I-75 in Sarasota via Fla. 72 ■ Best months Oct.-May ■ Camping, hiking, backpacking, walking, guided walks, boating, canoeing, fishing, biking, bird-watching, wildlife viewing, wildflower viewing, boat tours ■ Adm. fee ■ Park road may close due to flooding ■ Contact the park, 13207 Hwy. 72, Sarasota, FL 34241; phone 941-361-6511. www.myakka.sarasota.fl.us

SITUATED ALONG THE PICTURESQUE Myakka River a few miles from Florida's southwest coast, this immense state park covers 45 square miles of beautiful wetlands, palmetto prairies, pine flatwoods, and palm and oak hammocks. The watercourse that gives the park its name winds for 12 miles through this protected area, broadening into two lakes that attract a

Sunset, Myakka River

wealth of birds and other wildlife. The main park road presents views of forest and open marshland along **Upper Myakka Lake.** Wild turkeys, bobcats, deer, and feral hogs make homes in the woods, while wading birds, alligators, and turtles prefer the wetlands fringing the lake.

A designated wilderness preserve surrounds undeveloped **Lower Myakka Lake,** where wood storks and sandhill cranes convene to spend the winter months. Roseate spoonbills often dabble among the shallows here, and you might see an otter swimming quietly by or slinking along the muddy banks. Ospreys and bald eagles sometimes patrol the skies above the park's lakes in search of fish. One of the state's oldest reserves, Myakka River State Park highlights a particularly scenic section of Myakka River, one of only two Florida rivers afforded "wild and scenic" protection status by the state legislature.

What to See and Do

Start, at the **ranger station,** by picking up a brochure and any other literature that interests you. Just across the road on the left is the unstaffed but worthwhile **visitor center,** which holds taxidermed waterbirds and reptiles, five informative videos, and an enjoyable push-button display to help you identify the sounds of the pig frog, bullfrog, pinewoods tree frog, and other wetlands creatures.

For 7 twisting miles, you'll follow the **park road** northeast at a stately 25 miles per hour. You'll

Unwelcome Guests

Myakka River State Park is one of many places in South Florida where you may spot a feral hog or hear one snorting around in the underbrush. Some of these large, tusked creatures are descendants of pigs brought by Spanish explorers; others escaped or were released from domestic swine stocks. They all breed rapidly and upset a park's ecological balance by rooting up native plants, disturbing the soil, and competing with—or eating—indigenous wildlife. A quarter of their diet consists of amphibians, small rodents, and birds and their eggs. To maintain the natural ecosystem, the park service periodically removes them. Though generally shy of humans, feral hogs can be unpredictable, so it's always best to keep a safe distance from them.

want to go slower. It's surprising how much you can see right off the road. Deer and feral pigs sometimes browse along the edges of the woods and marshes. Few people take the unmarked **River Trail** at the first pullout on the right after you cross the bridge. It hugs the shore, giving you a good chance to see waterbirds dipping their beaks and perhaps turtles sunning on logs. The 0.6-mile **William Boyston Nature Trail** a little farther down the road takes you out into the green, scented hammock under rattling cabbage palms and old live oaks; markers explain the flora and fauna.

Continuing by car you'll find numerous places to pull over and hike into the woods on the right. Nearly 40 miles of trails, much of them along a power line or railroad grade, lace the palm hammocks and dry prairies. One of the prettiest and least visited spots in the park, **Deer Prairie Slough** lies some 10 miles east of the park road. Here an open prairie is fringed by towering oaks and maples that shelter an abundance of ferns and subtropical plants.

If you're not up for a 20-mile day, you can camp in one of six primitive sites along the trail system. Bring insect repellent and remember that the wet season (late spring to early fall) can mean soupy trails. Also be aware of heat exhaustion, especially on the shadeless prairies. But for the effort, you'll be rewarded with a lush wilderness that few get to see.

Take the left fork in the road to the **Boat Basin,** nerve center of the

Bird-watching on the Canopy Walkway, Myakka River State Park

park. Snacks, souvenirs, and fishing supplies are available from the concession stand, also the starting point for the popular tram safaris *(dry season only)*. Offered several times a day, they carry up to 50 people into the backcountry.

The concessionaire also rents canoes and bikes. Paddling a canoe along the lakeshore and over into the river gives you a great chance to study wading birds close-up and to see half-submerged alligators trolling along like armored submarines. You'll probably also see plenty of hydrilla, the green bottlebrush plants growing on the bottom. These exotic weeds have choked out many native species and reduced the fish population; they can also entangle propellers. Offshore breezes can pick up in the late afternoon, but if you hug the shore you'll find it easier going.

A bicycle is a good way to leisurely explore the park. From the boat basin, you can pedal about 3.5 miles to the north entrance along the flat, scenic park road. In 2 miles you come to the bird walk, where you can actually stroll through the treetops on the marvelous **Canopy Walkway.**

Great egrets, green herons, and white ibises are common year-round; they nest in the park and feed along the lakeshore. A panel here identifies the most common species. Rare park visitors include the black-shouldered kite, peregrine falcon, and cinnamon teal. If you turn right after the bridge 2 miles past the bird walk, and continue to the end of the road you'll find a pleasant little picnic spot by a creek on the right-hand side.

A relatively unknown area of the park, the 7,500-acre **wilderness preserve** spreads south of Fla. 72. The number of daily visitors is restricted, so register first at the ranger station, then go about a half mile east from the main park entrance and turn left to a parking area. A dirt track leads down to **Lower Myakka Lake,** where you'll see the same kinds of birds and wildlife as at Upper Myakka Lake. It's about 1.5 miles to the lake, and another half mile to **Deep Hole.** An intriguing natural phenomenon, this 140-foot-deep sinkhole at the southwest end of the lake is also a good bet for fishing. ■

Highlands Hammock State Park

■ 8,133 acres ■ 6 miles west of Sebring on Fla. 634 ■ Best months Nov.-April ■ Camping, hiking, backpacking, walking, guided walks, biking, mountain biking, bird-watching, wildlife viewing, wildflower viewing ■ Adm. fee ■ Contact the park, 5931 Hammock Rd., Sebring, FL 33872; phone 941-386-6094. www.dep.state.fl.us/parks/District_4/HighlandsHammock/index.html

ONE OF THE FOUR ORIGINAL state parks in Florida, Highlands Hammock started out in 1935 as a grassroots effort to save a scenic hardwood hammock from development as farmland. The Civilian Conservation Corps set up camp and went to work building bridges, roads, and water-control structures; their well-constructed facilities remain today. The park preserves a gloriously deep and dark virgin forest of giant live oaks, laurel oaks, cabbage palms, sweet gums, and red maples. Surrounding the hammock are pinewoods, a cypress swamp, scrub, and marsh, all of which shelter an abundance of birds, aquatic species, and other wildlife.

The **ranger station** and developed area of this thoughtfully planned park lie about a mile inside the park boundary. Pick up a map at the ranger station and visit the nearby **CCC Museum,** which houses good exhibits on the New Deal-era Civilian Conservation Corps. The park road then courses through a historic orange grove to begin a 3-mile loop. You can pull over at various places along the way to take short, but rewarding, nature trails out into the hammock.

Little blue heron, Highlands Hammock State Park

One not to be missed is the **Cypress Swamp Trail,** a leisurely 20- to 30-minute stroll on a narrow boardwalk around a floodplain creek whose still waters reflect tall trees hung with Spanish moss. Swamp lilies and blue pickerelweed add subtle splashes of color. In addition to the impressive cypresses, you're almost certain to see alligators lurking at water's edge, and herons and egrets flapping or squawking among the trees. Other birds commonly spotted here and elsewhere in the park include white ibises, red-tailed hawks, barred owls, and various warblers.

Highlands Hammock contains canopy trees typical of the temperate southeast, yet the understory looks more like a tropical forest. The 0.5-mile **Young Hammock Trail** on the north side of the park wends through an immature section of the hammock, while the 0.5-mile **Ancient Hammock Trail** on the south explores an older part. Found here in abundance, the cabbage, or Sabal, palm—Florida's state tree—got its common name because the heart, when cooked, tastes somewhat like cabbage.

The park road also makes an excellent bike loop. You can rent bicycles at the ranger station and park them at the trailheads to enjoy a variety of scenic hikes. More adventurous bikers will enjoy their own 8-mile off-road trail. You can also get into the denser backcountry on an interpretive tram tour (minimum five people), where you are sure to see alligators, wading birds, and other wildlife. Serious birders may pick up a bird checklist, also available at many other Florida state parks; nearly 200 species have been sighted in Highlands Hammock. ■

Airboat on Lake Kissimmee

Kissimmee Prairie State Preserve

■ 4,600 acres ■ 4 miles northwest of Okeechobee via US 441 and Fla. 724
■ Best months Sept.-April ■ Camping, hiking, backpacking, walking, guided
walks, fishing, biking, bird-watching, wildlife viewing, wildflower viewing ■ Roads
may be closed due to high water ■ Contact the preserve, 33104 NW 192nd
Ave., Okeechobee, FL 34972; phone 863-462-5360

ONE OF THE NEWEST and most remote preserves in Florida spreads over
a treeless prairie north of Lake Okeechobee. This vast tract, the largest
remaining piece of dry prairie in the world, opens from horizon to flat
horizon in a tawny tumble of wire grass, herbs, and low shrubs. Florida
grasshopper sparrows flit among hammocks; sandhill cranes stalk the
sloughs along the Kissimmee River; crested caracaras ride thermals in
search of prey. These and other endangered species find refuge here in
an ecosystem that can hold more than 40 plant species in a square meter.

Though much of the region's dry prairie was converted to vegetable
farms and citrus and pine groves starting in the mid-1800s, cattlemen
in this area were content to use controlled burns to keep the prairie open
for their livestock, thus preserving it the way lightning had for millennia.

Fires kept forests from encroaching upon the open grasslands. Ironically, the Army Air Corps helped prevent development by using the prairie during World War II as a B-17 training base and bombing range. In fact, signs at the visitor kiosk warn hikers about the possibility of encountering unexploded bombs and artillery shells. But bear in mind that the preserve has been carefully scoured and the chances of finding old ordnance are very slim. Nor will you likely see any evidence of bomb damage.

Kissimmee Prairie remains wild to the core. Acquired by the state in 1997, the preserve is currently undergoing some development, but it will be minimal. To get there you still travel 6 miles of unpaved road (off Fla. 724). A future unpaved road will lead nearly half the length of the 8-mile **Military Grade Trail** to a **visitor center.** The rest is wide open for explo-

Kites and Caracaras

Among birds of prey in South Florida, two have been hit particularly hard by habitat loss. The snail kite, found mostly in the Everglades, is a medium-size hawk with a hooked beak and a wingspan of about 45 inches. You can recognize the male by its black head, slate gray to black body, white tail patch, and orange legs; the female has a white face and dark brown body.

Snail kite clutching an apple snail

One curious feature about this bird is that it lives almost solely on freshwater apple snails. Flying over shallow sloughs and mudflats, the kite locates a snail, then carries it off to a perch where it can use its beak to extract the meat from the shell. Wetlands drainage has reduced their numbers drastically in recent decades. Nor has it helped matters that water hyacinth is infesting the marshes where the kite lives, thus limiting its ability to spot food. Today, fewer than 1,000 of these endangered birds remain.

The crested caracara, which inhabits Kissimmee Prairie and other places northwest of Lake Okeechobee, is a kind of falcon of about osprey size but with shorter wings. Look for its curved bluish beak, prominent white throat and neck, and large head. Named for its cackling cry, the caracara feeds on carrion, as well as insects, frogs, fish, lizards, snakes, and birds; pairs will sometimes work together to take an egret or a rabbit.

The proliferation of citrus groves, tree plantations, pasturelands, and other development threatens the crested caracara's population in Florida. Some illegal hunting and trapping and increasing collisions with traffic put further pressure on the species. Only time will tell whether these visually exciting birds will fall prey to South Florida's booming human population.

ration. Bikers and horseback riders especially enjoy exploring the back-country scrub and marshlands. Seven miles of the **Peavine Trail** heads straight north across the preserve, and it offers many possibilities for side trails as well as open-country rambling.

Animals you may spot include river otters, box turtles, eastern indigo snakes (nonpoisonous), wild turkeys, elusive bobcats, and rare Florida scrub jays. Gopher tortoises are often sighted lumbering across the trail. These brown-shelled land turtles can live more than 40 years; their 10-foot-deep burrows provide refuge for snakes, frogs, and other animals during fires or storms. Habitat loss and hunting have reduced their numbers to about 30 percent of their original population in the southeast.

But thanks to Kissimmee Prairie and Myakka River State Park (see pp. 224-27) to the west, large chunks of Florida prairie remain intact for the benefit of those native species that depend upon it. For humans, its value lies in its slow, aesthetic appeal. Take a walk knee-deep in autumn wildflowers; listen for the harsh cackle of the caracara; or simply stand under a broad sky engulfed in a sea of whispering grasses. ■

Hobe Sound National Wildlife Refuge

■ 1,000 acres ■ 8 miles north of Jupiter on US 1; Jupiter Island tract located 2 miles north, then east on Fla. 708 (Bridge Rd.) and north on North Beach Rd. ■ Best seasons fall, winter, and spring for cooler temperatures; summer for sea turtle walks and smaller crowds ■ Hiking, walking, guided walks, boating, canoeing, swimming, scuba diving, fishing, bird-watching, wildlife viewing, wild-flower viewing ■ Contact the refuge, P.O. Box 645, Hobe Sound, FL 33475; phone 561-546-614

OCCUPYING TWO SEPARATE TRACTS of coastal wilds, this refuge protects nearly 1,000 acres of beach dunes, mangrove swamps, and sand pine scrub. It was set aside in 1969 to provide safe nesting grounds for sea turtles at a time of rapidly expanding beach development. Endangered leatherback and green turtles, as well as threatened loggerheads, nest along the 2.5-mile beach. A good season will result in a half million hatchlings. Though most of those won't survive, the refuge does allow the turtles a quiet, dark place to continue their age-old ritual unmolested by the modern world. The beach stretches in unbroken splendor on the refuge's northern tract, a 735-acre chunk of **Jupiter Island.**

Hobe Sound and narrow **Peck Lake,** both part of the Intracoastal Waterway, separate the island from the mainland. Backing the dunes along the lake and sound, mangrove swamps provide nurseries for a huge variety of fish and shellfish. Farthest from the shore, the sand-pine scrub forest has also become vulnerable to loss by development; only about 10 percent of the original scrub remains. So Hobe Sound NWR and nearby

Sundappled cabbage palms

Jonathan Dickinson State Park (see pp. 234-36) have become more valuable to the wildlife that inhabit this community. The 232-acre mainland
tract harbors sand pine scrub where threatened skinks swim through
sand and scrub jays help feed their younger siblings for years. Here a
gopher tortoise makes his way across a trail; there a furtive bobcat sips
from a cool slough. The scrub looks like a series of sand gardens—dense
pockets of shrubs cut off from each other by large patches of white sand.
Plants and animals have learned to quickly use the rain that falls, before it
evaporates on the sand. Nearly 30 of the refuge's plant and animal species
are listed as threatened or endangered. Though few birds actually nest on
the refuge, thousands of migrating birds stop by to rest and feed.

Visitors will enjoy the opportunity to study and photograph plants
and animals in relative peace and quiet. Start out at the mainland tract
at the small but worthy **nature center,** which features a table of marine
artifacts—coral, tube sponge, whale skull, and the like—that you can
handle. Also here are tanks with snakes and fish, giving you names and
facts about animals you may have seen or will see. Outside, the short but
informative 0.5-mile **Sand Pine Scrub Trail** gets you out into the scrub
for an interesting lesson on the ecosystem in which so many beach
houses have been built. A stairway leads to a small beach on Hobe Sound,
framed by sea grapes and palmettos. Waves gently lap the shore here,
while across the sound stand expensive houses set back on green lawns.

Weekly **nature walks** explore the various biological communities and
the animals that inhabit them. During the April to October turtle nesting
season you can sign up for an educational nighttime turtle walk on the
beach. You'll learn that sea turtles have been known to migrate thousands
of miles and the largest, the leatherbacks, can weigh up to 1,300 pounds.
Turtles usually return to the same beach where they were hatched to dig
nests and lay their own clutches of eggs. ■

Jonathan Dickinson State Park

- 11,500 acres ■ 7 miles north of Jupiter on US 1 ■ Best season winter
- Camping, hiking, backpacking, walking, guided walks, boating, canoeing, fishing, biking, horseback riding, bird-watching, wildlife viewing, wildflower viewing, boat tour ■ Adm. fee ■ Contact the park, 16450 S.E. Federal Hwy., Hobe Sound, FL 33455; phone 561-546-2771. www.dep.state.fl.us/parks/District_5/ JonathanDickinson/index.html

LOCATED JUST INLAND from the Atlantic Ocean, this sprawling park sits on prime South Florida real estate, about 20 percent of which is "globally imperiled" sand pine scrub. Deep in the park, pine flatwoods give way to a cypress swamp along the federally designated wild and scenic **Loxahatchee River.** Although some areas were logged as recently as the 1940s, most of the park looks and feels like a precolonial coastal wilderness.

On the east side of the park, the sand pine scrub presents a desertlike appearance. Stands of short-needled sand pines and shrubby oaks are floored by open areas of sandy soil that seem barren. But look closely and you'll find prickly pear cactus and scrub mint with lavender blossoms, deer moss and low-lying gopher apple. Raccoons and gopher tortoises feed on the berries of the prevalent saw palmetto. Threatened scrub jays nest in scrub oaks; lizards and sand skinks slither through the hot sand.

It was through this harsh environment that Quaker merchant Jonathan Dickinson and his crew struggled in 1696. Shipwrecked on Jupiter Island, they spent months among the sometimes inhospitable Jobe Indians until finally being allowed to travel north to St. Augustine. Imagine, as you explore the park's trails, the 25 newcomers straggling up the coast, living by their wits and praying for deliverance from the elements, wild animals, and stinging insects that likely beset them every day.

Palm trees along the Loxahatchee River, Jonathan Dickinson State Park

What to See and Do

Pick up brochures and information in the small **ranger station** at the park entrance. Just off the parking lot begins the 0.5-mile **Sand Pine Nature Trail**—a sampler of the 1,000-mile Florida National Scenic Trail (see pp. 244-45)—that gets you out into the sand pine scrub. Big fires every 10 to 40 years in this community help maintain a healthy mix of plants, clearing the way for new growth. With the sand pine, the heat stimulates the release of seeds that may have been cone-bound for years.

Take time to watch for the dipping flight of the scrub jay, and to listen for its chirp. Scrub jays mate for life and stake out a territory of 10 to 50 acres. The Florida scrub jay is a distinct subspecies isolated from its western cousins.

Just down the road, take a short diversion to the right for the **Hobe Mountain Trail.** This five-minute walk climbs a high sand ridge, a relict dune. Now covered with

scrub vegetation, the ridge is topped by an observation tower that offers wonderful views of sweeping pine forests in three directions. To the east you can see the Intracoastal Waterway, the long strand of Jupiter Island, and the Atlantic beyond. The landscape to the west appears a seamless spread of scrub and forest; you cannot see the asphalt rivers of busy I-95 and the Florida Turnpike flowing only 5 miles away.

Traveling the park road gives you a sense of how big Florida's second largest state park really is. The road curves 4 miles back through the pine forests to a bend in the Loxahatchee River. The shady 1-mile **Kitching Creek Nature Trail** down here makes for a delightful way to explore the low pine flatwoods. If time is short, you can cut back along Wilson Creek. The thin pines, spaced far apart, give plenty of open views of wire-grass meadows, punctuated

Canoeing on the Loxahatchee River

with fan-shaped saw palmettos. Early morning and late afternoon sunlight filters through the pines, casting long shadows and tinting the edges of leaves with a luminous glow. Long-needled, scaly-barked slash pines shade an understory of wax myrtle, black-fruited gallberry, St. John's wort, and white tarflower.

Cabbage palms grow in the moist areas near Kitching and Wilson Creeks, as do a rank profusion of ferns. You might see an eastern diamondback rattlesnake coiled in the sun. Bear in mind that they are important to the local ecosystem and only very rarely bite people. They have the amazing ability to stay in one position for several days waiting for prey. Most experts think their numbers are in decline.

A park concessionaire *(561-764-1466)* offers two-hour **boat tours** *(fee)* on the Loxahatchee, a great way to learn about the area's natural and human history. Or you can rent a canoe and paddle about. Alligators patrol banks upon which turtles bask. Bald eagles, returning from the far north, roost in ancient mossy cypresses that print shadows on the dark water.

A woodpecker knocks unseen on a dead tree trunk, while a gentle breeze whispers through the leaves. Nonmigratory sandhill cranes preen and trumpet along the banks, their brilliant red heads flashing like diadems.

On a bend in the river, 4 miles south (upriver) of the boat dock, the remains of "wild man" Trapper Nelson's 1930s homestead are tucked away among the subtropical foliage. Downstream, the river heads north before looping back southeast, slowly becoming a saltwater mangrove system and emptying into the sea. ■

Arthur R. Marshall Loxahatchee National Wildlife Refuge

■ 150,000 acres ■ West of US 441, 3 miles north of Fla. 806 (Atlantic Ave.) at Boynton Beach ■ Best months Nov.-April ■ Hiking, walking, guided walks, boating, canoeing, fishing, biking, bird-watching, wildlife viewing ■ Adm. fee
■ Contact the refuge, 10216 Lee Rd., Boynton Beach, FL 33437-4796; phone 561-732-3684

A TREMENDOUS OVAL SOUTHEAST of Lake Okeechobee, this important wildlife refuge preserves the remaining bit of northern Everglades. Spreading west of the cane fields and busy beach communities north of Miami that tap into the precious water supply, the Loxahatchee exists because enough people spoke up before time ran out. Now, in a complex arrangement beneficial to both people and wildlife, the refuge's pumps, canals, and levees provide flood control and water storage, as well as habitat for wildlife. Though the majority of the refuge is closed to the public, a large section is open to daytime exploration.

The ecosystem comprises mostly open freshwater marshland, formed some 5,000 years ago on a limestone foundation upon which sits a spongy layer of peat up to 12 feet thick. Under the limestone is a vast and vital aquifer. On the surface live four distinct plant communities. Though the landscape is flat, the changes from one community to the next are pronounced. Backwaters called sloughs hold the deepest water in the Everglades—from a few inches to more than 2 feet, depending on the season. Wading birds poise on stilt legs among white water lilies and yellow-flowered spatterdock in the sloughs. The wet prairie, the largest community in the refuge, is covered with short rushes. Fringing the prairies and other wetlands are wide sweeps of rippling saw grass. Wax myrtles and dahoon hollies often grow in abundance alongside.

The fourth community may be hard to spot from the levees at the refuge headquarters, but tree islands are abundant throughout the Everglades. Small hardwoods grow in dense clusters on islands formed when underlying peat breaks loose and surfaces. Some islands actually float on the marsh and people have been known to step right through them. Tree islands offer the only high ground—and wildlife sanctuary during flooding or fire—so researchers consider them barometers of general Everglades health.

Epiphytes and Baton Rouge lichen

What to See and Do

The **visitor center** at the head-quarters area has all the fine exhibits and audio information stations that you'd expect of a national wildlife refuge. You'll no doubt see alligators in the ponds outside the visitor center, still as statues with menacing-looking grins. Thousands of gators live within the safety of the refuge.

Behind the visitor center, you'll find the 0.4-mile **Cypress Swamp Boardwalk,** which loops back into an atmospheric swamp buzzing with cicadas and the low grunting of the pig frog. A dis-tinct, though smaller, community from the four mentioned on the previous page, the cypress swamp has a canopy of bald cypress, striped with filtered sunlight and studded with epiphytes such as Spanish moss. Baton Rouge lichen paints the tree trunks red. You might see a snake slithering by a cypress knee, out through a wild garden of purple pickerelweed. Take your time here to absorb the closeness, which may at first feel almost claustrophobic.

For open views, head over to the **Marsh Trail,** a 0.8-mile turn around a water impoundment. You walk the dikes that enclose the impoundment, within which are numerous birds. Herons, egrets, ibises, and anhingas nest here, and at sunset they take to wing by the hundreds in a glorious splash of color, heading to their roosts.

A common and always spectac-ular sight is that of an anhinga perched on a branch, wings spread and long neck stretched to dry in the sun. Known as the "snake bird," the anhinga dives headlong into the water and spears fish with its stiletto beak. Then, since it needs to regulate its body temper-ature, it spends quite a bit of time drying out in that remarkable, crosslike pose. Related to the cormorant, the anhinga has a straighter beak and white-fringed dark wings. Find it on the bird list available at the visitor center.

About halfway around the path is an observation tower to give you a broader view of the refuge. In this section you will find nine other square-shaped impound-

Pioneer Preservationist

South Florida's residents—both animal and human—owe a great debt to Arthur R. Marshall. After serving in World War II, Marshall joined the U.S. Fish and Wildlife Service in Vero Beach. Early to spot the threats to the region's ecosystem, he declared, "There is an urgency in Florida environmental issues which compels those who are concerned to take prompt and decisive actions if the nat-ural attractions of the state are to survive." The "Repair the Everglades" program he put together with Marjory Stoneman Douglas and others was sometimes called "The Marshall Plan." In recognition, Marshall's name was officially added in 1986 to the title of the Loxahatchee National Wildlife Refuge.

Bird-watchers on the Marsh Trail, Arthur R. Marshall Loxahatchee NWR

ments that you can walk around. Water levels here are controlled to manage plant growth and create the optimal conditions for wildlife. In addition to the 50 species of birds that nest in the refuge, many more migratory birds stop here during the fall and winter.

To experience the marsh first-hand, you'll need a canoe. A 5.5-mile **canoe trail** loops out from the boat ramp just west of the Marsh Trail. You can rent canoes in Boynton Beach. One of the best things about the trail is that all you'll hear is the swirl of your paddle and the calls of birds; no motorized boats are allowed.

On the south end of the refuge, the **Hillsboro Area** *(12 miles S on US 441, then 6 miles W on Cty Rd. 827/Loxahatchee Rd.)* offers boat ramps, bank fishing, and some interpretive signs. A few miles east of headquarters, the **Wakoda-hatchee Wetlands** *(E of Jog Rd. between Woolbright Rd. and Atlantic Ave.)* makes creative use of a 50-acre tract below a water-treatment plant. The wetlands habitat further purifies the treated wastewater and proves that 21st-century industry can stand side by side with nature. A three-quarter-mile interpretive boardwalk wends its way among ponds that are inhabited by frogs and turtles, as well as some 120 bird species. ■

Corkscrew Swamp Sanctuary

Corkscrew Swamp Sanctuary

■ 11,000 acres ■ 15 miles northeast of I-75, Fla. 846 exit northeast of Naples
■ Best season winter ■ Walking, guided walks, bird-watching, wildlife viewing,
wildflower viewing ■ Contact the sanctuary, 375 Sanctuary Rd., Naples, FL
34120; phone 941-348-9151

ONE OF THE LARGEST and most acclaimed sanctuaries of the National
Audubon Society, this extensive parcel in the northwest corner of the
Everglades ecosystem protects the largest remaining stand of unlogged,
mature bald cypress on the North American continent. The undisturbed
tranquility of Corkscrew Swamp also serves as a safe haven and rookery
for great egrets and endangered wood storks. Hundreds of other species
find refuge here as well, including alligators, Florida black bears, otters,
white-tailed deer, and red-bellied turtles.

Within Corkscrew's bald cypress cathedral, magisterial trees hundreds of years old climb 130 feet in the air, tufted with mosses and air plants that flourish in the swamp's humid environment. Called bald because of their bare look in winter, the cypresses rise imposingly from quiet waters that support an astonishing profusion of life.

Pileated woodpeckers flash like rubies in the trees above ponds where turtles glide among ferns and water lettuce. An orb weaver's web shimmers in early morning light, tuned to the faintest touch of a passing insect. A green lizard slips along the boardwalk, while an egret fans its wings far back in the trees. On a half-submerged log near the boardwalk, a little blue heron is stepping gracefully along, its beak pivoting side to side as the bird stares into the water. With a sudden splash, the beak plunges and comes up with a crayfish or a small frog. These ancient rituals continue day after day in a primordial landscape that, but for the boardwalk, has changed little in 500 years.

Included among the favorites of the 200 bird species recorded here are secretive limpkins, colorful painted buntings, and 2-foot-tall barred owls. Songbirds, including warblers and yellow-billed cuckoos, begin passing through in fall, and swallow-tailed kites arrive from South America by mid-February. With the lowest water levels in late March and early April comes the highest concentration of fish and the easiest meals for wading birds. Mornings in the sanctuary are particularly busy as hundreds of birds partake of the bountiful seafood buffet.

Wood stork nesting season generally runs from December to March. The only stork species that hatches its offspring in the United States, wood storks build their nests in trees. During the breeding season, a pair of these large, long-legged birds can consume as much as 440 pounds of fish, which they catch by wading through shallow water with their bills open; when a fish hits, the bill snaps shut. Records show that the year 2000 wood stork nesting season was by far the best since 1994, with 2,538 fledglings compared with 300 or fewer for recent years.

The Audubon Society had its origins at the turn of the century when a few people began protesting the slaughter of birds for plumes to decorate women's hats. By 1912 a warden was employed in this area to guard egrets and other birds, but not until the 1950s was any acreage purchased. Even in today's climate of heightened environmental awareness, the fate of a 4,000-acre tract of wetlands and pasture within the Corkscrew watershed just west of the sanctuary is still uncertain, as developers and conservationists wage a legal battle of permits and studies.

Meanwhile, several local species are declining in number, and their continued survival or irrevocable demise may be settled within the next two or three decades. A mere 30-mile drive from downtown Naples, Corkscrew Swamp Sanctuary was once considered remote. But the last 20 years have witnessed an explosion of the human population and all its attendant development in southwest Florida, making wild places like Corkscrew Swamp Sanctuary even more rare. Their continued existence is vitally important to the region's ecology as a whole.

What to See and Do

Known far and wide as a birding paradise, Corkscrew Swamp attracts large numbers of serious bird-watchers armed with tripods, high-powered lenses, and other gear. These visitors tend to be a quiet, reverential lot. So even if the parking lot is crowded, the sanctuary will still feel like a sanctuary.

A new **visitor center,** scheduled to open on December 1, 2000, will offer several exhibits to help visitors better understand the swamp's ecology as well as identify its multitude of winged denizens. A 2.25-mile **boardwalk** snakes out into the sanctuary, passing first through pine flatwoods and a slice of wet prairie, edged with saw grass and dainty purple asters. Interpretive signs give background along with pleas for becoming involved in protecting your own local wetlands. The walk then enters the cypress "strand" and stays there for most of its length. There are plenty of cul-de-sacs and benches for quiet communing. Highlights include the wide views at the **central marsh** and the plentiful wildlife at the **Lettuce Lakes**. Volunteers are often on hand if you need a species identification. If you're interested in slogging out beyond the boardwalk to see what the swamp really feels like, inquire about special guided walks.

Everywhere on the sanctuary property are reminders of how humanity and nature can help each other, from the tropical hardwood boardwalk that requires no chemical treatment, to the swamp itself (it has mosquito fish to minimize mosquitoes), to the environmentally sensitive rest rooms. Called "living machines," the latter are self-contained water-treatment systems well worth a visit. They use sunlight, bacteria, fish, and green plants to decompose waste material and recycle water. ▪

Wood stork nest, Corkscrew Swamp Sanctuary

Arrowhead in Fakahatchee Strand State Preserve

Fakahatchee Strand State Preserve

■ 75,000 acres ■ West of Copeland between US 41 and Fla. 29; turn onto Jane's Drive ■ Best months Nov.-May ■ Hiking, walking, guided walks, canoeing, fishing, biking, bird-watching, wildlife viewing, wildflower viewing ■ Contact the preserve, P.O. Box 548, Copeland, FL 34137; phone 941-695-4593

A PRIMITIVE WILDERNESS within the Big Cypress Swamp, Fakahatchee Strand is a dense cypress forest running about 20 miles north to south and 5 miles east to west. The strand occupies a long drainage slough cut over the centuries by water slowly seeping across the toe of Florida to the Gulf of Mexico. Within this forbidding tangle of unchecked tropical growth lives the country's largest stand of native royal palms. Along with these tall, sleek monarchs grow a profuse variety of rare plants, including a remarkably abundant concentration of epiphytic orchids. Their eye-catching blooms decorate the trees in fantastic fashion.

Few trails penetrate the fastness of the strand, but the 2,000-foot **Big Cypress Bend Boardwalk,** 7 seven miles west of the junction of Fla. 41 and 29, will give you a taste of the Fakahatchee jungle, where shaggy-limbed trees take on weird, fairy-tale shapes. You'll behold woodpeckers and other birds illuminating the dark forest interior, alligators waiting for prey in deep water holes, and towering cypresses in the death grip of strangler fig vines. The strangler figs eventually kill their host and stand as one of the dominant trees in the swamp.

Just south and east of Copeland, unpaved **Jane's Drive** carves 11 deep miles into the interior of the forest (and continues into Picayune Strand State Forest). Dense forest walls both sides of the road. Pull over at one of the side tracks and get out for a short walk. Egrets and ibises trumpet in unseen swampy recesses, and the trail winds on, disappearing into a world of natural wonders where humans are still rare visitors. ■

Florida National Scenic Trail

WHEN REAL ESTATE BROKER Jim Kern set out to hike the 160 miles from the Tamiami Trail to Highlands Hammock State Park in 1966, he could not have foreseen how his efforts would ultimately pay off. Publicizing the state's lack of trails, Kern's hike was the beginning of a system that now includes more than 1,000 miles of them. Though the Forest Service originally doubted anyone would want to hike in Florida, the FNST today passes through all three of Florida's national forests, all well as many of its parks, refuges, state forests, and wilderness areas. Simply put, people do want to hike in Florida. When finished, the trail will run 1,300 miles from Big Cypress National Preserve in South Florida all the way to Gulf Islands National Seashore in the panhandle.

Starting in the subtropical wilds of Big Cypress country, the trail winds among old cypresses decked with bromeliads and orchids; it then courses around Lake Okeechobee and heads across central Florida's palm and oak hammocks, lakeshores, and springs; in the western part of the state the pathway takes on hilly forests and secluded rivers. Building the trails and keeping them cleared—a constant labor in Florida's vegetation-friendly climate—is the job not of any state agency but of the thousands of volunteers who recognize the crucial need for greenways amidst Florida's evergrowing corridors of asphalt.

The best time for hiking the trail is during the dry season, roughly from October to March. Florida is low on temperatures and bugs then, and high on migratory wildlife. Going in the latter part of the dry season will also avoid encounters with hunters. Things you should bring in any season: a hat, sunscreen, insect repellent, binoculars, a good bird book, and water, or chemicals to treat what you find. The FNST signs mark officially certified sections of the trail. In some cases the trail crosses private land, which may not yet be open to the general public.

Palms and longleaf pine in the twilight, Florida National Scenic Trail

One completed section of the trail circles Lake Okeechobee, the state's largest lake, in a 110-mile loop. Known mainly for its sugar mills and its old-fashioned fish camps, Okeechobee is increasingly popular with eco-tourists exploring Florida's interior. Some 50 access points lead to the trail, which follows a grassy levee 20 feet above the surrounding terrain. The scenery varies from open water to a marshy littoral zone. You have a good chance of spotting a bald eagle or other noble bird. Backpackers can camp along the levee or stay in one of the fish camps or motels nearby. Get information and maps from the Florida Trail Association, 5415 S.W. 13th St., Gainesville, FL 32608; 800-343-1882 or 352-378-8823. www.florida-trail.org. ■

Big Cypress National Preserve

■ 729,000 acres ■ Between Naples and Miami; visitor center 17 miles east of Ochopee ■ Best months Dec.-April ■ Camping, hiking, backpacking, walking, guided walks, canoeing, fishing, biking, off-road vehicle riding, bird-watching, wildlife viewing, wildflower viewing ■ Contact the preserve, HCR 61 Box 11, Ochopee, FL 34141; phone 941-695-4111. www.nps.gov/bicy

SWEEPING VISTAS OF WET PRAIRIES extending to far horizons humped with hardwood hammocks. Soggy forests where panthers prowl softly under broad-skirted cypresses that stood before Columbus was born. Mangrove thickets sheltering fish near the broken islands of the Everglades. These scenes belong to a preserve that encompasses 45 percent of the Big Cypress Swamp, the ecosystem buffering the north side of the Everglades.

An unusual white-tinged great blue heron

Nearly the size of Yosemite National Park, the preserve covers miles of prairies, sloughs, and cypress trees laden with orchids and pineapple-like bromeliads. About one-half of the remaining population of Florida panthers—numbering no more than 50—roam through here, their progress monitored with radio collars. Underpasses allow them to safely cross roadways; fences along highways and low nighttime speed limits further attempt to keep these elegant cats from extinction.

The construction of the Tamiami Trail (US 41) in 1928 made Big Cypress Swamp accessible to large numbers of people, and thus to economic exploitation. Logging and oil exploration in the '30s and '40s were followed by plans for draining and developing. Investors from far away bought up pieces of wetlands they knew nothing about, as a land speculation frenzy swept through like wildfire in the 1960s. Finally, plans for a major jetport—with its attendant noise and pollution—on the eastern

Fiberglass replica of a Florida panther along the Tamiami Trail, Big Cypress NP

fringe of the swamp brought together such diverse groups as conservationists, hunters, and off-road vehicle drivers to save Big Cypress.

In 1974 a compromise plan established Big Cypress National Preserve, which has looser regulations than a national park. Among the varied activities allowed here are hunting, trapping, fishing, airboating, oil drilling, cattle grazing, and some off-road driving. Privately owned camps still dot the backcountry. Yet with all this apparent activity, Big Cypress is far less developed and visited than Everglades National Park.

The creation of the preserve had one overriding advantage to South Florida wildlife. It protected a vast acreage through which fresh water flows from Lake Okeechobee down to the Everglades, and an unfettered Everglades watershed remains the key to a healthy South Florida ecosystem. Water does flow, albeit imperceptibly, across the swamp, at the rate of a half mile per day; the elevation drops a mere inch in that distance.

What to See and Do

The **visitor center** has interesting exhibits and a short film to get you excited about a plunge into the preserve. You can walk out along the **Florida National Scenic Trail** (see pp. 244-45), both north and south of the highway. Heading north, you'll see alligators in a fenced-off canal; then you skirt an airfield as you hike along fields of prairie grasses and wildflowers toward a distant line of trees. The going can get pretty muddy, especially in the wet summer season when you might find yourself up to your belt in water.

To the south are long views of sedge-filled prairie, speckled with islands of pine and cypress. Flights of white herons and ibises sweep overhead like long-necked angels, and the rare snail kite makes its shrill call. In all, 31 miles of the Florida National Scenic Trail pass through this preserve.

Two driving tours take you into the backcountry within a leisurely morning or afternoon. The 26-mile **Loop Road** begins 4 miles west of Shark Valley and heads west (Fla. 94). The pavement ends after about 8 miles. Stop at the education center and take the short **Tree Snail Hammock Nature Trail;** look for the brilliantly striped tree snail, clinging like a Christmas decoration to smooth-barked trees. The passion for snail collecting a century ago grew to such a pitch that to raise the value of their discoveries, collectors would burn the hammocks where they found them. Collecting of tree snails is now illegal in South Florida. The drive ends back on US 41, 15 miles northwest of your starting point.

On the western edge of the preserve, you can make a 20-mile scenic rectangle starting on **Birdon Road** (Fla. 841, west of Ochopee), then turning right on Fla. 837 and right again on Fla. 839. Two **canoe trails** meander out into the mangrove channels of Everglades National Park. Allow five to six hours to paddle these routes and expect to see untamed subtropical wilderness at its finest. *(But be sure to inquire first at the visitor center for water level and mosquito information.)* ■

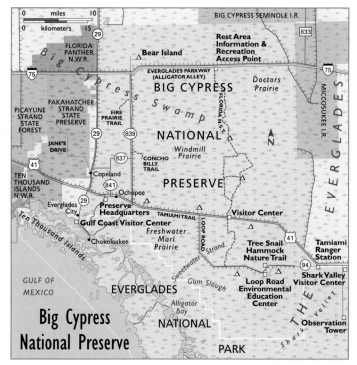

Fisherman at twilight

Everglades National Park

■ 1.5 million acres ■ Ernest F. Coe Visitor Center 10 miles southwest of Florida City on State Rd. 9336 ■ Best months Dec.-April ■ Camping, hiking, walking, guided walks, boating, canoeing, fishing, biking, bird-watching, wildlife viewing, wildflower viewing, boat tours (fee) ■ Adm. fee ■ Contact the park, 40001 State Rd. 9336, Homestead, FL 33034; phone 305-242-7700. www.nps.gov/ever

THEY SPREAD ACROSS THE TIP of the Florida peninsula in green and amber waves—the vast plains of saw grass embellished with islands of trees like ships in a verdant sea. On and on the Everglades run, down to the spindly mangroves that gird the broken coastline. An immense vault of sky over-arches the entire scene, an azure canvas for billowing clouds that can stack up like alpine ranges in the summertime.

Encompassing one-fifth of the original ecosystem, Everglades National Park contains the largest expanse of unsullied landscape in the Southeast—more than 85 percent of its acreage is designated as wilderness. An ark of rare birds, reptiles, and mammals, the park stretches more than 60 miles north to south, 40 east to west. Among the endangered species finding a foothold here are Florida panthers, manatees, Cape Sable seaside sparrows, wood storks, and American crocodiles. With the largest continuous stand of saw-grass prairie in North America, the park is recognized as a World Heritage Site, an International Biosphere Reserve, and a Wetland of International Importance.

Several times in the past million years, the Florida peninsula was covered by water, then exposed again as northern glaciers locked up the available water. About 100,000 years ago, an interglacial sea deposited the limestone beds now found near the surface of much of South Florida. To the west, a porous limestone bedrock became overlain with marl (organic mud) and peat on which the saw grass grows. Sprinkled throughout are bumps on the bedrock, some as large as a few hundred acres. These are now hardwood hammocks, streamlined in the direction of the water flow across the marsh. In some places, the limestone shows through—for example, on Long Key Pine—and you can see solution potholes made by weak organic acids. Water fills these holes and creates little self-contained tanks of small plants and animals. So even though the hammocks appear to have more solid footing than the soupy marshes, you can believe that blazing a trail across this pitted, scrubby terrain is tough work.

A wide sheet of water averaging a mere 6 inches deep flows slowly across the Everglades, sustaining life. Pioneering environmentalist Marjory Stoneman Douglas aptly titled her 1947 book *The Everglades: River of Grass.* From May to October, thunderstorms and the occasional hurricane rake the land, replenishing the water supplies; during the dry season, sloughs and ponds shrink, trapping aquatic life and providing easy meals for hordes of hungry wading birds.

In addition to the southwesterly flow, the water tunnels underground southeast to the Atlantic. The pressure created by this freshwater flow prevents salt water from intruding inland; thus the Everglades system provides bountiful quantities of drinking and irrigation water to coastal cities. In a misguided effort to divert even more water to sustain the region's booming human population, engineers built some 1,400 miles of canals in the mid-1900s. But with massive die-offs of birds and other animals, local officials realized that the three keys to the South Florida ecosystem were water, water, and water. The last couple of decades have seen attempts to undo some of the damage (see p. 256).

Goals for the near future include restoration of freshwater flows into the park and Florida Bay without destroying more wetlands with canals; restoration of Lake Okeechobee by reducing pollutants and letting the water level fluctuate naturally; requiring polluters (mainly agricultural interests) to pay for cleanups; and limiting the amount of phosphates running from farms into protected areas, since fertilizers trick marsh vegetation into growing out of control. In 1988 the federal government had to sue the state of Florida for not enforcing its own water quality standards. A hard-fought campaign continues against exotic invaders such as water hyacinth, Brazilian pepper, Australian pine, and the melaleuca tree, the latter planted in the 1930s to dry up the wetlands.

How much has been lost? Recent studies suggest a 93 percent decline in the wading birds that nest in the southern Everglades—from a quarter million in the 1930s to somewhat under 20,000. You can just imagine what it must have been like—the sky filled from horizon to horizon with birds, the air thundering with their wingbeats. It can be maddening to think about what you missed by being 70 years too late.

Following pages: Ten Thousand Islands, Chokoloskee Bay

What to See and Do

There are very few places in the coastal southeast where you get the kind of heartbreakingly beautiful panoramas of sinuous marshland that you find in the Everglades. Especially lovely in the soft, bent light of dawn and dusk, the estuaries and saw grass plains have a simple, primal quality: Breezes make rippling patterns across the water and the grasses. A large silence, broken only by mating calls, hangs over everything.

It's not a landscape that draws your eye in any particular direction the way, say, a snowcapped peak does. Some people find it hard to love, at least the first time. The park road has been called "38 miles of nothing." True, the austere flatness is relieved only by the scattered tree islands. Nature here is subtle, the land gentle. But on a trail just off the road you may witness something as spectacular as an alligator leaping for an unsuspecting heron, or as routine as a butterfly lighting upon a wildflower. Take your time. Meander as slowly as the river of grass, and learn to feel its rhythm.

Ten Thousand Islands Area

In the northwest corner of the park, a convoluted maze of emerald mangrove islets fans out from Chokoloskee Bay to form an ideal haven for dolphins, manatees, ospreys, terns, cormorants, herons, and roseate spoonbills. The islets, as you'll see if you take a canoe or tour boat among them, are densely packed with red mangroves whose reddish aboveground roots filter salt out of the water they thrive in.

Mangroves mass together in low bunches, giving them the ability to withstand almost any wind or tide. Like cages, their root systems trap soil and detritus, so that one beanlike seedling, dropping and floating from a parent branch, may end up starting its own island. Once considered nuisance plants blocking off beach access, these hardy trees are now admired for their ability to stabilize shorelines and provide breeding and feeding grounds for hundreds of fish and crustacean species.

The **Gulf Coast Visitor Center** (*Fla. 29, 1/2 mile S of traffic circle in Everglades City. 941-695-3311*) is the place to go for **cruises** (*fee*) and **canoe rentals.** On the way through town, you'll pass numerous tour boat operators, some offering old-fashioned airboat rides. These will not enter the boundary of the national park, where they are not allowed because of their noise and tendency to destroy saw grass.

The concession at the national park visitor center generally, though not always, includes a park ranger on cruises. Non-ranger guides may not present as well-organized a narration but will at least be able to identify what you're seeing. The 90-minute cruises thread the heart of the Ten Thousand Islands archipelago, where you're practically guaranteed sightings of beautiful and rare birds, possibly including bald eagles that winter here. Another cruise travels inland up the dark and mysterious **Turner River,** past Calusa shell mounds, wading

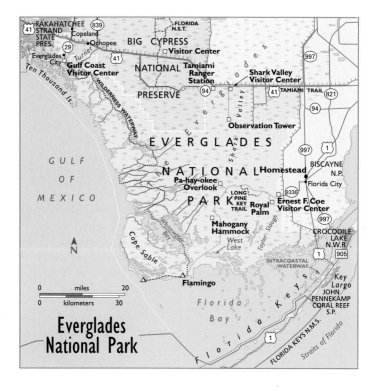

Everglades
National Park

birds, and alligators. While waiting for your tour you can picnic under the thatched shelter at the dock adjacent to an expanse of Bermuda grass and listen to the lazy slap of water on boat hulls and the call of hungry gulls.

For a self-paced browse through the mangrove channels, you can rent a canoe. Chokoloskee Bay is the northern terminus of the wild and adventurous **Wilderness Waterway,** a circuitous 99-mile route from Everglades City to Flamingo in the southern end of the park. The complete journey takes 5 to 10 days by canoe, 6 to 8 hours by motorboat. Campsites are strung out along the way. You can also start from Flamingo and paddle up the other way, and there's

a shuttle service if you want to leave your car at one end.

(On all outings, long and short, be aware of poisonous plants and animals, including paisley-barked poisonwood trees, poison ivy, coral snakes, water moccasins, and pygmy and diamondback rattlers. Remember, most snakes in the park are not poisonous, but all are protected. Do not approach alligators closer than 15 feet. Summer brings clouds of salt marsh mosquitoes; avoid grassy, shady areas and wear repellent.)

Shark Valley

Up in the northeast part of the park lies Shark Valley, which gets its name from Shark River Slough. A freshwater channel, the slough winds through mangroves before

Tamiami Trail through the Everglades

Keeping the Wetlands Wet

Water is the lifeblood of the Everglades. All the wonderful variety of plant and animal life depends upon this wide, shallow current, which until the 1920s flowed unrestricted from Lake Okeechobee to Florida Bay. The Glades back then were an obstacle: People needed to travel, sugar fields required water, sunseekers wanted dry ground for homes. Work crews blasted away the limestone, building roads and dredging channels to divert water from the Everglades. After all, there were innumerable miles of Everglades, endless amounts of water, and birds past counting.

Except that there weren't. Instead, there were endless numbers of people, needing space and water. The billions of gallons siphoned off the Everglades annually by a system of canals and levees over a half century has reduced the original ecosystem by half.

Only in recent decades have wetlands risen in status from worthless swamp to vital resource. Wetlands, we now know, purify water in an efficient way, while acting to stabilize shorelines. As natural reservoirs they can help in flood control by holding excess rainwater. The value of wetlands to plant and animal life is well known; for many migratory and endangered species, the marshes, bogs, and swamps are absolutely necessary. Meanwhile, recreational usage grows yearly as more people seek quiet places to hike, canoe, fish, and bird-watch.

With the Everglades as a bellwether for wetlands across the country, a new program, years in the planning, is seeking to restore the Everglades' natural water flow. The 8-billion-dollar restoration plan calls for the removal over 20 years of some dikes and other barriers that fragment the region. Taking them all out would involve moving too many people to drier ground. Instead, the Army Corps of Engineers, responsible for the original dikes, plans a massive replumbing, with underground reservoirs that will periodically release water and thus imitate the natural wet and dry cycles of the Glades. Whether this project will work on such a large scale is a subject of much debate. Meanwhile, the population of South Florida grows, wading birds still flock at sunset, and water keeps slipping softly to the sea.

emptying into the Shark River. Sharks have been spotted where the river merges with Ponce de Leon Bay. The valley is a basin lying a few feet lower than the rest of the Everglades. Aerial photographs show a saw-grass prairie landscape dotted with tree islands.

Mangroves from farther south have tried to stake positions here, clinging to the edges of these life-giving creeks. But alligators do an efficient job ripping the mangroves out by the roots, clearing the channels and consequently making them open for other wildlife. Down on the ground, views are hemmed in by the profligate growth of saw grass—up to 12 feet tall in this part of the park. The saw grass is so strong and resilient here that only a fierce hurricane can push it over.

Stop in at the **Shark Valley Visitor Center** (US 41. 305-221-8776). Popular open-air tram tours (fee) will take you about 7 miles deep into the saw grass. Here you will have an opportunity to see herons, alligators, garfish, and rare snail kites. Built in part by early oil seekers, the road leads to a 65-foot **observation tower** that will get you above the grassy plains for long and wonderful views of the hammock-studded wetlands stretching far into the distance. There are also bikes for rent and short **trails** that explore the saw-grass marsh and a tropical hardwood hammock.

Southern Everglades

Holding a cross section of the major Everglades communities, the southern part of the park follows the general flow of Taylor Slough southwest through gaps in a pine-laden ridge, across saw grass- and cattail-lined creeks, to the mangroves at the edge of Florida Bay. Entering the park from the **Ernest F. Coe Visitor Center** puts you on this pineland ridge, though you'd scarcely realize it. The elevation here is only about 6 feet above sea level. Over the gradual course of about 15 miles, the land slowly levels to the sea, tilting the water out through a capillary network of creeks.

The driest ecological zone in the park, the pineland stays above water the year-round. The park road tracks through this zone, and you can get out and explore it in any season. The going is rough, though, because of the exposed limestone, its porous surface corrugated into sharp crags and pocked with water holes. Fires, prescribed and natural, periodically sweep through the pines, the largest remaining stand of slash pine in South Florida. Though the trunks may char, the pines survive, while interloping hardwoods get killed off. Other survivors include moon vines, coonties, and saw palmettos; though the tops burn, the roots remain alive.

You can learn about the pinelands and other communities inside the Coe Visitor Center, the most recently updated of the park's information stations. There are several worthwhile exhibits and films here to get you primed. You'll also begin to understand that at least part of the Everglades experience is a shared one. Because most of the park is a daunting, high-grass, wet wilderness, there is only one main park road.

Anhinga chicks

With a count of more than one million visitors annually, the park funnels quite a few cars down its midriff. March attracts the highest number—an average of about 4,500 a day—and September the lowest with less than 1,700 a day. A visit in winter or early spring practically ensures that you'll see the most wildlife, the best weather, and the fewest mosquitoes.

When you consider the fact that a metropolitan area of more than 3.5 million people reaches almost to the park's borders, you realize what a unique and fragile life raft Everglades National Park is. Oddly enough, though, after the first few miles, the park can seem almost empty; most people, it seems, drive nonstop down to Flamingo, at the end of the road.

Heading southwest from the pinelands, you descend about 2 feet to the saw-grass plain, the actual Everglades. Out here elevation variances of only a few inches can mean the difference between tropical hardwood islands and swamp vegetation that needs slightly more water. Beyond the grasslands lies the coastal prairie, anchored by the former fishing village of **Flamingo.** The apron of Florida Bay spreads south from here, dotted with keys and filled with game fish. All but four of the keys are bird sanctuaries, off-limits to humans. At the marina you can join boat tours (*fee*) that take you either out onto the bay or back up Buttonwood Canal. The shallow bay—never more than 9 feet deep—occupies one-third of the park's territory. Out on the bay you can behold ospreys nesting on channel markers and great white herons stalking among the mangroves of the keys. One of several species once hunted nearly to extinction for its plumes, the great heron has made a comeback. You can distinguish the slightly smaller great egret—actually a species of heron—by its black legs. At sunset huge flocks of birds take wing as they leave their mainland feeding grounds for the safety of the keys, where they have no predators.

You can also rent bikes, canoes, and kayaks here at Flamingo and explore on your own. Going up Buttonwood Canal into the mangrove backcountry you have a good chance of seeing the endangered American crocodile. This area and the Upper Keys constitute its sole remaining habitat. Crocodiles and alligators have similar habits, but crocs prefer saltier water, have a more tapered snout, and are gray-green—lighter in color than alligators.

Several interesting hiking trails wind through this environment. The 2-mile (one way) **Snake Bight Trail** courses through a mangrove forest, hardwood area, and coastal prairie. A boardwalk takes you out to Florida Bay. A more adventurous walk, the 6-mile (one way) **Coastal Prairie Trail,** heads west into wide-open views of prairie laced with saltwort and delicate sea oxeye daisy. The trail ends at the beach on **Cape Sable,** a wild sweep of coconut palms and

crushed-shell shore accessible only by boat and this trail. Closer to Flamingo, **Eco Pond** is well worth a stroll around. Built for sewage treatment, this small, unsmelly pond brims with plant life and animals. Gator bulls bellow like boat motors near the shore, while heedless coots and moorhens chuckle and whinny and roseate spoonbills encrimson the water in rippled reflections.

Coe Visitor Center to Flamingo

Seeing the Everglades by car involves taking the main park road, a 38-mile, one-way trip. Add about 10 miles for side excursions, plus a couple of extra hours for short hikes, and you've spent a half day getting to Flamingo. Time well spent, because this road is more than just a quick way to Florida Bay; a slow cruise through the heart of the park gives you a chance to savor the various Everglades ecosystems—pinelands, river of grass, hardwood hammocks, and mangrove estuary—and their associated wildlife. Easing off the gas pedal will help you spot points of interest and avoid hitting animals on the road.

The road starts out in the pine rocklands, along a ridge that separates Shark River Slough to the north from Taylor Slough. You won't notice the ridge, because it's only a few feet higher than the surrounding land. Broad views of high tawny grasses are punctuated by islets of pines and hardwoods. An African savanna comes to mind as you travel the road, the views growing ever longer as you head southeast. After 4 miles, turn left at the sign for **Royal Palm.** The star attractions here are the two half-mile trails, one ambling around a freshwater slough and the other investigating a hardwood hammock. From the boardwalk on the former trail you get open views and an appreciation for the variations a few inches in elevation can make. First look west to the lush palms on Paradise Key Hammock, then turn around and study the landscape a few hundred yards away. The thickets of willow, which need more water, indicate a slightly lower terrain.

About 3 miles past the Royal Palm turnoff, pull to the right for **Pinelands,** where a half-mile stroll through tall, thin pines illustrates the value of forest fires. Many of these pine trunks are blackened by fires that beat back the encroachment of hardwoods and impenetrable undergrowth. Deer and other mammals find homes in this 20,000-acre slash-pine forest, a mere 10 percent of what existed before the region was settled.

Six miles farther on, **Pa-hay-okee Overlook** is a must for a real appreciation of the beauty of the Everglades. A short boardwalk here leads to an observation platform that gives horizon-to-horizon views of the grassy waters ("pa-hay-okee" in Seminole). Discerning eyes can pick out different kinds of tree islands—tropical hardwood hammocks and palms mean raised ground; "cypress domes" (cypress and other swampy growth), on the other hand, take root in depressions.

While other trails are marked with fact-filled panels, park officials chose to interpret this boardwalk through quotations; words from Thoreau, Loren Eiseley, Rachel Carson, and other naturalists are all you really need. The quiet rustle of acres and acres of saw grass speaks for itself.

To step out onto a tree island, take the right turn for **Mahogany Hammock** (7 miles beyond Pa-hay-okee). An elevated trail bores into the humid recesses of a subtropical jungle. The nation's largest mahogany trees grow here, filtering meager shards of sunlight into the hammock, where zebra butterflies flit by rare orchids and strangler figs clasp host trees in a slow but deadly embrace.

About 11 miles south, a left-hand pull-off offers quick access to a quarter-mile boardwalk out to lovely **West Lake.** At the edges of this brackish lake a mangrove forest thrives. Indeed, from here south, you encounter much the same environment, the shrubby salt-resistant trees forming the gateway to Florida Bay. Three species of mangroves are found here—white, black, and red (in order from inland to coast). White and black mangroves excrete salt from their leaves, while reds filter it out of their roots. Take your time here, listening to the trill of frogs and the squawk of herons, and watching gangly birds pad the water's surface as they build momentum to take flight.

Anhinga and Gumbo-Limbo Trails

This easy, paved 1-mile walk combines the two trails at the Royal Palm area, each offering a very different picture of the Everglades. Starting with the Anhinga Trail, you begin on a wide walkway, part

Bird-watching on the Anhinga Trail

of an old road, alongside a man-made canal at the edge of Taylor Slough. You can watch egrets moving with balletic precision among the saw grass, while alligators lie out on the grassy banks or swim slowly along with only their eyes above water. If the wading birds seem oblivious to the gators, it's because alligators eat only about once a week. During the dry season, life perforce focuses on these watery sloughs, and the small risk of becoming food for a larger animal is worth it.

Follow the looping boardwalk out over the open wetlands, where you can see turtles, fish, and sometimes otters. The trail takes its name from the anhinga, or snake bird, which swims underwater to skewer fish. It then flips the fish into the air and swallows it whole. Look for dark-winged anhingas perched on low branches.

The adjacent Gumbo-Limbo Trail goes practically unnoticed by the large number of people who take the Anhinga Trail. This short loop penetrates a lush subtropical hammock, giving you a taste of the close spaces of the Everglades. A hothouse garden of wild coffee, ferns, strangler fig vines, and air orchids that cling to trees only for support, this jungly environment has the rank odor of decaying vegetation, mixed with the refreshing perfumes of luxuriant growth.

Along with the tropical trees are more temperate-climate hardwoods like live oak and sumac. Touch the wrinkled "sunburned" red skin of the amazingly versatile gumbo-limbo. Its wood was once used for carousel animals, its inner bark for flavoring soups, its resin for sealing canoes and to treat bee stings and poisonwood rashes.

Parts of the trail that were shaded a few years ago were opened up to new growth by Hurricane Andrew in 1992. The storm tore down huge moss-covered live oaks that had taken centuries to grow. Before leaving the trail, take a moment to step into the unpaved hammock. You might not get very far in this dense jungle, but you'll get a sense of its real mystery. ■

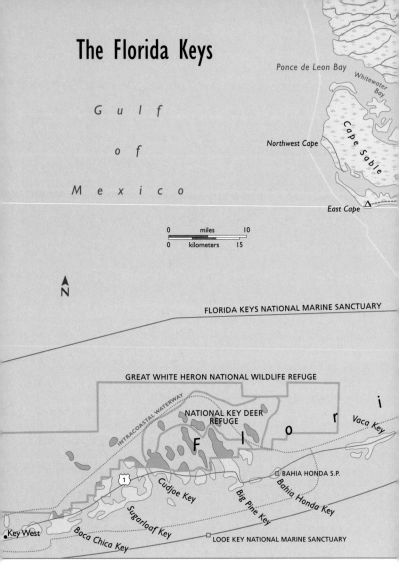

The Florida Keys

Gulf

o f

M e x i c o

Ponce de Leon Bay

Whitewater Bay

Cape Sable

Northwest Cape

East Cape

0 — miles — 10
0 — kilometers — 15

N

FLORIDA KEYS NATIONAL MARINE SANCTUARY

GREAT WHITE HERON NATIONAL WILDLIFE REFUGE

INTRACOASTAL WATERWAY

NATIONAL KEY DEER REFUGE

F l o r i

Vaca Key

BAHIA HONDA S.P.

Bahia Honda Key

Cudjoe Key

Big Pine Key

Sugarloaf Key

Key West

Boca Chica Key

LOOE KEY NATIONAL MARINE SANCTUARY

The Keys

CURVING 220 MILES from Biscayne National Park to the Dry Tortugas, the Florida Keys hold the third largest coral reef tract in the world. The glittering islands in this splendid chain began forming about 100,000 years ago. During various ice ages that followed, the sea level rose and fell, alternately submerging and exposing the growing keys. From Big Pine Key north, islands are composed of layers of fossilized coral, while those farther down are actually ancient sand shoals.

After the last ice age ended, the sea level continued its steady rise, filling Florida Bay about 5,500 years ago and making swamps out of land that had been high and dry. The Keys began taking on their present

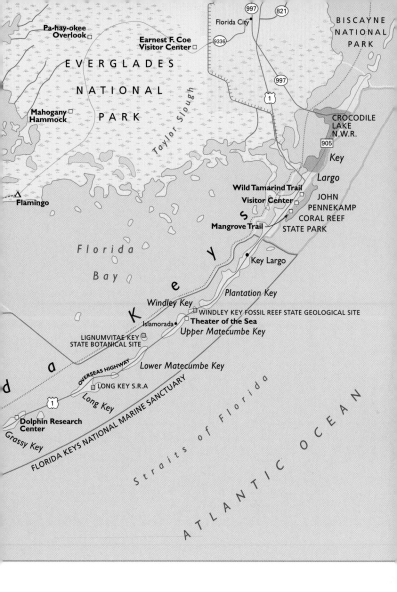

look—tropical hardwood hammocks, encircled by saltwater-loving man-groves. Beyond the mangroves, sea grass waved on sandy bottoms, and hosts of birds, turtles, manatees, tropical fish, and other creatures filled the Keys with warm-weather life. Most miraculous of all was the jewel-box chain forming parallel to the islands, a dazzling barrier reef bursting with corals and fish in all manner of colors and shapes.

Today the 2,800-nautical-square-mile **Florida Keys National Marine Sanctuary** *(305-743-2437)* attempts to safeguard the living treasures of the Keys' marine ecosystems. It's a tough job: Nearly four million people come here every year, many to boat and dive on the reef. Other local parks and sanctuaries shelter such rare and endangered species as the bay cedar and the mahogany, the wood stork and the diminutive Key deer. ∎

Biscayne National Park

■ 172,000 acres ■ Fla. Tpk. south to Speedway Blvd. exit, south on Speedway Blvd. 4 miles to S.W. 328th St., east on S.W. 328th St. 9 miles to Convoy Point ■ Season year-round ■ Camping, hiking, walking, guided walks, boating, canoeing, swimming, scuba diving, fishing, bird-watching, wildlife viewing, boat tour ■ Contact the park, 9700 S.W. 328th St., Homestead, FL 33033; phone 305-230-7275. www.nps.gov/bisc

ONLY 18 MILES EAST OF Everglades National Park lies a sanctuary protecting the reefs and barrier islands that fan out south of Miami. Set aside in 1968, Biscayne National Park is unusual in that 95 percent of it is covered by the warm, blue-green waters of Biscayne Bay. A mangrove-fringed shoreline, sea-grass and hard-bottom bay communities, a cluster of small islands, and the coral reefs constitute the ecosystems of this subtropical

Coral reef, Biscayne National Park

marine park. From the middle of the park, far out on the bay, the land recedes to a penciled line of green, and the world becomes a wide circle of water domed by an impossibly big sky.

On keys where developers once imagined million-dollar homes, life in its myriad forms continues as it has for thousands of years. Yet from just about anywhere in the park, you can see the compact skyline of Miami on the horizon, an inescapable reminder of just how tenuous is this water wilderness in the shadow of millions of people.

On the park's mainland, the mighty mangrove predominates. Holding the shoreline in place and bearing the brunt of fierce storms, the ranks of mangroves also act as safe havens for resting, feeding, and breeding marine life. Bacteria feed on decaying leaves, which are consumed by microorganisms. They, in turn, are eaten by larger creatures—and so it goes on up the food chain. Among the labyrinthine prop roots, fish and crustaceans find both shelter and nourishment.

Fiddler crab

Dotting the bay are more than 40 keys large and small, the only other bits of land in Biscayne National Park. The top of the 150-mile-long chain of Florida Keys, these islands began slowly accumulating as coral colonies, then emerging as islands when sea levels dropped. Ancient coral rock is exposed in some places. Seeds from the tropics, broadcast by the wind or dropped by migrating birds, took root and turned the islands into thick jungles of mahogany, gumbo-limbo, strangler fig, and Jamaican dogwood. Though loggers cleared out many old mahoganies and other hardwoods, particularly on Elliott Key, much has been preserved. Fishing birds such as pelicans, cormorants, and frigatebirds swoop low along the shore, while the interiors are inhabited by reptiles, a few small mammals, and plenty of insects.

Surrounding the keys, the shallow waters of Biscayne Bay support a wondrous diversity of bird and marine life. Manatees float among the shallows, grazing in sea grass meadows. More than 250 species of fish make this a fisherman's and snorkeler's paradise. Birds also partake of the natural bounty. One of the most thrilling sights is to watch a patrolling brown pelican spot its prey, fold its great wings, and dive from as high as 30 feet, hitting the water with tremendous force. Snowy egrets, little blue herons, and others nest on the protected Arsenicker Keys; white ibises are often seen policing the mudflats in search of crabs and little fish.

Gin-clear only on windless days, the bay waters still possess a remarkable purity, thanks in large part to conservationists whose efforts culminated in the creation of this sanctuary. The large amount of dredging, land filling, and boat traffic from the 1950s to the 1970s stirred up so much sediment that photosynthesis on the reefs was nearly impossible and the coral stopped growing. A temporary halt in dredging helped, but rain runoff carrying everything from pesticides and fertilizers to sewage, detergents, and oil still threatens the health of the bay and its reefs.

For now the underwater world remains intact. Below the surface, amid the intricate, colorful beauty of the reefs, the park blossoms into an exquisite landscape of tropical fish and corals. The northernmost coral reef in the country grows here in a finely tuned environment; the water is no cooler than 68°F, shallow enough to receive plenty of sunlight, and has the proper salinity. Only a few miles north, coral reefs cannot grow. At Biscayne, billions of polyps have over the eons built a megalopolis of tiny tube-shaped exoskeletons that serve as the reef foundation. Soft corals like sea fans and sea whips adhere to this solid base, feeding on microscopic plankton. Fish dart among the corals, finding food and shelter.

In the shallow patch reefs close to shore, snorkelers will find calm water for viewing brain and star corals, spiny lobsters, shrimp, sponges, and a variety of tropical fish. Some schools pass in glittering mirages of light, swept in synchronous motion by an invisible force. Others, like angelfish and the curious parrotfish, swim alone; parrotfish chew on the coral itself, extracting the polyps and algae. Spotted moray eels wait in secluded holes for hapless fish to pass, then spring out like pistons.

Beyond the barrier islands, about 10 to 12 miles out, the outer reefs contain huge branching corals, like elkhorn and staghorn. Exposed to the waves and currents, these reefs are home to a bustling variety of life that includes sea turtles, rays, squid, triggerfish, and barracuda.

What to See and Do

If you do not have your own boat, drive to the **Dante Fascell Visitor Center** at Convoy Point and view the displays and film. A concessionaire *(305-230-1100)* operates three-hour glass-bottom boat tours *(fee)*. More adventurous souls can sign up for snorkeling and scuba diving trips *(fee);* equipment rentals are available. A three- to four-hour trip gives you about 75 minutes of water time.

There are also occasional jaunts to the keys for hiking and picnicking. **Elliott Key** has a nature loop through a hardwood hammock filled with ancient trees and rare air plants, and a 7-mile trail traverses the length of the island. **Boca Chita** and **Adams Keys** offer short nature trails. It's a good idea to make reservations for these trips, especially in high season.

If you arrive too late for an excursion, you can walk out onto the **jetty** at Convoy Point for fine views of the bay and the shoreline. The concessionaire rents canoes and kayaks for close-up exploration of the mangroves. The adjacent **Homestead Bayfront Park** *(305-230-3034)* has a full-service marina. Elliott Key has drinking water and first-come, first-served camping; for more primitive camping try Boca Chita.

Elliott and Adams Keys offer overnight anchorages. Fishing is excellent for marlin and sailfish on the ocean side, while grouper and snapper are more likely in the bay. Boaters should take special care not to damage reefs that have taken thousands of years to develop—be especially alert near the shallow patch reefs. ■

Glass-bottom boat tour

John Pennekamp Coral Reef State Park

■ 178 nautical square miles ■ Key Largo, US 1 at Milepost 102.5 ■ Season year-round ■ Camping, walking, guided walks, boating, canoeing, swimming, scuba diving, fishing, bird-watching, boat tour ■ Adm. fee ■ Contact the park, P.O. Box 487, Key Largo, FL 33037; phone 305-451-1202. www.dep.state.fl.us/parks/District_5/JohnPennekamp/index.html

THE COUNTRY'S FIRST UNDERWATER PARK spreads for roughly 22 miles along Key Largo and 3 miles out into the Straits of Florida, preserving a popular and beautiful piece of the Keys' coral reef. The adjacent **Florida Keys National Marine Sanctuary** extends protection to some of the best sections of the reef—marked by yellow buoys—resulting in a swath of clear, shallow water where multihued corals and tropical fish live unmolested.

Though 95 percent of the park's acreage is submerged, a significant parcel of low-lying land holds mangrove swamps and tropical hammocks that offer refuge to wading birds, mammals, and rare plants. Wedged between the reef and the shore, luxuriant beds of sea grass wave in gentle currents, constituting yet another ecological community favored by man-atees, sea turtles, fish, and crabs. The warm currents of the Gulf Stream and gentle trade winds keep this entire bountiful ecosystem a year-round haven for a richly diverse pool of wildlife.

The present reef took about 5,000 to 7,000 years to grow to full matu-rity. Like the Keys themselves, the reef is built upon the skeletons of tiny polyps. But unlike the dry rock of the islands, the reef is still alive, its thousands of polyps continuing to add to the sprawling underwater housing complex. Whips, sea fans, and plumes anchor to the hard mass, undulating in currents and providing shelter and feeding grounds for a kaleidoscopic array of crabs, sponges, shrimp, and 600 species of fish.

It was common practice before the establishment of the park for visi-tors to break off pieces of the reef to take home as souvenirs. But like cave formations that take millennia to grow, the souvenirs were irreplaceable. In the late 1950s Gilbert Voss of the Marine Institute of Miami, noticing the destruction that was occurring, began working to protect the reef. His most outspoken ally, *Miami Herald* assistant editor John Pennekamp, lent Voss's research the power of the press. Pennekamp had played a key role in the founding of Everglades National Park, so he knew just what needed to be done. In 1960 the preserve was finally established.

What to See and Do

The **main concession building** is the place to go first to sign up for glass-bottom boat and snorkel tours *(fee)*. On days of calm, clear weather, there are usually three of each tour, and they provide the easiest way to see the reef, which lies 6 to 8 miles out in the ocean. The 2.5-hour tours provide about 90 minutes of reef time. In the glass-bottom boat you'll have a guide to point out what's what, but since the boat rolls a bit you may get a little dizzy staring at the wonders below. If so, look up for a while at a point on the horizon, or take a breather out on deck.

Whether you see it wet or dry, the reef promises an entrancing visual feast. Schools of blue-striped grunts swing through a forest of elkhorn coral; neon-blue parrotfish nibble on coral rock for its algae; brilliant Daliesque

wrasses clean other fish for a free meal of parasites and dead skin.

Look sharply for moray eels skulking down in hidden recesses, pink plume worms decorating dark corners, and huge sponges standing like thrones in a mer-maid's palace. In addition to the wonders of the natural world, you'll also probably see at least one of the many wrecked ships that lit-ter the Straits of Florida. On some pieces of wreckage colonies of coral have begun to grow.

On the way to and from the dock, your boat will navigate the narrow mangrove channels that buffer the shoreline and provide sanctuary for creatures of the air and sea. Dolphins and manatees sometimes surface close enough for a good view. The meadows of sea grass that grow along here may not be as visually stunning as the

Sex Under the Sea

You may at some point in your underwater explorations come across a parrotfish, wrasse, or other reef fish that looks twice as big as the others. Don't bother adjusting your mask. For little-understood reasons having to do with population dynamics, groups of fish will sometimes produce a "supermale" that is bigger, more colorful, and . . . just plain different from all the others of its gender. These buffed hunks of the fish world lord it over harems of females and establish a well-defined territory off-limits to other males.

The concept of the supermale, however, is mild in comparison with what many parrotfish do at some point in their lives: They undergo a hormonally induced sex change. When you dip your head below the surface in the Keys, you have to abandon the whole idea of normal.

The coral reefs themselves are created by several different kinds of sexuality. A pioneer reef begins when polyps on an existing reef create a new polyp by "normal" sexual reproduction; that is, male polyps spew out sperm cells, which are then taken in by female polyps. But in some corals, male and female polyps are the same—both sexes produce sperm *and* eggs.

In either case, the immature polyp, called a planula, is pushed out of its parent's mouth and swims through the ocean for hours or days. If the planula survives, it will latch onto a hard surface—no deeper than 150 feet—and secrete limestone to form a protective shell. Now permanently anchored, the new polyp begins building its own colony—asexually, in a process called budding. A single polyp thus eventually multiplies into a cooperative community of thousands.

reefs, but they do attract a sizable number of the same marine creatures that frequent the coral.

Among the few plants that flower underwater, the sea grasses help keep the water clear by trapping sediments. They also provide food and habitat for a wealth of marine life and are thus more than just a nuisance for propeller blades. From the water's surface you can see scars along the shoreline where boats have worn paths through the sea grass shoals.

Since it's illegal to harm protected sea grass, coral, or any other plants or animals, tread with care. If you plan on boating, steer for blue or green water, avoid brown

patches, and use navigation charts. On the reefs, use the park's mooring buoys instead of dropping an anchor. And don't ever stand on or handle the coral! Remember that of all the ecosystems in the country, this is one of the most delicate and most heavily visited. More than a million people come here every year—about the same number that visit Everglades National Park, which is 25 times larger.

While on shore, take a turn around the two short nature trails. The .25-mile **Wild Tamarind Trail** provides a nice introduction to a hardwood hammock. Markers explain the historical uses of trees such as Spanish stopper (tea from

Windsurfing in the Keys

White ibis at John Pennekamp Coral Reef State Park

its leaves was drunk as a treatment for diarrhea), Jamaica dogwood (Indians used the poison bark and leaves to stun fish), and soapberry (sap and orange berries make a good lather). Dawdle along this aromatic trail and marvel at the botanical variety a small tropical hammock can pack. By the water's edge, the .25-mile **Mangrove Trail** boardwalk crosses tidal creeks to an observation platform overlooking the dense mangroves.

To learn more, you can stop by the **visitor center,** which has a 30,000-gallon saltwater aquarium full of fish, coral, anemones, and sponges. And if you have the urge, return to the concessionaire and inquire about their scuba courses and tours. They also rent fishing boats, kayaks, canoes, and diving equipment. A **canoe trail** of about 2.5 miles gives you a chance to see the mangrove wilderness up close.

After your more strenuous adventures, kick back at **Cannon Beach** on Largo Sound. For some easy snorkeling, swim out about 130 feet and take a look at the reconstructed Spanish shipwreck. You can also enjoy a quiet swim at the **Far Beach** area. There are several areas within the park where you can fish, but you'll need a saltwater license. Don't worry if you forget to bring food—there's a good snack bar in the main concession building. Pennekamp's less-than-wild ibises will linger nearby, waiting to pounce on any scraps you leave behind. ■

Lignumvitae Key State Botanical Site

■ 280 acres on land; 10,000 acres submerged ■ Two tours a day (fee), Thurs.-Mon., by boat from Robbie's Marina at Milepost 77.5 ■ Best months Nov.-April ■ Guided walks, canoeing, bird-watching, wildlife viewing, wildflower viewing, boat tours ■ Contact the site, P.O. Box 1052, Islamorada, FL 33036; phone 305-664-2540. www.dep.state.fl.us/parks/District_5/LignumvitaeKey/index.html

SITUATED IN THE CALM WATERS of Florida Bay off Lower Matecumbe Key, this tiny island's fossilized coral rock supports a vibrant virgin forest of gumbo-limbo, strangler fig, poisonwood, mastic, pigeon plum, and the rare lignum vitae. Meaning "wood of life," the lignum vitae was used as a remedy for gout, syphilis, and other disorders. Though about 1,500 grow on the island, the numbers here and on the nearby Upper and Middle Keys are dropping because of competition from taller trees.

The three-hour tour includes a one-hour guided walk through hardwood forest and into a clearing containing the coral-rock Matheson House, built in 1919 by a wealthy resident of Key Biscayne. Long sleeves and insect repellent are good precautions against the island's mosquitoes.

Nearby **Windley Key Fossil Reef State Geological Site** *(Milepost 88.5. 305-664-2540. Thurs.-Mon.)* is an interesting complement to the living coral reefs found elsewhere. One of the highest of the Upper Keys, Windley rises to 18 feet above sea level. From the early 1900s to the 1960s, Windley's limestone was mined for "keystone," a popular decorative facing. The stone was shipped by rail until a 1935 hurricane destroyed the railroad, then by the Overseas Highway.

A short trail through the quarry lets you stand inside a fossilized coral reef and marvel at its complex structure. Packed together in high walls are petrified brain corals, star corals, snails, clams, green algae, and other organisms, cemented in place by calcite sediment. Though you can't see its full thickness, the reef extends in places down to 180 feet. A side trail traverses a hammock of cactus, palms, and hardwoods. ■

Lignum vitae

Beach at Bahia Honda State Park

Bahia Honda State Park

■ 524 acres ■ US 1 at Milepost 37 ■ Best season fall ■ Camping, hiking, guided walks, boating, swimming, scuba diving, fishing, biking, bird-watching, wildlife viewing, boat tours ■ Contact the park, 36850 Overseas Hwy., Big Pine Key, FL 33043; phone 305-872-2353. www.dep.state.fl.us/parks/District_5/BahiaHonda/index.html

THOUGH OFFSHORE REEFS SHIELD most of the Keys from ocean waves, Bahia Honda with its wide sandy beach is a notable exception. The island hooks out into the open Atlantic at a place favorable for catching sand-carrying currents. Here you can soak up long views of glassy turquoise water, properly outlined by sand and stately rows of royal palms with long pin-wheel fronds. Roseate spoonbills and other wading birds add grace notes to the tropical intermezzo. For even better views, walk out on a section of the old **railroad bridge** at the south end of the park.

Also consider taking a turn around the **Silver Palm Nature Trail** at the end of Sandspur Beach. Rimming the shore of a tidal lagoon, the trail explores some of the island's rare and lovely flora, many species of which originate in the Caribbean, their seeds carried here by hurricanes, birds, and waves. Among the unusual plants are Jamaica morning glory, orange-flowering Geiger trees, sealavender, white Key spiderlily, and wild alamanda. Bahia Honda also contains the national champion specimens of the yellow satinwood and silver palm.

If you want to increase your activity level even further, more vigorous pursuits available in the park include bicycling and kayaking. The conces-sionaire *(305-872-3897)* rents equipment and runs daily snorkeling tours out to **Looe Key National Marine Sanctuary.** ■

Dry Tortugas National Park

■ 85 acres on land; 64,572 submerged ■ 70 miles west of Key West by plane or boat ■ Best seasons spring and early summer ■ Camping, walking, boating, swimming, scuba diving, fishing, bird-watching, wildlife viewing ■ For full-day boat trips call the Yankee Fleet at 305-294-7009 or 877-327-8228 or Sunny Days Catamarans at 305-292-6100 or 800-236-7937 ■ Seaplanes of Key West offers half- and full-day trips; phone 800-950-2359 ■ Contact the park, P.O. Box 6208, Key West, FL 33041; phone 305-242-7700. www.nps.gov/drto

AS FAR OUT AS YOU CAN GO in Florida, this beyond-the-end-of-the-road island group basks in solitary splendor, its seven small keys surrounded by shoals, reefs, and miles of limpid aquamarine water. Among the Tortugas (Spanish for "turtles"), sea sponges and fans sway like gossamer, while tropical fish flash their colors and sea turtles glide with an ancient grace to beaches where their kind have laid eggs for thousands of years.

Sooty terns numbering 100,000 turn **Bush Key** into a bustling rookery as they arrive from the Caribbean for the spring-to-summer nesting season. (For this reason the key is closed to visitors from February through September.) Frigatebirds with 7-foot wingspans pick off some hatchlings; more die from other natural causes; the rest fly off when they are big enough. You might also see double-crested cormorants, roseate terns, brown and masked boobies, brown pelicans, and gulls.

The islands are called dry for good reason: They have no fresh water. Nor does the park provide water, or services of any kind. You're on your own, unless you come with a tour. The reefs have some fine beaches and areas for snorkeling and scuba diving, and you can ramble around the battlements of the tremendous 19th-century brick **Fort Jefferson** on Garden Key. From atop the wall there are serene views of the fort, the nearby keys, and the huge, lonely, windswept heart of the Gulf of Mexico at this tail end of the great American outdoors. ■

Male frigatebirds   *Following pages:* Old railroad bridge, Bahia Honda State Park

Other Sites

The following is a select list of other Southeast sites.

Appalachian Mountains

Buck's Pocket State Park

Just north of Grove Oak in northeast Alabama, a remote 2,000-acre park sprawls over a deep box canyon gouged out by South Souty Creek. Contact the park, 393 Cty. Rd. 174, Grove Oak, AL 35975; 256-659-2000.

Glassy Mountain Heritage Preserve

Though only 65 acres, this off-the-beaten-path site is worth a visit for its crenulated 400-foot cliffs and granite outcrops that harbor such rare plants as the thousand-leaf groundsel. A winding trail offers views of both the Blue Ridge and the Piedmont. The preserve is located east of Pickens, off S.C. 183. Contact South Carolina Dept. of Natural Resources Heritage Trust, P.O. Box 167, Columbia, SC 29202; 803-734-3894.

Oak Mountain State Park

Approximately 10,000 acres, Oak Mountain offers some 35 miles of trails through hardwood bottoms and pine-topped ridges, as well as cottages and a golf course. Contact the park, P.O. Box 278, Pelham, AL 35124; 205-620-2520.

Ruffner Mountain

Eight miles northeast of Birmingham, this 1,000-acre preserve and education center has exhibits on local geology, biology, and history. A wildflower garden showcases native blooms, and trails explore the forest. Contact the center, 1214 81st St. S., Birmingham, AL 35206; 205-833-8264 or 205-833-8112 (weekends). www.ruffnermountain.org

Piedmont

Heggie's Rock Preserve

A Nature Conservancy site near Appling, this granite outcrop has many niche-specific plants and animals. Cedars and flowering hardwoods provide shade for rare mosses and worts, while deer, wild turkeys, and beavers live in the woods and around the creek. Contact the Nature Conservancy, 1330 Peachtree St., Suite 410, Atlanta, GA 30309; 404-873-6946.

Stevens Creek Heritage Preserve

The 434 acres of bluffs and floodplain forest protect rare plants, such as the Mickoukee gooseberry. Investigate wildflowers and trees along the creek and bluff. The preserve is located off County Road 88, south of the Sumter National Forest. Contact the South Carolina Dept. of Natural Resources Heritage Trust, P.O. Box 167, Columbia, SC 29202; 803-734-3894.

Sweetwater Creek State Conservation Park

About 15 miles west of Atlanta, south of I-20, 2,035-acres of piedmont woodlands offer hiking, camping, and a lake with boating and fishing. Trails course through oaks, sycamores, magnolias, sourwoods, river birches, and wildflowers. Contact the Georgia Parks, Recreation and Historic Sites Division, P.O. Box 816, Lithia Springs, GA 30122; 770-732-5871.

Tuskegee National Forest

Off I-85 between Montgomery and Auburn, this 11,054-acre woodland along the Fall Line features an 8.5-mile section of the Bartram National Recreation Trail, as well as bike and horse trails. Camping permits are free from the ranger station. Alabama fishing licenses are needed. Contact the District Office, 125 National Forest Rd. 949, Tuskegee, AL 36083; 334-727-2652.

Coastal Plain

Broxton Rocks Preserve

Schedule a tour with the Nature Conservancy to visit this consortium of rare plants harbored upon the back of an extruded layer of sandstone. Rocky Creek courses through the preserve's ravines, which hold shoestring and filmy ferns, greenfly orchids, and endangered silky creeping morning glories. Owls hunt here at night; indigo snakes and gopher tortoises live in a remnant longleaf–wire grass forest. The preserve is in Coffee County, off US 441. Contact the Nature Conservancy, 1330 Peachtree St., Suite 410, Atlanta, GA 30309; 404-873-6946.

Cedar Key National Wildlife Refuge

South of the Lower Suwannee National Wildlife Refuge, this group of 12 sand-fringed islets lies in the Gulf of Mexico, surrounding Cedar Key. Among the many species that nest here are cormorants, ibises, pelicans, herons, egrets, and ospreys. Contact the U.S. Fish and Wildlife Service, 16450 N.W. 31st Pl., Chiefland, FL 32626; 352-493-0238.

Chickasaw State Park

Four miles north of Linden, off US 43, the 520-acre park offers hiking in the west-central part of the state. Near the Tombigbee waterway, the park features a full roster of southeast flora and fauna. Contact the park, 26955 US 43, Gallion, AL 36742; 334-295-8230.

The Estuarium

Forty aquarium tanks focus on the four main ecosystems: Delta, Mobile Bay, Barrier Island, and the Gulf. Dauphin Island Sea Lab. Contact the estuarium, 101 Bienville Blvd., Dauphin Island, AL 36528; 334-861-7515. www.disl.org

Gulf State Park

This park on the Gulf offers freshwater fishing and boating off a white-sand beach. A nature center includes trails and shore ecology exhibits. Contact the park, 20115 Ala. 135, Gulf Shores, AL 36542; 334-948-7275.

Meaher State Park

Just off I-10 east of Mobile, this 1,327-acre park at the mouth of the Tensaw River has two scenic nature trails, one with a boardwalk providing fine views of the Mobile Delta. The river offers access to 185,000 spectacular acres of protected Mobile-Tensaw Bottomlands, a landmark of wildlife-filled swamps and marshes. Contact the park, P.O. Box 7826, Spanish Fort, AL 36577; 334-626-5529.

Stone Mountain Park

On Ga. 78, 16 miles east of downtown Atlanta, this 3,200-acre park has fishing, camping, and hiking and biking trails. It also has a scenic railroad, an antebellum plantation, a sky lift museum, and a riverboat. Contact the park, P.O. Box 778, Stone Mountain, GA 30086; 770-498-5690 or 800-317-2006

South Florida

Archie Carr National Wildlife Refuge

On a barrier island south of Melbourne Beach, this refuge hosts up to 25 percent of all the loggerhead

sea turtles that nest on U.S. Atlantic beaches. An undeveloped dune ridge, graced by prickly pears, sea grapes, and daisies, gives way to a pristine shoreline. Contact the U.S. Fish and Wildlife Service, Merritt Island National Wildlife Refuge, P.O. Box 6504, Titusville, FL 32780; 407-861-0667.

Florida Keys Refuges

The National Key Deer Refuge, Great White Heron National Wildlife Refuge, Key West National Wildlife Refuge, and the Crocodile Lake National Wildlife Refuge (temporarily closed) offer visits to their wildlife havens. Contact the refuges c/o Headquarters, Winn-Dixie Shopping Center, P.O. Box 430510, Big Pine Key, FL 33043; 305-872-2239.

J. N. "Ding" Darling National Wildlife Refuge

At more than 6,300 acres, this popular Gulf Coast birding site embraces mangrove forests, cordgrass marshes, and West Indian hardwood hammocks as well as walking and canoeing trails. A 5-mile drive offers views of gators, roseate

spoonbills, herons, ospreys, and more. Contact the U.S. Fish and Wildlife Service, 1 Wildlife Dr., Sanibel, FL 33957; 941-472-1100.

Pelican Island National Wildlife Refuge

This two-acre island of mangroves in the Intracoastal Waterway hosts 10,000 birds in the winter, including great blue herons and brown pelicans. Evening tours leave from Sebastian, west of the refuge. Contact the U.S. Fish and Wildlife Service, Merritt Island National Wildlife Refuge, P.O. Box 6504, Titusville, FL 32780; 407-861-0667.

Pelican Man's Bird Sanctuary

Adjacent to the Mote Marine Aquarium on the northern end of Lido Key, this facility rescues more than 7,000 birds a year, many injured by cars or fishing lines. A boardwalk passes pens with pelicans, crows, cormorants, sandhill cranes, herons, hawks, ospreys, kestrels, owls, and others. Contact the sanctuary, 1708 Ken Thompson Pkwy., Sarasota, FL 34236-1000; 941-388-4444.

Resources

The following is a select list of resources. Contact state and local associations for additional outfitter and lodging options. For chain hotels and motels in Alabama, Florida, Georgia, and South Carolina, see p. 283.

ALABAMA

Federal and State Agencies

Alabama Bureau of Tourism and Travel
    401 Adams Ave.
    Montgomery, AL 36103
    334-242-4169 or
    800-252-2262
    Lodgings, activities, and visitor information.

Division of Parks
    Alabama Department of Conservation and Natural Resources

64 North Union St.
Montgomery, AL 36130
334-242-3333
www.dcnr.state.al.us

Division of Wildlife and Freshwater Fisheries
    Alabama Department of Conservation and Natural Resources
    64 North Union St.
    Montgomery, AL 36130
    334-242-3469 (hunting and management area)
    334-242-3465 (fisheries, state lakes, and boat ramp)
    334-242-3826 (licensing)
    334-242-3467 (rules, regulations, and law enforcement)
    334-242-3623 (outdoor sports and nonconsumptive wildlife recreation)
    www.dcnr.state.al.us

Outfitters and Activities

Biophilia Nature Center
    12695 County Road 95
    Elberta, AL 36530

334-987-1200
Biologist-guided tours on preserving and restoring nature.

DeSoto Caverns
    5181 DeSoto Caverns Pkwy.
    Childersburg, AL 35044
    256-378-7252
    800-933-2283
    Guided tours daily with laser, light, and water shows.

Morgan Outfitters
    P.O. Box 26766
    Birmingham, AL 35260
    800-788-7070
    Canoe rentals and equipment for Bear Creek and the Locust Fork of the Blade Warrior River.

Subsealevel Dive and Aquatic Center
    474 E. Beach Blvd.
    Gulf Shores, AL 36542
    334-948-6883
    Diving instruction and rentals and boat charters.

The Trading Post
11312 Ala. 33
Moulton, AL 35650
Canoeing and kayaking
on the Sipsey River and
Bear Creek.

Wiley Outdoors
1820 6th Ave., S.E.
Gateway Shopping Center
Decatur, AL 35602
256-351-8603
Camping, canoeing, and
fishing merchandise.
Kayaking rentals for use
on the Sipsey River
and in Bankhead National
Forest.

Lodgings

Alabama Hospitality
Association
P.O. Box 241715
Montgomery, AL 36124-
1715
334-213-2526
Hotel and motel informa-
tion and reservations.

Bed and Breakfast
Association of Alabama
P.O. Box 707
Montgomery, AL 36101
256-329-3717
For locations and
availability throughout
the state.

Camping

To make reservations for
state parks campsites, as
well as cabins and chalets,
through the Central
Reservation Service, call
800-252-7275. For more
information, go to www.dcnr.
state.al.us/parks.

Cheaha State Park
19644 Ala. 281 S.
Delta, AL 36258
256-488-5111
Mountainous site for
camping; park offers pedal
boating, fishing, and a lookout tower on Cheaha
Mountain.

DeSoto State Park
13883 Cty. Rd. 89
Fort Payne, AL 35967
256-845-0051
Tent, trailer, and RV sites;
hiking, swimming, and
scenic drive.

Joe Wheeler State Park
201 McLean Dr.
Rogersville, AL 35652

256-247-1184
Improved campsites
and primitive camping;
boating and fishing on lake.

FLORIDA

Federal and State Agencies

Department of
Environmental Protection
3900 Commonwealth Blvd.
Tallahassee, FL 32399-3000
904-488-1554
904-488-3701 (Office of
Greenways and Trails)
904-488-6131 (Division
of Recreation & Parks)
www.dep.state.fl.us/parks/
index.html
Find out about state parks
and local flora and fauna.

Florida Fish and Wildlife
Conservation Commission
620 S. Meridian St.
Farris Bryant Building
Tallahassee, FL 32399-1600
904-488-4676
Fishing and hunting infor-
mation statewide.

Outfitters and Activities

Adventures Unlimited
Fla. 6, Box 283
Milton, FL 32570
850-623-6197
Canoeing, kayaking, and
tubing on Coldwater
Creek; ropes course.

Blackwater Canoe Rentals
10274 Pond Rd.
Milton, FL 32583
850-623-0235
Canoes, kayaks, and tubes
for the Blackwater River.

Blackwater Heritage
State Trail
7220 Deaton Bridge Rd.
Holt, FL 32564
850-983-5363
An 8.5-mile trail for hikers,
bikers, and in-line skaters,
starting in Milton.

Bob's Canoeing Company
4569 Ploughman Lane
Milton, FL 32583
850-623-5457
Canoes, tubes, and kayaks;
day and overnight trips on
the Coldwater Creek.

Everglades NP Boat Tours

P.O. Box 119
Everglades City, FL 34139
800-445-7724
Tours of the mangrove
forests with a chance to
see dolphins, manatees, and
bald eagles. Canoe rentals.

Florida Bay Outfitters
104050 Overseas Hwy.
Key Largo, FL 33037
305-451-3018
Kayak rentals, instruction,
and tours of mangroves, the
Everglades, and Keys.

Kayak Amelia
2701 Lesaber Place
Fernandina Beach, FL 32934
904-321-0697
Kayak trips through creeks
and marshes of Talbot
Island SP and Amelia Island.

Keys Divers Inc.
99696 Overseas Hwy.,
Unit #1
Key Largo, FL 33037-2432
305-451-1177
Masks, fins, and other snorkeling equipment rentals.

Seadwellers Dive Center
99850 Overseas Hwy.
Key Largo, FL 33037
305-451-3640
Instruction on scuba diving;
related equipment rentals.

Shark Valley Tram Tours
P.O. Box 1739
Tamiami Station
Miami, FL 33144
305-221-8455
Four daily tram ride trips
into the saw-grass prairies
and hammocks of the
Everglades.

Lodgings

Call the State of Florida
Hotel and Restaurant Com-
mittee at 305-470-5680.
Or call Florida Bed and
Breakfast Inns at 281-499-
1374 or 800-524-1880, or go
to www.florida-inns.com.

Camping

To make reservations at state
parks, call the parks or go to
www.dep.state.fl.us/parks.

Anclote Key State Preserve
c/o Gulf Islands Geopark
1 Causeway Blvd.
Dunedin, FL 34698
727-469-5918
Primitive camping on
the island's north end;

swimming and fishing in the Gulf.

Bahia Honda State Park
36850 Overseas Hwy.
Big Pine Key, FL 33043
305-872-2353
Tent and motor home sites; swimming and snorkeling.

Blackwater River State Park
7720 Deaton Bridge Rd.
Holt, FL 32564
850-983-5363
Camping, canoeing, and hiking.

Everglades NP
4001 Fla. 9336
Homestead, FL 33034
305-242-7700
Campsites in Flamingo and Long Pine Key. Canoeing, kayaking, biking, and fishing.

Gulf Islands National Seashore
1801 Gulf Breeze Pkwy.
Gulf Breeze, FL 32561
850-934-2635
Sites at Fort Pickens campground open daily; nearby hiking and scuba diving.

Highlands Hammock
State Park
5931 Hammock Road
Sebring, FL 33872
863-386-6094
Regular, primitive, and horse sites. Horseback riding, bicycling, and bird-watching.

John Pennecamp Coral Reef State Park
P.O. Box 487
Key Largo, FL 33037
305-451-1202
Wooded campsites near the water. Snorkeling, diving, kayaking, and glass-bottomed boat tours.

Jonathan Dickinson
State Park
16450 S.E. US 1
Hobe Sound, Florida 33455
561-546-2771
Sites for tents, trailers, and RVs. Canoe rentals and bike trails.

Little Talbot Island State Park
12157 Heckscher Dr.
Jacksonville, FL 32226
904-251-2320
Shaded campsites in a beachside park; bird-watching, fishing, hiking, and nearby horse riding.

Myakka River State Park
13207 FL 72
Sarasota, FL 34241
941-361-6511
Tent, trailer, and RV sites.

St. Joseph Peninsula State Park
8899 Cape San Blas Rd.
Port St. Joe, FL 32456
850-227-1327
Wilderness area with camping, swimming, canoeing, hiking, and a boat ramp.

Torreya State Park
Fla. 2, Box 70
Bristol, FL 32321
850-643-2674
Campsites and trails offer views of the hardwood forests, rivers, and ravines, as well as primitive camping. Canoeing, birding, and wildlife tour.

GEORGIA

Federal and State Agencies

Department of Industry, Trade and Tourism
285 Peachtree Center Ave. N.E.
Suite 1000
Atlanta, GA 30303
404-657-0563 or
800-847-4842
www.georgia.org
Statewide accommodations and attractions, as well as festivals and fairs.

Georgia Department of Natural Resources
205 Butler St. S.E,
Suite 1352
Atlanta, GA 30334
404-656-3530 (state parks)
770-918-6406 (fishing)
770-918-6404 (hunting)
www.gastateparks.org
For information on parks, historic sites, and special events.

Outfitters and Activities

Appalachian Outfitters
24 N. Park St.
Dahlonega, GA 30533
706-867-6677
Rentals for canoeing, kayaking, and tubing on the Chestatee and Etowah Rivers. Climbing and kayaking instruction.

SouthEast Adventure Outfitters
313 Mallory St.
St. Simons Island, GA 31522
912-638-6732
Kayak tours of the Satilla and Altamaha Rivers. Kayaking and camping equipment sales and rental.

Southeastern Expeditions
50 Executive Park S., Suite 5016
Atlanta, GA 30329
800-868-7238
White-water rafting trips on the Chattooga and Oconee Rivers.

Tallulah Adventures
P.O. Box 84
Tallulah Falls, GA 30573
706-754-4318
Canoe, inflatable kayak, and mountain bike rentals for use in the Tallulah Gorge State Park.

Wilderness Southeast
711 Sandtown Rd.
Savannah, GA 31410
912-897-5108
Nonprofit educational outfitter offering half- and full-day programs around the Savannah area.

Wildwater
P.O. Box 309
Long Creek, SC 29658
800-451-9972
South Carolina-based outfit offering white-water rafting on the Chattooga River.

Lodgings

Contact the Department of Industry, Trade and Tourism (see above) for accommodations. Or contact the Northeast Georgia Mountains Travel Association at 404-231-1820 or P.O. Box 464, Gainesville, GA 30503. Or call the Great Inns of Georgia at 404-843-0471 or 800-501-7328, or write to 541 Londonberry Rd., N.W., Atlanta, GA 30327.

For information on lodgings around Okefenokee, contact Waycross Tourism Association at 912-283-3744 or 315 Plant Ave., Waycross, GA 31501. For lodgings around Chattahoochee, contact Dahlonega/Lumpkin County Chamber of Commerce at

706-864-3711 or 13 S. Park
St., Dahlonega, GA 30533.

Camping

For reservations in Chata-
hoochee National Forest
call 877-444-6777, or go to
www.reserveusa.com.

For state parks, contact
the Georgia Department
of Natural Resources at
770-389-7275 or 800- 864-
7275. Or go to www.dnr.
state.ga.us/dnr/parks. You
can also contact the parks
below directly.

Cloudland Canyon
State Park
  122 Cloudland Canyon
  Park Rd.
  Rising Fawn, GA
  30738
  706-657-4050
  Tent, trailer, walk-in, and
  primitive campsites. Tennis
  and swimming.

Stephen C. Foster
State Park
  Ga. 177, Box 131
  Fargo, GA 31631
  912-637-5274
  Tent, trailer, and RV sites;
  boat rentals and ramp.

Unicoi State Park
  P.O. Box 997
  Helen, GA 30545
  706-878-2201 or
  800-573-9659
  Camping sites, as
  well as mountain biking,
  hiking, fishing, and sea-
  sonal canoe and pedal
  boat rentals.

Vogel State Park
  7485 Vogel State Park Rd.
  Blairsville, GA 30512
  706-745-2628
  Sites and trails in Georgia's oldest state park.

SOUTH CAROLINA

Federal and
State Agencies

Department of Parks,
Recreation & Tourism
  205 Pendleton St.
  Columbia, SC 29201
  803-734-1700
  www.travelsc.com
  Visitor information on
  statewide activities.

Department of Natural
Resources
  Rembert C. Dennis
  Building
  1000 Assembly St.
  Columbia, SC 29201
  803-734-3888
  Licenses, rules, and regu-
  lations information, and
  educational courses.

Outfitters
and Activities

Adventure Carolina
  1107 State St.
  Cayce, SC 29033
  803-796-4505
  Guided canoe and kayak
  trips on the Congaree and
  Saluda Rivers.

Barrier Island Ecotours
  P.O. Box 343
  Isle of Palms, SC 29451
  843-886-5000
  Biologist-led trips to
  Capers Island Wildlife
  State Heritage Preserve
  and other excursions.

Bohicket Boat: Adventure
and Tour Company
  1880 Andell Bluff
  John's Island, SC 29455
  843-768-7294
  Custom tours, boat rentals, and dolphin-watching
  around ACE Basin and the
  North Edisto River area.

Fish Incorporated
  15071 North S.C. 11
  Salem, SC 29676
  864-944-9292
  Customized fishing or
  touring excursions on
  Lake Jocassee.

Great Wide Open
Outfitters
  35 Grier St.
  Sumter, SC 29150
  803-775-6103
  Tours and equipment for
  canoeing, kayaking, and
  rock climbing around the
  Lake Santee area.

Hoyett's Bait and Tackle
  516 Jocassee Lake Rd.
  Salem, SC 29676
  864-944-9016
  Boat rentals and fishing
  trips on Lake Jocassee.

Kayak Farm
  1289 Sea Island Pkwy.
  St. Helena Island,
  SC 29928

843-838-2008
  Guided kayak tours and
  introduction to paddling
  around the ACE Basin.

Nature Adventures
Outfitters
  1900 Iron Swamp Rd.
  Francis Marion National
  Forest
  Awendaw, SC 29429
  843-928-3316
  or 800-673-0679
  Biologist-guided
  sea kayaking, Blackwater
  Swamp and river
  tours, and canoe, kayak,
  and mountain bike
  rentals.

River Runner
  905 Gerdais St.
  Columbia, SC 29201
  803-771-0353
  Canoe and kayak rentals
  and sales. White-water
  clinics on the Saluda River.

Second Nature Sports
  86 Holmsan Way
  Suite 204
  Hilton Head Island,
  SC 29920
  843-341-5590
  Offers parasailing, hang
  gliding, kayaking, and
  guided ecotours around
  Hilton Head and Dau-
  fuskie Islands.

Wildwater
  P.O. Box 309
  Long Creek, SC
  29658
  800-451-9972
  White-water rafting on
  the Chattooga River.

Lodgings

Contact the South Carolina
Bed and Breakfast Association at 888-599-1234 or
P.O. Box 1275, Sumter, SC
29150-1275. Or contact
the Department of Parks,
Recreation and Tourism
(see above) for inn, hotel,
and motel information.

Camping

For private campground
information, call 800-344-
4518 for a free brochure or
go to www.sccamping.com.
For information and reservations for state parks, call
803-734-0156 or 888-
887-2757, or go to www.
southcarolinaparks.com.

Caesars Head SP
8155 Geer Hwy.
Cleveland, SC 29635
864-836-6115
Trailside sites and moun-
tain panoramas.

Devils Fork SP Campground
161 Holcombe Circle
Salem, SC 29676
864-944-2639
Facilities include paved
sites with hookups;
angling and boating.

Edisto Beach SP
8377 State Cabin Rd.
Edisto Island, SC
29438
843-869-2156
Ocean-side sites and sites
near the salt marsh.

Hunting Island SP
2555 Sea Island Pkwy.
Hunting Island, SC 29920
843-838-2011
A waterfront park with
camping and kayak events.

Myrtle Beach SP
4401 South Kings Hwy.
Myrtle Beach, SC 29575
843-238-5325
Oceanfront park with
campsites, hiking trails,
and a nature center.

Santee State Park
251 State Park Rd.
Santee, SC 29142

803-854-2408
Campsites on or
near Lake Marion;
pedal boat rentals, boat
tours, and nature and
bike trails.

Table Rock SP
158 East Ellison
Pickens, SC 29671
864-878-9813
Packed-gravel tent and RV
sites; strenuous hikes.

Hotel and Motel Chains in the Southeast

Best Western International
800-528-1234

Choice Hotels
800-424-6423

Clarion Hotels
800-252-7466

Comfort Inns
800-228-5150

Country Inn & Suites
800-456-1578

Courtyard by Marriott
800-321-2211

Days Inn
800-325-2525

Doubletree Hotels and
Guest Suites (not Alabama)
800-222-6733

Econo Lodge
800-446-6900

Embassy Suites
800-362-2779

Fairfield Inn by Marriott
800-228-2800

Hampton Inn
800-426-7866

Hilton Hotels
800-774-1500

Howard Johnson
800-654-2000

Hyatt Hotels and Resorts
(not Alabama)
800-233-1234

Key West Inn and Suites
(not South Carolina)
800-833-0555

Marriott Hotels
Resorts Suites
800-228-9290

Motel 6
800-466-8356

Quality Inns-Hotels-Suites
800-228-5151

Radisson Hotels, Inc.
800-333-3333

Ramada Inns
888-298-2054

Sheraton Hotels and Inns
800-325-3535

Super 8 Motels
800-843-1991

Westin Hotels and Resorts
800-228-3000

About the Author and the Photographer

John Thompson has traveled on assignment to more than 35 states for numerous National Geographic books. He is currently on the road researching the Central Appalachia volume for this series on America's Outdoors. John's home base is
in Charlottesville, Virginia, where he lives with his wife and two children.

Freelance photographer **Raymond Gehman** specializes in outdoor and natural
history subjects. His fascination with the woods and wetlands of the Southeast
grew out of a stint as an award-winning photographer for the *Virginian-Pilot* news-
paper in Norfolk, Virginia. A frequent contributor to *National Geographic* and *Traveler* magazines, he now lives in central Pennsylvania with his wife and two sons.

Illustrations Credits

Photographs in this book are by Raymond Gehman except for the following:

p. 23 - Eric Horan
p. 58 - Earth Scenes/Dale Sarver
p. 223 - Tony Stone/Stuart Westmorland
p. 275 - Animals Animals/John Pontier

Index

Abbreviations

National Historic Landmark =
NHL
National Monument = NM
National Park = NP
National Recreation Area =
NRA
National Wildlife Refuge =
NWR
State Forest = SF
State Park = SP
State Reservation = SR

National Geographic Guide to America's Outdoors: Southeast
by John Thompson
Photographed by Raymond Gehman

Published by the National Geographic Society
John M. Fahey, Jr., *President and Chief Executive Officer*
Gilbert M. Grosvenor, *Chairman of the Board*
Nina D. Hoffman, *Executive Vice President*

Prepared by the Book Division
William R. Gray, *Vice President and Director*
Charles Kogod, *Assistant Director*
Barbara A. Payne, *Editorial Director and Managing Editor*

Guides to America's Outdoors
Elizabeth L. Newhouse, *Director of Travel Books*
Cinda Rose, *Art Director*
Allan Fallow, *Senior Editor*
Barbara A. Noe, *Associate Editor*
Caroline Hickey, *Senior Researcher*
Carl Mehler, *Director of Maps*
Roberta Conlan, *Project Director*

Staff for this Book
Jim Lynch, Jarelle S. Stein, *Editors*
Joan Wolbier, *Designer*
Greta Arnold, *Illustrations Editor*
Caroline J. Dean, Victoria Garrett Jones,
  Jane Sunderland, *Researchers*
Linda Averitt, *Editorial Consultant*
Thomas L. Gray, Joseph F. Ochlak, Nicholas P. Rosenbach, *Map Editors*
  Matt Chwastyk, Jerome N. Cookson, Sven M. Dolling, Thomas L. Gray,
  Nicholas P. Rosenbach, Martin S. Walz, National Geographic Maps,
  Mapping Specialists, *Map Research and Production*
Tibor Tóth, *Map Relief*
R. Gary Colbert, *Production Director*
Gillian Carol Dean, *Assistant Designer*
Sharon K. Berry, *Illustrations Assistant*
Mark A. Wentling, *Indexer*
Angela George, Robert Della Vecchia, *Project Assistants*
Deb Antonini, *Contributor*

Manufacturing and Quality Control
George V. White, *Director;* John T. Dunn, *Associate Director;* Vincent P. Ryan, *Manager;*
  Phillip L. Schlosser, *Financial Analyst*

Library of Congress Cataloging-in-Publication Data
Thompson, John M. (John Milliken), 1959-
  Guide to America's Outdoors. Southeast / by John Thompson ; photography by Raymond Gehman.
    p. cm. -- (National Geographic guides to America's outdoors)
  ISBN 0-7922-7752-X
    1. Southern States--Guidebooks. 2. National parks and reserves--Southern States--Guide books. 3.
  Outdoor recreation--Southern States--Guidebooks. I. Gehman, Raymond. II. National Geographic Society
  (U.S.) III. Title. IV. Series.
    F207.3 .T47 2000
    917.504'44--dc21   00-060539
                                                                            CIP

The information in this book has been carefully checked and is accurate as of press date.
However, details are subject to change, and the National Geographic Society cannot be
responsible for such changes, or for errors or omissions. Assessments of sites are based on
the authors' subjective opinions, which do not necessarily reflect the publisher's opinion.
The publisher cannot be responsible for any consequences arising from the use of this book.